*Beaumarchais and the War
of American Independence*

Elizabeth Sarah Kite

Contents

HISTORICAL INTRODUCTION	7
CHAPTER I	18
CHAPTER II	40
CHAPTER III	52
CHAPTER IV	69
CHAPTER V	86
CHAPTER VI	98
CHAPTER VII	116
CHAPTER VIII	128
CHAPTER IX	143
CHAPTER X	157
CHAPTER XI	176
CHAPTER XII	187
CHAPTER XIII	204
CHAPTER XIV	219

BEAUMARCHAIS AND THE WAR OF AMERICAN INDEPENDENCE

BY

Elizabeth Sarah Kite

HISTORICAL INTRODUCTION

THE primary cause of discontent among the American colonies, which led to the Declaration of Independence in 1776, was the proclamation by the King of England after the evacuation of America by the French in 1763, forbidding the colonists to extend their settlements west of the Alleghenies[1].

This proclamation instantly roused the ire of the men of the New World, for the war waged for so many years in the wilderness against the French and the Indians had taught the settlers the incomparable value of their vast "Hinterland," and having won at so great cost and by such effort a footing on the coast, they were by no means willing to be dictated to in the matter of expansion. Like stalwart sons of a mighty race, grown to manhood in heroic struggle with the forces of nature, brought to self-consciousness by the conflict they had endured, these men of the New World felt within themselves the power, and therefore believed in their right, to conquer the great and almost unexplored wilderness lying beyond them. From the moment they were made to feel a restriction to their liberty in this direction, there was nothing wanting but a pretext for breaking with the mother country. Nor had they long to wait. One petty act of tyranny after another showed the determination of the English King still to treat as a child the son now grown to manhood. At length the time was ripe and the outbreak came.

Righteous indignation and personal prowess, however, are of themselves unable to win battles or to insure victory. To be effective they must rest upon a material basis, and in the contest of the colonies with England this material basis was

---

1 Sec Bancroft, Vol. III, p. 62.

conspicuously wanting.

Sparingly provided with munitions of war, possessing no central government, and lacking unity among themselves, the colonies seemed at the first to be leading a forlorn hope. The feeling of resentment roused by the arbitrary interference of England was indeed great, yet the jealousy that existed between the colonies themselves was, if possible, greater still[2].

Nor wag this surprising. Up to the time of forming the determination to break with England there had been no common interest to unite them. Neither habits of life nor uniformity of opinion bound them together; on the contrary, the causes which had brought them into being were just so many forces tending to keep them widely apart. It was this spirit of jealous fear that made of the Continental Congress a body so conspicuously devoid of dignity and incapable of commanding respect either at home or abroad. Composed of delegates representing the colonies, this improvised body found itself, when assembled in Philadelphia, practically without power. It could advise and suggest, but it had no authority to tax the people or even to levy troops.[3]

The presence of members representing different party factions was a fertile source of discord. More than once the whole cause was brought to the brink of ruin through the injudicious actions of this incompetent body[4]. Once it was put to flight by a handful of drunken soldiers and during the entire course of its existence it remained a living demonstration of the fact that where there .is no authority, no respect can be commanded, no law enforced.

In this state of affairs help from outside was imperatively needed and eagerly sought. The question that presented itself was, to whom could the Americans turn in their dilemma. Naturally to no second-rate European power, for in combating England, England so lately victorious over all her enemies, powerful support was necessary; and for powerful support to whom could she turn but to France? (Geo.

2   See John Fiske's American Revolution, Vol. I, p. 244.

3   J. Fiske's American Revolution, Vol. I, p. 943.
4   J. Fiske's American Revolution, Vol. II, pp. 27-32.

Bancroft, Vol. IV, p. 360.) It is not therefore surprising that we find her looking in this direction. Nor was France herself indifferent to the situation for she was still smarting under the humiliating treaty of 1763. The blood of every true-born Frenchman boiled with indignation when he realized the position to which his proud nation had been brought through the frivolity and egotism of Louis XV. From her place among the nations France had been east down. She had fallen, not because her own courage or strength had failed her, but because she had been foully betrayed by those who placed the satisfaction of their immense egotism before their country's honor; she was burning with desire to vindicate herself before the nations of the earth, and to reconquer her place among them. No wonder, then, that she hailed with joy the first symptoms shown by the Americans of resistance to British rule.

On the part of the colonists, however, there was no feeling of real sympathy uniting them with the French. Eng-lish still at heart, though for the moment fighting against England, the descendants of the Puritans looked with a half disdain upon what they considered the light and frivolous French. More than this, the war terminated by the treaty of 1763 had left many bitter memories:—Indian massacres, and midnight atrocities, all laid at the door of England's historic foe. Moreover, the disinterestedness of her offers of help seemed to the colonists at the beginning to be open to question. Had France for a moment shown signs of a desire to regain her footing upon the western continent, there was not an American but would have scorned her proffered services. Upon this point, indeed, they were one—their "Hinterland." For this they would fight, and in regard to this they would make no compromises.

Perhaps even better than they themselves, France understood the instinctive attitude of the Americans towards their own continent, and her first care was to assure the colonists that in case she should decide to come to their assistance it would be with no intention of laying claim to any part of the New World. (See **Recommendations to Bonvotdoir,** by the Comte de Vergennes—"Canada," he says, "is with them le point jalotux; they must be made to understand that we do not think of it in the least.")⁵

But however great her interest in the struggle, however enthusiastic her admiration of the heroic part played by the colonists, she was yet far from desiring to enter prematurely into the contest by openly espousing their cause at the moment. As a people, she might give them her moral support, but as a body politic she was forced to act with extreme caution, for not only was the treasury exhausted, the army and navy demoralized,[6] but above all the irresolute character of the young Monarch, his settled aversion to war, his abhorrence of insurrection, were almost insurmountable obstacles which had to be overcome before the French Government could attempt to send aid to the insurgent colonies.

The interests of France were, however, too deeply involved to permit the ministry to look on as idle spectators, and early in 1775 Bonvouloir had been sent to Philadelphia with secret instructions to sound the attitude of Congress in regard to France, but bearing positive orders to compromise the Government in no wise by rousing in the colonies hope of assistance.

As soon, however, as it became known that a kindly interest was felt for them by France, the secret committee of Congress began to investigate how far this interest could be relied upon for the benefit of their cause[7].

Early in the summer of 1776, Silas Deane was sent to Paris with a commission to secure the urgently needed mili-tary supplies and also to enlist foreign officers, especially engineers, for the war. He was received at Versailles in a friendly manner, and though no open support was given him, a secret agent of the Government was pointed out, and Deane was made to understand that there would be no interference with any proceedings that might go on between them. The direct result of

---

5   H. Doniol, Vol. I, p. 129.

6   Sec Turgors Address to the King; Bancroft, Vol. IV, p. 369.

7   See Durand's New Material for the History of the American Revolution, p. 6.

these negotiations was that during the spring of 1777, ammunition, guns, and the complete military equipment for twenty-five thousand men, amounting in value to no less than five million French livres, were landed on the American coast. The joy of the colonists knew no bounds, for by this time they were not only practically destitute of all munitions of war, but they were quite without means of securing them. The timely arrival of these immense cargoes permitted the vigorous carrying on of the campaign of 1777 which ended in the decisive victory of Saratoga. This proved the turning-point of the war. Emboldened by the success of our arms, Congress began forming plans for urging upon the French Government the open espousal of our cause. The delicate mission of securing this recognition was entrusted to Franklin, while the entire hope of our ultimate victory over the British rested with the success of his endeavors.

Notwithstanding the victory which terminated the campaign of 1777, the winter that followed was in reality the darkest period of the war. While the fate of the new nation hung in the balance at the court of Versailles, the forlorn remnant of the American Army, half-clothed and half-fed, was wintering under the command of Washington at Valley Forge, and the incompetent Congress, unable to supply men or money to the public cause, was exerting what influence it possessed in undermining the authority of Washington, the one man who in this time of general depression, by his quiet strength and unwavering faith, was able to infuse hope and courage into the hearts of the forlorn upholders of the cause of independence. Had Congress possessed the power, it would have supplanted him in command by the mock hero of Saratoga, the scheming Gates, who had succeeded in having himself named to the command of the forces of the north, at the moment when the scattered divisions of the army under Herkimer, Schuyler, and Arnold, had been able to unite their forces and entrap Burgoyne at Saratoga. The subsequent career of Gates in the South showed him to have been a man of unprincipled character and devoid of real ability, so that the danger to the country was very great. Fortunately Congress did not possess this power and Washington remained Commander-in-Chief of the American Army[8].

---

8 For an account of the cabal formed for replacing Washington in his command, see Fiske's American Revolution, Vol. II, p. 32.

With the spring, however, fresh hope came to the budding nation. The winter passed so painfully at Valley Forge had not been spent in vain; the men had grown used to camp life, and under the excellent discipline of Baron von Steuben, they had become the nucleus of a formidable army that was ready to take the field. With the spring, too, came news of the alliance which Franklin had been able to consummate at the Court of Versailles. Already victory seemed assured for the cause of independence. Not only had the colonies become more united in interest and better trained in the art of war, but England found herself confronted by a new and formidable enemy which gave to the war a different aspect. Millions of money at once began to pour into the treasury of the new nation, while armies and fleets were sent to help fight her battles and to guard her coasts. From this time forward, the aid rendered by France was openly avowed; no more mystery was necessary, and the results are too generally known to need dwelling upon here. It is sufficient to recall that after two more years of fighting, came the brilliant victory of De Grasse over the English fleet off Cape Henry, at the moment when Cornwallis had taken up his position on the peninsula of Yorktown, confidently relying upon the English supremacy of the seas; that later through the masterful tactics of Washington, aided by the genius of Rochambeau, the combined American and French forces were rapidly moved southward, cutting off the retreat of Cornwallis; and two years later, that peace was declared which deprived England of her American Colonies.

The very important role played by France in this gigantic drama never has received due recognition even in her own annals. Its significance was dwarfed by the stupendous events which followed so soon after, known as the French Revolution.

Naturally England has taken little public notice of French achievement in this war; like all nations, she dwells upon her victories more than upon her defeats, so that the entire subject of the War of American Independence has received scant attention from her historians.

The conspicuous lack of recognition among Americans of the value of French aid is certainly less pardonable. Real gratitude is so rare and fine a quality that it is hardly to be expected from aggregates of mankind, yet from America, indeed, we have the right to expect it, for she is a country preeminently based upon high ideals. Her children always have been taught to sound the praises of her national heroes, especially those of 76 who won for us liberty and independence. But shall America stop here and refuse to tell them the whole truth about our national existence? There" can be no danger to the patriotism of our children in giving them a correct idea of what we as a nation owe to France, for the actions of our own heroes can lose none of their lustre by a generous recognition of what we owe others.

In giving the rising generation a true understanding of what we as Americans owe the nation that stood by us in our time of trial, we shall be training them to an ideal higher than that of mere patriotism, namely, that of justice.

A decided step in this direction was taken a few years ago, when Theodore Roosevelt, then President of the United States, caused a statue of the French General Rochambeau to be erected at Washington and in so doing opened the way to a more general recognition of a great historical truth.

In 1917, the arrival upon our shores of the Allied Missions has struck a new note in our national consciousness. Resentment towards England has died away long ago and warm friendship has taken its place. For France nothing but the most enthusiastic admiration exists, and men's minds everywhere are opening to a new realization of the part that that country has always played in the grand epic of human emancipation.

But America's debt of gratitude to France never can be fully repaid until she has been brought to consider the claims of the one Frenchman who was the first of all Europeans to recognize the importance of the uprising among the colonists. This is no other than Caron de Beaumarchais, the secret agent to whom Silas Deane had been directed by the French Ministers in 1776. That his claim to the gratitude of Americans has so long been neglected is due to a complexity of causes, chief of which is the fact that not until 1886 were the archives of the French Government touching this period, given to the public[9]. Among these archives may be found the complete outline of the help given by France to America during the period which elapsed between the arrival of Deane in 1776 and the open recognition by France of American Independence in 1778, all of which aid passed through the hands of Beaumarchais. After a careful study of these documents it must be conceded that to him belongs the credit of having roused the French Government to a realization of the honorable part it might play in the great conflict. Long before the historic dinner at Metz, where Lafayette conceived his chivalrous design, before even the Signing of the Declaration of Independence, Beaumarchais had planned and worked out the details of the aid to be rendered by France and then literally had forced the cautious and conservative government of France into acquiescence with his plans.

The earliest authentic biography of this remarkable man was from the pen of his ardent admirer and lifelong friend, Gudin de la Brenellerie. It was intended to be prefixed to the first edition of the works of Beaumarchais which appeared in 1809. This biography was suppressed, however, for Gudin, it would seem, was an old philosopher of the eighteenth century who had outlived his time. In writing the life of his friend, the spirit of freedom revived in his breast. The Declaration of Independence called from him imprudent outbursts of enthusiasm. Almost every page gave expression to the ideas that filled men's minds in the days before the Revolution. In 1809 such expressions were not only out of place: they were dangerous. Madame de Beaumarchais felt that it was wiser to suppress the work, dreading lest it should bring upon her family the hostile attention of the emperor. It was therefore set aside. Although many of its pages after-wards appeared in the remarkable life of Beaumarchais by Monsieur de Loménie, it was not until many years later that Gudin's work as a whole was given to the public[10].

By far the most important of the many lives of Beaumarchais, which have ap-

---

9 H. Doniol, La Participation de la France dant l'établissement des Etas-Unis, Paris, 86-'92, in five folio volumes,

10 Histoire de Beaumarchais, by Paul Philippe Gudin de la Brenellerie. Edited by Maurice Tourneux, Paris, 1888.

Beaumarchais and the War of American Independence 15

peared, is the Study by Louis de Lo-ménie, from unedited letters and documents preserved in the family, which was published in 1855. In this work Beaumar-chais's participation in the cause of American independence was first made known to the French public. It is incomplete, however, because in 1855 the Secret Archives of the French Government relative to this period, were not accessible. The German biography by Bettleheim published in 1886, lays more emphasis upon the importance of Beaumarchais's aid in the War of American Independence than has come from any other recent writer. But it, too, is only fragmentary. In 1887 came the master work by E. Lintilhac—which is chiefly, however, a critical analysis of Beaumarchais's literary productions, barely touching upon his other activities, and making no attempt to penetrate his political career. This is natural; recognition of the services rendered by Beaumarchais in the War of Independence rightly should come first from America, since it was primarily America that was benefited by those services.

But until recently the Hon. John Bigelow is the only American who has rendered anything like adequate justice to the merits of this great Frenchman in advocating our cause. During the. years that Mr. Bigelow was minister to France, he made the acquaintance of descendants of Beaumarchais and was given free access to family papers dealing with the subject. In 1870, in an article entitled Beaumarchais, The Merchant read before the New York Historical Society, Mr. Bigelow says: "To him (Beaumarchais) more than to any other person belongs the credit of making Louis XVI comprehend the political importance of aiding the Colonies in their struggle with Great Britain; he planned and executed the ingenious scheme by which the aid was to be extended; he sent the first munitions of war and supplies which the Colonists received from abroad and he sent them too, at a time when, humanly speaking, it was reasonably certain that without such aid from some quarter, the Colonists must have succumbed. He, too, was mainly responsible for sending them forty or fifty superior officers, some of whom not only rendered incalculable service in the field, but a still greater service, perhaps, in enlisting for the Colonies the sympathies of continental Europe."

In making a close survey of the part played by Beaumarchais in the cause of American independence, it would seem that we as a nation owe to him not only a debt of gratitude, but also one of reparation[11]. Surely this is not because we are incapable of gratitude. The young and chivalrous Lafayette, throwing himself heart and soul into our cause, won an undying place in the hearts of the American people. We shall learn, however, that even Lafayette owed something to Beaumarchais.

Universal gratitude is felt also for the inestimable services rendered by Baron von Steuben; and here it is primarily to Beaumarchais that we are indebted for those services. It is easy to give honor where nothing else is required to be paid; neither Baron von Steuben, nor any other officer, received from us money for their services; they did not need to ask it, for the purse of Beaumarchais was ever open to aid the friends of America when other means were wanting; but because Beaumarchais expected tobacco and indigo in return for the several million dollars' worth of ammunition and other supplies which he had furnished the American cause, he was denied all claims to gratitude, although it was his own boundless energy and enterprise that had overcome all obstacles in sending those supplies upon which success depended. More than this, his financial claims were long ignored and he himself was stamped with the character of a dishonest adventurer.

It cannot be denied, however, that Beaumarchais's own character lent itself to misrepresentation. The very bril-liancy and versatility of his genius was a snare to him, while the expansiveness of his nature gave such an air of adventure to his most sober acts, that they often were regarded with suspicion by those whom he most desired to serve. The misunderstandings which arose from these innate qualities were keenly felt by Beaumarchais. Moreover, he early realized that the ministry, while making use of his rare abilities, intended to keep him in the background.

---

11   A similar debt of reparation is still owed by America to the memory of Silas Deane. As his part in the great conflict was closely interwoven with that of Beaumarchais, the suspicions that fell upon one were necessarily shared by the other—and both rested under the same Impossibility of justifying themselves before the world. The publication of the French archives has done for both men what they could not do for themselves, and though the treatment accorded Silas Deane by Congress drove him to such despondency that he subsequently lost faith in the American cause, no shadow rests upon the patriotism which inspired his early efforts in that cause. Charlemagne Tower, Jr., in his The Marquis de La Fayette in the American Revolution has given to the public all the essential documents which show the claim to gratitude which Silas Deane has upon the American people

Beaumarchais was neither willing to forego recognition nor resigned to the obscurity in which he was left. The gay philosophy of his nature enabled him to laugh at his misfortunes, although it was only as he himself has said through his creation, Figaro, "that he might not be obliged to weep/' Stung to the quick on finding himself thrust aside in the midst of his almost superhuman exertions in the American cause, he turned for relief to lighter matters and found distraction by writing **Le Mariage de Figaro,** the gayest comedy perhaps ever put upon the stage, and one so full of political significance that it was condemned by the authorities, though in the end he succeeded in bringing it before the public, in spite of the King and his ministers. Such a man was Beaumarchais, that it is no wonder that he failed to receive recognition for his serious labors, or that many people refused to believe him in earnest at all. If his own nation regarded him somewhat in the light of an adventurer, surely the men of the New World, bred in stern necessity, accustomed to deal only with hard facts and unyielding realities, may be judged with less severity if they failed in comprehending the true nature of their benefactor and friend. He himself was the first to forgive them, and no spirit of enmity or personal resentment was ever to be observed in his subsequent attitude towards them. To the end he called them "My friends, the free men of America."

When, during the French Revolution, Beaumarchais, finding himself an exile, reduced to a beggarly garret in an obscure quarter of Hamburg while his wife, his daughter, and his sisters were languishing in a French prison, his property confiscated, and his credit ruined, addressed a final desperate appeal to the American people, begging for justice, not a voice was raised in his favor. Since Robert Morris, the Philadelphia financier, was allowed to remain for years in a debtor's prison, it is not surprising that little interest was roused by the claims of a foreigner, in whose existence even, people refused seriously to believe.

Tardy and very partial justice was at last rendered the heirs of Beaumarchais by the United States Government, when in 1885 their claims were settled by the payment of a portion of the debt owed to him; but as a personality he still remains unknown to us. The study which follows aims at portraying this unusual character in its true colors; it does not attempt to make of him an ideal hero, faultless and blameless; but it endeavors to show him as he was, full of violent contrasts, of limitless resource and energy, raising constantly about him a whirlwind of opposition, loved by his family and friends, hated by those whom he outstripped in the rapidity of his advancement, plunging from one gigantic enterprise into another, never at rest; ready at all times to come to the aid of distress which presented itself in any form, entering with sympathetic interest into the minutest details, always with time for everything, but above all, with persistent determination demanding justice, and in the pursuit of this aim, rousing the antagonism of all classes; attacking fearlessly time-honored institutions,—literary, social and judicial,—so that he becomes one of the most powerful undermining forces which finally brought about the total collapse of the old regime.

In his adventurous career, the part which he played in the War of American Independence forms but an incident. Though the primary object of this book is to show what that part really was, yet it is necessary to study his life and character in order to understand why Beaumarchais was interested in our cause, and how it came about that he was able to render us such signal service.

CHAPTER I
BEAUMARCHAIS
AND THE WAR OP AMERICAN INDEPENDENCE

Formed by nature for fun and frolic, the little "Pierrot" as he was called had the merriest possible childhood. His mother gentle, loving, and indulgent shielded her favorite from his father, who at times was somewhat stern, while his elder sisters petted and spoiled him, and the younger ones entered heartily into his games and pastimes. Two of the girls were younger than he, the one nearest his age, Julie, was his favorite, and was also the one who most resembled him by her talents and her native wit and gaiety. It is from her pen that we have most of the details of their early life. In some of her youthful rhymes Julie tells us how "Pierrot" commanded a band of little good-for-nothings, roving about either to plunder the larder of Margot, the cook, or returning at night to disturb the slumber of the peaceful inhabitants of the rue St. Denis. Again in inharmonious verse she recounts how—

"*Upon* an *incommodiouss seat*
Arranged in *form* of a *pagoda*
Caron presents *a* magistrate,
By his *huge* wig *and* linen *collar*
Each one *pleads* with *might* and *main,*
Before that judge inexorable
That nothing *will* appease,
Whose only *pleasure* is *to* rain
Upon his *clients* ever *pleading*
Blows of *fist* and *tongs* and *shovel;*
And the *hearing* never *ends,*
Till wigs *and* bonnets *roll* away
In dire *confusion* and *disorder.*"

But it must not be thought that the elder Caron approved of too much levity. Although he was himself witty and gifted with a keen literary and artistic sense, he was above all A serious man with an earnest purpose in life. He was descended from Huguenot ancestors who had managed to live in France after the revocation of the Edict of Nantes, although they no longer possessed a legal existence. Their religious exercises were performed in caves or dark woods or in some desert spot. Here their marriages were solemnized by wandering ministers. The grandparents of Pierre-August, Daniel Caron and Marie Fortain, had been thus united, but their son, Andre-Charles Caron, shortly before his marriage with Louise Picheon in 1722, abjured his faith and joined himself to the Catholic Church. He retained, however, his Calvinistic character.

Andre-Charles Caron, like his father, was a watchmaker by profession. He was one of those exquisitely skilled French workmen who had done so much for the advancement of science in their own country, and who, when driven into exile, made the fortune of the people among whom they sought refuge, notably the Swiss. Not content with the exercise of his profession alone, the penetrating mind of Andre-Charles Caron led him into extensive scientific investigations so that he came to be looked upon as an authority in many branches of mechanics.

At ten years of age the young Pierre-August was sent by his father to a professional school at Alfort, where he learned the rudiments of Latin, but three years later his father brought him home intent on his becoming a watch-maker.

In the years that followed there was a period of stress and storm during which father and son wrestled for mas-tery. Always when the latter worked he showed a dexterity of touch, an ingenuity of invention which astonished the father; but, on the other hand, his escapades away from home were the despair of the stern watchmaker. The young Caron, full of wit, of song, skillful in tricks and gay of humor, attracted a following of youths whose tendencies were toward a loose life and low morals.

For five long years the struggle continued between the father and his brilliantly gifted son. Promises of amend-ment on the one hand and paternal pardon on the other had led to nothing. Finally, since remonstrance proved in vain, the elder Caron resorted to sterner measures: he turned his son into the street and closed his doors against him. He left open to the boy, nevertheless, one way of return. Friends of the family in secret communication received the lad, who soon showed a sincere desire to be restored to the good graces of his father. The Père Caron, at first inexorable, at length relented so far as to write the following letter, which is still in existence:

"I have read and re-read your letter. M. Cottin has shown me the one which you have written to him. They seem to me wise and reasonable. The sentiments which you therein express would be entirely to my taste if it were in my power to believe them durable, for I suppose that they possess a degree of sincerity with which I should be satisfied. But your great misfortune consists in having entirely lost my confidence; nevertheless, the friendship and esteem which I entertain for the three respectable friends whom you have employed, the gratitude which I owe them for their kindness to you, force from me my consent in spite of myself, although I believe there are four chances to one against your fulfilling your promises. From this, you will judge the irreparable stain upon your reputation if you again force me to drive you away.

"Understand then thoroughly the conditions upon which you will be allowed to return; . . . I require full and entire submission to my will and a marked respect in words, actions, and expression of countenance; do not forget that unless you employ as much art to please me as you have shown in gaining my friends, you hold nothing, absolutely nothing, and you have only worked to your harm. It is not simply that I wish to be obeyed and respected, but you shall anticipate in everything that which you imagine will please me.

"In regard to your mother, who has twenty times in the past fortnight implored me to take you back, I will put off to a private conversation on your return what I have to say to make you thoroughly understand all the affection and solicitude which you owe to her. Here then are the conditions of your return:

"First,—you shall neither make nor sell, nor cause to be made or sold, directly or indirectly, anything which is not for my account; and you shall succumb no more to the temptation of appropriating to yourself anything, even the smallest matter, above that which I give you. You shall receive no watch to be repaired under any pretext whatever, or for any friend, no matter whom, without notifying me; you shall never touch anything without my express permission—you shall not even sell an old watch key without accounting for it to me.

"Second,—you shall rise at six o'clock in the summer and at seven in the winter and you shall work till suppertime without repugnance at whatever I give you to do; I do not propose that you shall employ the faculties which God has given you, except to become celebrated in your profession. Remember that it is shameful and dishonorable to be the last and that if you do not become the first in your profession, you are unworthy of any consideration; the love of so beautiful a calling should penetrate your heart, and be the unique occupation of your mind.

"Third,—you shall take your suppers always at home, and shall not go out evenings; the suppers and evenings abroad are too dangerous for you, but I consent that you dine Sundays and holidays with your friends, on condition that I know always to whom you are going and that you are absolutely never later than nine o'clock. And furthermore I exhort you never to ask permission contrary to this article and I advise you not to take it to yourself.

"Fourth,—you shall abandon totally your *maudite musique,* and above all the company of idle people. I will not suffer any of them. The one and the other have brought you to what you are. Nevertheless, in consideration of your weakness, I permit the violin and the flute, but on the express condition that you never use them except after supper on working days, and never during the day; and you also never shall disturb the repose of the neighbors, or my own.

"Fifth,—I shall avoid as far as possible sending you on errands, but in cases where I shall be obliged to do so, re-member that above everything else I shall accept no poor excuses for your being late. You know in advance how much this article is revolting to me.

"Sixth,—I will give you your board and eighteen livres a month which will serve for your expenses and little by little enable you to pay your debts. It would be too dangerous for your character and very improper in me to count with you the price of your work and require you to pay me board. If you devote yourself as you should, with the greatest zeal to the improvement of my business, and if by your talents you procure me more, I will give you a fourth part of the profits of all that comes to me through you. You know my way of thinking; you have experienced that I never allow myself to be surpassed in generosity; merit therefore that I do more for you than I promise; but remember that I give nothing for words, that I accept only actions.

"If my conditions suit you—if you feel strong enough to execute them in good faith, accept them and sign your acceptance at the bottom of this letter which you shall return to me; in that case assure M. Paignon of my sincere esteem and of my gratitude; say to him that I shall have the honor of seeing him and of asking him to dinner to-morrow, so dispose yourself to return with me to take the place which I was very far from believing you would occupy so soon, and perhaps never."

Beneath is written:

"Monsieur, very honored, dear father;—I sign all your conditions in the firm desire to execute them with the help of the Lord; but how sadly all this recalls to me a time when such laws and such ceremonies were unnecessary to engage me to do my duty! It is right that I suffer the humiliation that I have justly merited, and if all this, joined to my good conduct, may procure for me and merit entirely the return of your good graces and of your friendship, I shall be only too happy. In faith of which, I sign all that is contained in this letter.

A. Caron, fils"

During the three years which followed the young man's return to his father's house he made such rapid progress in the art of watchmaking that we find him in 1753 making his first appearance in public in the defense of an escapement for watches of which he claimed to be the inventor.

In the December number of **Le Mercure** of that year, the following letter was published, which needs no commentary to show how thoroughly his father's conditions had been understood by the youthful genius and with what serious purpose he had set to work.

"I have read, Monsieur," he says, "with the greatest astonishment, in your September number, that M. Lepaute, watchmaker to the Luxembourg, there announces as his invention, a new escapement for watches and clocks which he says he has the honor of presenting to the King and to the Academy.

"It is of too much importance to me in the interests of truth and of my reputation to permit him to claim this in vention by remaining silent on the subject of a breach of faith.

"It is true that on the 23rd of July last, in the joy of my discovery I had the weakness to confide this escapement to M. Lepaute, allowing him to make use of it in a clock which M. de Julienne had ordered of him, and whose interior he assured me would be examined by no one, because of the arrangement for winding of his own invention, and he alone had the key to the clock.

"But how could I imagine that M. Lepaute would ever undertake to appropriate to himself this escapement which it will be seen I confided to him under the seal of secrecy?

"I have no desire to take the public by surprise, and I have no intention to attempt to range it on my side by this simple statement of my case; but I earnestly beg that no more credence be extended to M. Lepaute than to me, until the Academy shall have decided who is the author of the new escapement. M. Lepaute evidently wishes to avoid all explanation, for he declares that his escapement resembles mine in no way; but from the announcement which he makes, I judge that it is entirely conformable to it in principle.

"Should the commissioners which the Academy names discover a difference it will be found to proceed merely from some fault in his construction, which will help to expose the plagiarism.

"I will not here give any of my proofs; our commissioners must receive them in their first form; therefore whatever M. Lepaute may say or write against me, I shall maintain a profound silence, until the Academy is informed and has decided.

"The judicious public will be so good as to wait until then; I hope this favor from their equity, and from the pro-tection which they have always given the arts. I dare flatter myself, Monsieur, that you will be kind enough to insert this letter in your next issue.

"Caron, son, watchmaker, rue 'St. Denis, near Sainte-Catherine, Paris, November 15th, 1753."

Two days before the writing of this letter the ardent young inventor had addressed a lengthy petition to the Royal Academy of Sciences, in which the following passage occurs, permitting us to judge how completely watchmaking had become, as the father had hoped, the sole occupation of his son's mind. He says: "Instructed by my father since the age of thirteen in the art of watchmaking, and animated by his example and counsels to occupy myself seriously with the perfecting of the art, it will not be thought surprising that from my nineteenth year, I have endeavored to distinguish myself therein, and to merit the public esteem. Escapements were the first object of my reflections. To diminish their defects, simplify and perfect them, became the spur which excited my ambition. . . . But what sorrow for me if M. Lepaute succeeds in taking from me the honor of a discovery which the Academy would have crowned! I do not speak of the calumnies which M. Le-paute has written and circulated against my father and me, they show a desperate cause and cover their author with confusion. It is sufficient for the present that your judgment, Gentlemen, assures to me the honor which my adversary wishes to take from me, but which I hope to receive from your equity and from your insight.

Caron, fils

At Paris, November 13th, 1758"

The following February, two commissioners were appointed to investigate the matter. In the registry of the Royal Academy of Sciences, under the date of February 23rd, 1754, a lengthy report is given, a short extract from which will suffice to show the results of the investigation.

"We therefore believe that the Academy should regard M. Caron as the true inventor of the new escapement and that M. Lepaute has only imitated the invention; that the escapement of the clock presented to the Royal Academy on the 4th of August by Lepaute, is a natural consequence of the escapement for watches of M. Caron; that in its application to clocks, this escapement is inferior to that of Grabain, but that it is in watches the most perfect that has been produced, although it is the most difficult to execute."

Signed, "Camus and de Montigny."

"The Academy has confirmed this judgment in its assemblies of the 20th and the 23rd of February. In consequence of which I have delivered to M. Caron the present certificate with a copy of the report, conformable with the deliberations of March 2nd at Paris."

This, March 4, 1754—

Signed, "Grand-Jean de Fouchy, Perpetual Secretary of the Royal Academy of Sciences,"

This lawsuit from which the young watchmaker issued triumphant, proved for him a valuable piece of advertising, for it gained him the attention of the king himself who happened to have a passion for novel devices in time-pieces. It was not long before the young Caron received an order from His Majesty to make for him a watch having the new escapement.

In a letter to a cousin in London dated July 31st, 1754, less than five months after receiving the certificate, he writes:

"I have at last delivered the watch to the King by whom I had the happiness to be recognized at once, and who remembered my name. His Majesty ordered me to show the watch to all the noblemen at the levée and never was artist received with so much kindness. His Majesty wished to enter into the minutest details of my invention. The watch in a ring for Madame de Pompadour is only four lines in diameter; it was very much admired although it is not entirely finished. The King asked me to make a repeater for him in the same style. All the noblemen present followed the example of the king and each wishes to be served first. I have also made a curious little clock for Madame Victoire in the style of my watches; the King wished to make her a present of it. It has two dials, and to whatever side one turns, the hours always can be seen.

"Remember, my dear cousin, that this is the young man whom you have taken under your protection and that it is through your kindness that he hopes to become a member of the London Society."

Even as late as June 16th, 1755, the ambition of the young watchmaker had not extended itself as is clearly shown in a letter addressed to Le Mercure by the young horloger du roi as he now styles himself. In this letter he modestly defends himself against the envy which his success has awakened. He writes:

"Monsieur, I am a young artist who has only the honor of being known to the public by a new escapement for watches which the Academy has crowned with its approbation and of which the journals have spoken a year ago. *This success fixes me to the state of watchmaker, and I limit my whole ambition to acquiring the science of my art.* I never have thrown an envious eye upon the productions of others of my profession, but it is with great impatience that I see others attempting to take from me the foundation which by study and work I have acquired. It is this heat of the blood, which I very much fear age will never correct, that made me defend with so much ardor the just pretentions which I had to the invention of my escapement when it was contested eighteen months ago. Will you allow me to reply to certain objections to my escapement which in numerous writings have been made public? It is said that the use of this escapement renders it impossible to make flat watches, or even small ones, which if it were true would make the best escapement known very unsatisfactory.

After giving numerous technical details the young watchmaker terminates thus: "By this means I make watches as thin as may be desired, thinner even than have before been made, without in the least diminishing their good quality. The first of these simplified watches is in the hands of the king. His Majesty has carried it for a year and is well satisfied. If these facts reply to the first objection, others reply equally to the second. I had the honor to present to Madame de Pompadour a short time ago a watch in a ring, which is only four lines and a half in diameter and a line less a third in thickness between the plates. To render this ring more convenient I contrived in place of a key a circle which surrounds the dial plate bearing a tiny projecting hook. By drawing this hook with the finger nail about two thirds of the circuit of the dial the watch is wound up and goes thirty hours. Before taking it to her I watched this ring follow exactly for five days the second hand of my chronometer; thus in making use of my escapement and my construction, excellent watches can be made as thin and as small as may be desired.

"I have the honor to be, etc.,

Car on, fils, horloger du roi."

Although the vision of the young man was still hemmed in by the walls of his father's shop, yet his ardent spirit was eager for flight and was waiting only for opportunity to test its powers. He was now twenty-three years of age; the unparalleled success which had attended his efforts had taught even the stern father the need of a wider field for the genius which had so easily outstripped him in his own calling. Satisfied now with the solid foundation in character which his own hand had helped to lay he had no desire to stand in the way of his son's advancement. As not infrequently happens, it was a woman's hand that opened the door and liberated the captive. Speaking of this period, his friend Gudin says: "Attracted by the celebrity of his academic triumph, a beautiful woman brought a watch to his father's shop, either to have it repaired, or perhaps with the design of meeting the young artist of whom so much was said. The young man solicited the honor of returning the watch as soon as he had repaired the disorder, and this event, which seemed so commonplace, changed the purpose of his life and gave it a new meaning.

"The husband of this woman was an old man possessed of a very small office at court, whose age and infirmities almost incapacitated him for the performance of his duties, he therefore sought to pass them on to the young Caron."

Here indeed was an opening which, if embraced, would lead him into a world wholly outside that by which heretofore he had been surrounded. It meant for him opportunity. Instantly all the latent desires within him surged into consciousness. Springing with joy from the low bench of his father's dimly lighted shop, the youthful genius cast forever aside his workman's frock and with one bound entered the service of the king, becoming an inmate of the vast and splendid palace of Versailles.

November 9, 1755, a warrant was issued in the name of Louis XV, King of France from which the following is an extract:

"Great Stewards of France, high stewards and ordinary stewards of our household, masters and controllers of our pantry and account room, greetings! Upon good and praiseworthy report which has been made to us of the person of M. Pierre-August Caron, and his zeal in our service, we have this day appointed him and by these presents, signed with our hand do appoint him to the office of one of our ***clerc-controleurs*** of the pantry of our household, vacant by the dismission of Pierre-August Franquet, last possessor thereof, that he may have and exercise, enjoy and use, the honors, authorities, prerogatives, privileges, liberties, salary, rights, etc.

"Given at Versailles under the seal of our secret,

Louis."

The exchange being thus officially made, Pierre-August Franquet, the aged man in question, ceded his office, and in return was to receive a yearly pension which was guaranteed by the elder watchmaker. Although this office was too insignificant to admit its possessor to the dignity of bearing a title of nobility, yet certain it is that in his own estimation at least, the brilliant young contrôleur of the pantry was already a member of the aristocracy and with the same ardor which he had shown at watchmaking, he set about acquiring at once, and to perfection, all the external marks of one born to that station.

His duties as contrôleur clerc d' office **were not arduous; he was one of sixteen similar** contrôleurs who served the king's table, four at a time, alternating quarterly. His duty was to walk in grand livery, his sword by his side, in the long procession which preceded the king's meat; when arrived at the table, he took the platter and placed it before the king. Ample time was thus left him to develop those graces of mind and of person which nature had so lavishly bestowed upon him. For the first time he began to feel the lack of that classical education which had been denied him in his youth. The practical training which he had acquired under his father's roof enabled him, however, readily to turn the force of his intellect in this new direction, so that in an incredibly short time he acquired such a knowledge of literature, grammar, geography, history, and geometry as served for the basis of the important literary work he was afterward to accomplish.

Amongst the vast collection of manuscripts from the pen of Beaumarchais left after his death, M. de Loménie discovered very many belonging to this period which show that the young contrôleur of the pantry already was exercising himself in the art of writing and that from the first he formed the habit of noting as he read such passages as struck him forcibly, to which he freely added impressions of his own.

But the many-sided nature of the young man did not permit him to indulge exclusively his taste for study. The gay world into which he had entered enlisted much of his time and talents although it never absorbed them. It gave him the opportunity of cultivating his rare social gifts which he soon learned to display to advantage. As soon as Beaumarchais appeared at Versailles, to quote Gudin, "The ladies were struck with his high stature, the elegance of his form, the regularity of his features, his vivid and animated countenance, the assurance of his look, with that dominating air which seemed to elevate him above all his surroundings, and, in a word, with that involuntary ardor which illuminated him at their approach." But he adds, "Before going farther let us observe that it was in the work-shop of his father that his soul was made strong and inaccessible to vice or adversity. If he had been born in luxury or grandeur it would have been softened like wax in the rays of the sun."

Less than two months after relinquishing his duties at court, Pierre-August Franquet died suddenly of apoplexy leaving his widow a considerable fortune. Before the year was out she consoled herself by marrying the brilliant young contrôleur, although she was six years his senior. Thus it would seem that the young man was at last settled in his career, having a beautiful wife who idolized him, and a sufficient fortune at his disposal. Their married happiness, however, was of short duration. In less than a year she was attacked by typhoid fever and died after a short sickness, although attended by four of the best physicians of the capital.

Gudm, in speaking of her sudden death, says that Beaumarchais was at that time so inexperienced in the ways of the world and so grieved at the loss of his wife that he allowed the term permitted by law to expire before he thought of taking steps to secure to himself the succession to his wife's property, so that after her death he was re-duced to the small income from his office at court; and it would seem that he never gained from this connection any material advantage except his footing at court and the name of Beaumarchais which he took from a small landed property belonging to his wife and which was in itself a fortune. At twenty-five we find him again free and awaiting eagerly the opportunity to push his fortunes further. He had not long to wait.

We have seen already that Beaumarchais was very fond of music and that according to his father it was this same **_maudite musique_** that had in his early youth brought him so near the brink of ruin. Little did his father dream that this was to become later the means of his son's most rapid advancement.

Gudin says: "He loved music and played upon several instruments, amongst others the harp and the flute. The harp was at that time disdained, but when Beaumarchais applied to it his mechanical knowledge, he perfected it and brought it into vogue.

"Having won a wide celebrity by performances in numerous salons at Paris and

Versailles, the fame of his skill reached the ears of the Princesses of France, who were four in number and who all had a taste for music.

"They desired to hear the young musician, who was only too flattered to be permitted to play before them."

The dignity and charm of his person, his manners which though polished and respectful retained a certain frankness such as rarely penetrated to those august presences, joined to his brilliant talents, completely won for him the favor of Mesdames who insisted upon being permitted to have Beaumarchais for their instructor. From this moment, dates what in a certain sense might almost be called an intimacy between the young man who was so recently seated on his workman's bench behind the window looking out on the rue St. Denis and the four Princesses who were separated by so profound a gulf from even the highest of the nobility in the court about them. It must be understood that these women took no part whatever in the gay licentious existence which disgraced the court of their father, Louis XV. Trained by their mother, the admirable Queen Marie Leczinska, to a life of sincere piety, they passed their time with her in the performance of the really arduous duties of their rank. As queen and daughters of France they belonged to the nation and not to themselves. So long as they performed these duties, the nation cheerfully allowed them the prerogatives of their rank, and the means of gratifying their luxurious tastes.

It was therefore into this august family circle that Beaumarchais entered, to be for several years the central figure of all its pastimes and amusements. Gudin tells us that at this time Mesdames were in the habit of giving a weekly concert at which the King, Queen and Dauphin were present and to which a very select compapy was invited.

These concerts were arranged and superintended by Beaumarchais who seems to have been treated by all with marked favor and esteem. The Dauphin took great pleasure in his company, and on one occasion said of him, "He is the only man who speaks frankly with me." The Dauphin, as is well known, was of an austere nature, and for that reason, doubtless, valued the honest character of Beaumarchais at its true worth.

In dealing with his royal pupils, Beaumarchais exercised great tact and knew how to make them satisfied with themselves and with him. La Harpe says of him: "I have seen few men more favored by nature. His countenance and the tone of his voice were equally ardent, the former illuminated by eyes full of fire; there was as much expression in the accent and the look, as delicacy in the smile, and above all, a kind of assurance which was inspired by a consciousness of power."

These personal gifts, this assurance and skill, even more than the favor of Mesdames, quickly attracted to him the enmity of those whose high birth alone assured them a reception at court. No better idea of the snares set for him, nor of his skill in avoiding them can be given than by quot-' ing a few pages from Gudin.

"One morning as he presented himself to be admitted to Mesdames, one of their women ran to meet him.

" 'Oh my dear friend you are lost, some one has persuaded Mesdames that you are on very bad terms with your father, that he has driven you from his house and that, indignant at the tricks you have played him, he will not see you any more.'

" 'Oh, is that all? Then I do not count myself dead. Don't disturb yourself.' He said this and hurried back to Paris.

You have always wished to see Versailles; I have an excellent opportunity today to show you the palace in detail. Father and son then returned with all possible speed. Beaumarchais took pains that they should be seen by the Princesses at the celebration of the mass, at their dinner, at their promenade, everywhere they were to be found.

"In the evening, still accompanied by his father, whom he left in an antechamber, he entered the apartments of the Princesses; he found them cold, dreamy, embarrassed, and not wanting to look at him, trying to show more annoyance than they really felt.

"The most vivacious of them said to him with impatience, With whom have you been all day?'

'Madame, with my father.'

" His father, Adelaide, that isn't possible, we were told that they had quarreled.'

" I, Madame. I pass my life with him. He is in the ante-room—I have come for your orders; he is waiting for me, if you will deign to see him he will testify to the attachment which I have never ceased to have for him.'"

The Princesses, as Beaumarchais had well guessed, were anxious to see the father of their instructor and he was bidden to enter. As the elder Caron possessed, amongst his other qualities, scarcely less sense of a situation and power of adaptability than his son, he was at once at his ease. His personal dignity and sincerity of manner could not fail to produce a pleasing impression upon the young women who, as we have seen, demanded merit as the ground of their favor, so that in its results this intrigue which was intended to ruin the young man, really served to heighten the esteem in which he was held.

At another time on leaving their apartments, Beaumarchais was intercepted by a crowd of youthful noblemen one of whom had wagered to cover him with confusion. Approaching him, the nobleman said,—to quote from Gudin, "Monsieur, you who are so clever with watches, will you tell me if this is a good one?'

" 'Monsieur,' replied Beaumarchais, looking at the company, 'since I have ceased to work at that trade I have be-come very awkward.'
" 'Ah, Monsieur, do not refuse me.'

" 'Very well, but J warn you that I have lost my art,' Then taking the watch he opened it, raised it in the air feigning to examine it, and suddenly let it fall from that elevation; then, making a profound reverence, he said, 'I warned you, Monsieur, of my extreme awkwardness,' and walked away leaving his provoker to gather up the debris of his watch while the assembly burst into laughter."

But the insults did not stop here.

They became so frequent and their tone grew so malignant that Beaumarchais felt the time had come to put a stop to them. Seriously outraged by a courtier whom Gudin calls the Chevalier du C-he accepted the provocation.

They mounted their horses and rode off to a secluded spot in the woods behind Meudon. In the words of Gudin, "Beaumarchais had the sad advantage of plunging his sword into the bosom of his adversary; but when on withdrawing it he saw the blood issue in a copious stream he was seized with terror and thought of nothing but helping him. He took his handkerchief and attached it as well as he could over the wound, to arrest the flow of blood and to stop fainting.

" 'Save yourself said the fallen man, 'you are lost if any one sees you, if any one learns that it is you who have taken my life.

'You must have help, I will get it for you'—Beaumarchais mounted and rode to Meudon, found a surgeon, and indicating the spot to him, where the wounded man lay, he went off at full gallop to Paris to see what was to be done. His first care was to inform himself if the Chevalier du C still lived. He found that he had been brought to
Paris but that his life was despaired of—he learned that the sick man refused to name the one who had wounded him so seriously.

" 'I have only what I merit,' he said, 'I have provoked All honest man who never gave me any offense, to please people whom I do not esteem,'

"His relatives and friends were not able to draw any other reply from him during the eight days which he lived. He carried the secret to the tomb, leaving to Beaumarchais the regret of having taken the life of a man who proved so generous an enemy.

" 'Ah, young man,9 Beaumarchais said to me one day when I was joking over some duel which was then much talked about, 'you do not know what despair a man feels when he sees the hilt of his sword upon his enemy's breast!' It was then that he related to me this adventure which was still afflicting him, although many years had elapsed since it had taken place. He never spoke of it without grief, and I should probably never have heard of it, if he had not thought it right to make me feel how dangerous it might be to joke about such fatal affairs, the number of which is increased much more by frivolity than by bravery."

It may be well to add, in relation to the death of the Chevalier du C that the protection of Mesdames, who personally interceded with the King, prevented an investigation being made so that Beaumarchais was secure.

But while he was still holding his own in the envious crowd of courtiers at Versailles, his position was in reality far from desirable. Monsieur de Lomenie says: "Having no other resource than the small income from his charge of ***controleur,*** not only was he obliged to put his time gratuitously at the disposal of the Princesses, without speaking of the cost of keeping up appearances, but he even at times found himself under the necessity of proceeding like a great lord, and of making advances for the purchase of costly instruments which they scarcely thought of promptly paying back. Very desirous of enriching himself, he was too clever to compromise his credit by receiving pecuniary recompense, which would have put him in the rank of a mercenary; he preferred to wait for some favorable occasion, when he might obtain a real advantage from his position, reserving the right to say later: 'I have passed four years in meriting the good graces of Mesdames by the most assiduous and most disinterested pains bestowed upon divers objects of their amusements.'

"But Mesdames, like all other women and especially princesses, had sufficiently varied fancies which it was necessary to satisfy immediately. In the correspondence of Mme. du Deffant is the very amusing story of a box of candied* quinces of Orleans, so impatiently demanded by Madame Vic-toire that the King, her father, sent in haste to the minister, M. de Choiseul, who sent to the Bishop of Orleans, who was awakened at three o'clock in the morning to give him, to his great affright, a missive from the King, running as follows:

" 'Monsieur the bishop of Orleans, my daughters wish some *cotignac*; they wish the very small boxes; send some.. If you have none, I beg you ... [in this place in the letter there was a drawing of a Sedan chair, and below] to send immediately into your episcopal city and get some, and be sure that they are the very small boxes; upon which, Monsieur the bishop of Orleans, may God have you in His holy keeping. Louis.' Below in postscriptum is written: 'The sedan chair, means nothing, it was designed by my girls upon the paper which I found at hand.' A courier was immediately dispatched for Orleans. 'The *cotignac*,' says Madame du Deffant, 'arrived the next day, but no one thought anything more of it.'

"It often happened that Beaumarchais received missives that recalled somewhat the history of the *cotignac,* with this difference, that the young and poor master of music, had not, like the bishop of Orleans, a courier at his disposal. Here, for example, is a letter addressed to him by the first lady in waiting of Madame Victoire:

" Madame Victoire has a taste, Monsieur, to play to-day on the tambourine, and charges me to write instantly that you may get her one as quickly as will be possible. I hope, Monsieur, that your cold has disappeared and that you will be able to attend promptly to the commission of Madame. I have the honor of being very perfectly, Monsieur, your very humble servant,
De Boucheman Coustillier.'

"It became necessary instantly to procure a tambourine worthy to be offered to a princess; the next day it was a harp; the day after a flute; and so on and so on."
When the young Beaumarchais had completely exhausted his purse, very thin at that time, he very humbly sent his note to Mme. Hoppen, the stewardess of Mes-

dames, accompanying it with reflections of which the following is a sample :

"I beg you, Madame, to be so good as to pay attention to the fact that I have engaged myself for the payment of 844 livres, not being able to advance them, because I have given all the money that I had, and I beg you not to forget that I am in consequence, absolutely without a sol.

> Besides the   1852 livres
> Madame Victoire owes me   15
> Then for the book bound in morocco with her
> arms and gilded   36
> And for copying the music into said book   36 "
> Total   1939 livres
> Which makes a sum of 80 louis, 19 livres.

"I do not count the cab fares which it cost me to go among the different workmen, who nearly all live in the suburbs, nor for the messages which all this occasioned, because I have never had the habit of making a note of these things or of counting them with Mesdames. Don't forget, I beg you that Madame Sophie owes me five louis; in a time of misery one collects the smallest things.

"You know the respect and attachment which I have for you. I will not add another word."

Four years spent in petty services of this kind was a severe test to the earnestness of purpose of a man fired with lofty ambitions and full of restless energy. Although at times suffering from secret irritation he remained master of himself and steadily refused to compromise his hope of great fortune by yielding to the dictates of present necessities. At last his patience was rewarded in a way worthy of the sacrifices he had made.

There was at this time a celebrated financier, named Paris du Verney, who for years had been organizing a great work, the ***Ecole Militaire,*** actually in existence to-day on the Champs de Mars in Paris, but which Seemed likely to languish at its beginning owing to the lack of Royal recognition.

As Paris du Verney had been the financial manager for Madame de Pompadour, and as he had been protected by her, a settled aversion was directed against him by all the members of the Royal family. The disasters of the Seven Years War had notably diminished the influence of the Marquise so that the ***Ecole Militaire,*** considered as her work was regarded with an evil eye by the people of France. Nothing less than the official recognition of the school by the King's visiting it in person, could lift it out of the disfavor into which it had fallen. But how could that indolent monarch be induced to honor the old financier with a visit? This was the problem that for nine years occupied the mind and heart of Paris du Verney. All his efforts in this regard had however been in vain. The King was indifferent, the Princesses prejudiced; there seemed left no avenue through which approach could be made.

Matters were at this pass when the attention of du Verney was attracted by the young music master of Mesdames, now growing restless under the tedium of his showy but irksome charge. The shrewd mind of du Verney was quick to discover the latent business capacity which lay hidden under the exterior of a gay courtier. He determined to make a final effort for the accomplishment of his project by employing the mediation of the favorite of the Princesses, to whom he promised, if success should crown his efforts, an open pathway to the rapid acquisition of a brilliant and independent fortune.

CHAPTER II

"On dira que l'amour des lettres, des plaisirs, n'exclut point une juste sensibilité dams tout ce qui regarde l'hon neur." Marsolier—"Beaumarchais à Madrid.

Induces the Princesses to Visit the *Ecole* Mitiaire Established by du Verney—First Financial Successes—Certain Great Lords *mis hors du combat*—"The *Frere* Charmcmt"—the Devoted Son—Preparations for Trip to Spain.

PARIS DU VERNEY, who had pushed his way upward from an origin even more obscure than that of Beau-marchais, was a man of wide experience in life, and of rare energy of character.

Although a certain shadow rested upon his name in connection with the protection accorded him by Madame de Pompadour and the management of the Seven Years war, yet no doubt can be entertained of his mastery of the science of finance or of the breadth and liberality of his views.

Clear sighted and keen in business matters, Paris du Verney was at the same time a close observer of men, and one not easily deceived as to their real merits. It was the innate qualities of heart and mind added to the acquired habit of doing thoroughly and well whatever he undertook, that du Verney had detected in the young man of bourgeois extraction, so conspicuous at court, and it was upon him that he now fixed his hopes. In speaking of it later, Beau-marchais says:

"In 1760, M. du Verney, in despair at having employed vainly for the last nine years, every means at his command to engage the Royal family to honor with a visit the Ecole Militaire, desired to make my acquaintance; he offered me his heart, his aid and his credit, if I was able to effect that which everyone had failed to accomplish for him."

It is easy to understand how readily Mesdames were persuaded to confer this much coveted honor upon the old financier, understanding as they very well did that in this way they could repay the years of faithful service of their young protégé.

The joy of du Verney may be readily imagined. His heart overflowed with gratitude toward the one who had done him this great service. It was an event as La Harpe has said, "That brought to the old man's eyes the sweetest tears of his life."

The day for the visit was therefore appointed, and Beau-marchais was permitted the honor of accompanying the distinguished guests. They were received with great pomp and the impression made upon the Princesses was so agreeable, that on their return to Versailles, as had been hoped, the account they gave so stimulated the curiosity of the indolent King, that in a few days he followed the example of his daughters, thus entirely fulfilling the desire of the founder of the school.

Du Verney was not slow on his side in fulfilling his promise to the ardent young man who asked for nothing better than the privilege of learning all that the experienced financier could teach him.

Dating from this moment Beaumarchais entered a new world, where new ideas, new possibilities opened themselves before him. To quote La Harpe again, "Depository of the entire confidence of the old man, charged with the handling of his capital, Beaumarchais learned the science of vast commercial operations and applied himself to it with all the vivacity of an ardent, enterprising, and indefatigable nature."

Speaking of du Verney, Beaumarchais has said, "He initiated me into financial matters of which as everyone knows he had a consummate knowledge; I worked at my fortune under his direction and undertook by his advice a number of enterprises; in several of these he aided me by his capital and credit, in all by his advice."

Of du Verney's feeling for Beaumarchais, we have the following testimony from his own pen.

"Since I have known him and since he has become an intimate in my restricted circle of friends, everything convinces me that he is an upright young man, with an honest soul, an excellent heart, and cultivated mind, which merit the love and esteem of all honest people; proved by misfortune, instructed by adversity, he will owe his advancement if he succeeds to his good qualities alone."

Du Verney also aided Beaumarchais in the acquiring of certain functions at court which gave him a legal claim to his title of nobility. In 1761 he bought for 85,000 francs the very noble but very useless charge of Secretary to the King. An attempt was made afterwards to bring him into a still higher place by securing for him the very important and very lucrative charge of Grand Master of the Waters and Forests of France. M. de Loménie says in speaking of this matter that had it been successful, the whole career of Beaumarchais might have been changed. As it proved, however, so much opposition was aroused by the almost meteoric rapidity with which he had arrived at so great for-tune that for the first time in his life, and notwithstanding the warm recommendations of Mesdames, Beaumarchais was forced to change the direction of his solicitations and to content himself with the less lucrative but even more honorable charge of ***lieutenant*-general *des chasses* aux *bail-liage* et capitainerie *de* la *varenne* du *Louvre.***

For a young man of bourgeois extraction, not yet thirty years of age, his complete transformation had come about with an almost incredible rapidity. The new office, which will be treated in detail later, placed him on the level with the ancient aristocracy of France and gave him a social position which his ever increasing fortune enabled him more and more effectively to support.

Not content, however, with his own rise in the world, he desired to share his fortune with his whole family. We shall soon see him uniting them all under his roof in Paris, but for the moment we must picture him continuing to live at Versailles, and though occupied for the most part with his new business operations, he still has time to superintend, as of old, the pastimes and amusements of the Princesses, as well as to cultivate his rare social gifts. No man ever made a more amiable or a more brilliant figure in a salon. His music, his songs, his jests and repartees, the gaiety and ardor of his nature, made him everywhere a favorite.

Gudin says of him at this period, "He never forgot his old comrades and almost never came to Paris without stay-ing with his father, going to see and embracing his neighbors, and those who had been witnesses of his first efforts. Showing himself as far removed from the silly vanity which blushes at its origin as from the pride which pretends to be what it is not; by his gaiety and affability he made those about him forget the change in his fortune and even at times the superiority of his talents. In the bosom of his family his manners were simple, he was even what one calls a ***bonhomme.***" Characterizing him a little further on, Gudin says, "For frivolous people Beaumarchais was only a man of the world; for the ladies, a man attractive by his figure and his wit, amusing by his talents, his dress, his imagination and a host of amiable adventures such as the gayest and most interesting romance can scarcely furnish; but for the old du Verney he was an excellent citizen, a truly manly genius, zealous for his country, full of liberal ideas, of grand and useful conceptions. He possessed pre-eminently all the talents which form the charm of society, he put into everything a piquant originality which made him more loved and prized than others. In verses or couplets which he composed, there was always a turn, an idea, a striking feature, another would have missed. His conversation, mixed with new ideas, jests, lively but never bitter, unexpected repartee, always founded upon reason, made him singularly attractive.",

It can not be thought surprising that while these amiable and brilliant qualities endeared Beaumarchais to the hearts of his friends, and to the ladies into whose society he came, the effect produced by the same qualities upon men of rank and position, who possessed no such attractions was of a very different nature.

The hatred which his first entry into the service of Mes-dames had so bitterly aroused was now redoubled since the old financier, du Verney, had fixed his affections upon the young plebeian, and had helped him to the amassing of a fortune and the procuring of a high position at court.

This hatred did not hinder these same noblemen from receiving favors from him which is proved by the numerous lawsuits, quarrels, and disasters which came to thwart his career, nearly all of them the result of some debt owed to him, or money not returned of which he demanded restitution.

We shall have occasion in the course of this study to show from innumerable instances that no man was ever more ready to come to an amiable adjustment, or when necessary completely to forgive a debt, but it will be found that this was always on condition that a just and fair statement be admitted first. When this was refused, as in the famous Goezman trial, we shall see that though it be only a question of fifteen louis, Beaumarchais is ready to stake reputation, happiness, fortune, and, as the event proves, his civil existence even, in demonstrating before the whole world that his adversary is completely in the wrong.

To quote Fournier, "These gentlemen who did not wish to accept Beaumarchais as a nobleman, but to whom he had so well proved that at least, the courage was not lacking to be one, had very much more agreeable ways with him, when it was a question of some service to be asked, service of money almost always, but which from lack of restitution made of almost every debtor an enemy."

As an illustration of the arrogance of some of these courtiers who were gentlemen in name only, as well as of the cool assurance of Beaumarchais, Monsieur de Loménie has given a series of letters exchanged apropos of a small debt owed the latter, and contracted at a card table.

It must be stated before going further, that among the peculiarities of Beaumarchais, was a pronounced distaste for any sort of gambling. This trait was the more unusual as gaming was at this period the recognized amusement of all the upper classes while lotteries were recognized by law.

Later Beaumarchais used his influence for the suppression of what he clearly saw to be an institution ruinous to the prosperity of the country. As a young man at Versailles and later at Madrid he was frequently witness of disasters resulting from the chance of a card, and his whole mind turned toward the procuring of more solid pleasures. But to return to the matter of the debt contracted at a card table. M. de Loménie says: "Beaumarchais found himself in 1763 at a ball at Versailles where there was playing. He was standing by a table looking on. A man of quality named M. de Sablières borrowed of him, although he was a complete stranger, thirty-five louis. At the end of three weeks Beaumarchais hearing nothing of the thirty-five louis wrote to the gentleman in question who replied that he would send them the next day, or the day after. Three more weeks passed. Beaumarchais wrote a second time; no reply. He grew impatient and addressed to M. de Sablières the third letter which follows:

" 'Since you have broken the written word which I have received from you, Monsieur, it would be wrong for me to be surprised at the fact of your not replying to my last letter; the one is the natural consequence of the other. This forgetting of yourself does not authorize me to reproach you. You owe me neither any civility, nor any regard. This letter is written only to remind you once more of the debt of thirty-five louis which you have contracted with me at the home of a mutual friend without other title required but the honor of the debt, and that which is due from both of us to the house where we met. Another consideration which is of not less weight is that the money that you owe me has not been taken from me by the chance of a card, but I loaned it to you from my pocket, and perhaps I deprived myself by that of the advantage which it was permitted me to hope, if I had wished to play instead of you.

"'If I am not happy enough to produce upon you by this letter the effect that would be made upon me were I in your place, don't take it amiss that I place between us two a third respectable person, who is the natural judge in similar cases.

" 'I shall await your reply until day after tomorrow. I shall be very happy if you judge by the moderation of my conduct of the perfect consideration with which I have the honor to be—Monsieur, etc.,

De Beaumarchais.'"

See now the reply of M. de Sablières, man of quality addressing Himself to the son of the watchmaker, Caron. Lo-ménie says, "I reproduce literally the letter with the mistakes in spelling and grammar with which it is decorated. [Unfortunately the effect is spoiled by translation.] 'I know that I am unhappy enough to owe you thirty-five louis, and I deny that this can dishonor me when I have the will to pay them back. My manner of thinking, Monsieur, is known, and when I shall no longer be your debtor, I will make myself known to you by terms which will be different from yours. Saturday morning I shall ask a rendezvous in order to acquit myself of the thirty-five louis, and to thank you for the polite things with which you have had the goodness to serve yourself in your letters; I will attempt to reply in the best possible manner and I flatter myself that between now and Saturday you will be good enough to have a better idea of me. Be convinced that twice twenty-four hours will seem very long to me; as to the respectable third, with which you menace me, I respect him but no one could care less for threats, and I care even less about your moderation. Saturday you shall have your thirty-five louis, I give you my word, and I know not whether for my part I shall be happy enough to reply with moderation. While awaiting to acquit myself of all that I owe you, I am, monsieur, as you desire, your very humble. Sablières.'

"This missive announcing not very pacific intentions was replied to by Beaumarchais (who it will be remembered had recently killed a man at a time when the laws against duels were very rigorous) in a letter in which he begins by assurances of having had no intention to wound the honor of that petulant M. de Sablières, and he closes the letter thus: 'My letter explained I have the honor of announcing to you that I will wait at my house all Saturday morning the effect of your third promise; you say you are not happy enough to vouch for your moderation; from the style of your letter it is easy to judge that you are scarcely master of yourself in writing, but I assure you that I shall not exaggerate in any way an evil of which I am not the cause, by losing con-trol of myself, if I can help it. If after these assurances, it is your project to pass the limits of a civil explanation and to push things to their utmost, which I do not wish in the least, you will find me, Monsieur, as firm to repulse an insult as I try to be on my guard against the movement which brings it into being. I have no fear, therefore, to assure you again that I have the honor to be with all possible consideration, Monsieur,

" 'Your very humble, etc.,

" 'De Beaumarchais.

" 'P. S. I keep a copy of this letter as well as of the first, in order that the purity of my intentions may serve to jus-tify me in case of misfortune; but I hope to convince you Saturday that far from hunting a quarrel, no one should make greater effort than I to avoid one. I cannot explain myself in writing.'"

Upon the copy of the same letter is written with the hand of Beaumarchais the following lines which explain the post-scriptum and which treat of the duel with the Chevalier du C. of which we have spoken already. "This happened eight or ten days after my unhappy affair with the Chevalier du C, which affair would have ruined me but for the goodness of Mesdames who spoke with the king. M. de Sablières asked for an explanation of the postscriptum of my letter from Laumur, at whose house I lent him the money, and what is amusing is that this explanation took away all his desire to bring the money himself."

We have chosen this instance among numerous others to show the difficulty of the position in which Beaumarchais found himself placed. Gudin says, "The efforts of envy against him, fortified the character to which nature had given so much energy. He learned to watch unceasingly over himself, to master the impetuosity of his passions, to conserve in the most perilous and unexpected circumstances, a perfect coolness united with the most active presence of mind. Everything which seemed prepared to destroy him turned to his advantage and enabled him to rise superior to circumstances."

It was very soon after acquiring the foundations of a fixed fortune, that Beaumarchais carried into execution the cherished dream of his life, which was to gather all the members of his family under his own roof and to lavish upon them all those comforts of life, in which the limited means of the elder Caron had not permitted them to indulge. His mother was no longer living but there remained his father and two unmarried sisters at home. The elder Caron had, two years before, at his son's request given up his trade of watchmaker, receiving from the latter a lifelong pension and a considerable sum of money to cover certain heavy losses which had come to him in the way of business.

We have formed already the acquaintance of Julie whom Beaumarchais especially loved and who shared with him to the end all the vicissitudes of his career.

Julie is spoken of as charming, witty,.and vivacious; a good musician, speaking Italian and Spanish with fluency, improvising songs and composing verses, "more remarkable by their gaiety than by their poetic value." Later in life she appeared before the public in a serious little volume entitled ***Reflections*** on ***Life,*** or ***Moral*** Considerations ***on*** the ***Value*** of ***Existence,*** but at the present time—1763—the tone of her letters distinctly betokens one not yet disenchanted with the gay world of which her brother formed the center.

The youngest sister of all, Jeanne Marguerite Caron, seems to have received a more brilliant education than the rest. M. de Loménie says of her that, "She was a good musician, playing very well on the harp, that she had a charming voice and more than that she was very pretty. She loved to compose verses like her sister Julie, and without being equally intelligent she possessed the same vivid, gay esprit which distinguished the family. In her infancy and girlhood she was called 'Tonton.' When her brother, now a courtier, had associated Julie with the graceful name of Beaumar-chais, he found an even more aristocratic name for his youngest sister, he called her Mademoiselle de Boisgarnier, and it was under this name that Mlle. Tonton appeared with success in several salons.

"In her correspondence as a girl, Mlle. Boisgarnier appears to us as a small person, very elegant, slightly co-quettish, slightly indolent, somewhat sarcastic, but still very attractive. The whole tone of her letters is that of the ***petite*** bourgeoise, ***of quality, very proud to have for a brother a*** Secretaire ***du*** roi, ***Lieutenant***-general ***des*** chasses***, and in relation to whom she says in one of her letters,*** 'Comment ***se*** gouverne ***la*** petite societé? ***Le*** frère ***charmant*** en ***fait***-il ***toujours*** les délices?"

An older sister, Françoise, already had married a celebrated watchmaker of Paris, named Lépine, with whom the family tie was never broken. Her home served as a place of rendezvous for the scattered members of the family during those cruel years, of which we shall have to speak, when the property of Beaumarchais was seized and he himself degraded from his rights as citizen.

A son of this sister afterwards served as an officer in the American army under the name of "Des Epinières."

The eldest sister of all, Marie-Josèphe, had left her father's house when her brother was a young lad just returned from the school at Alfort. She had married an architect named Guilbert and had settled at Madrid in Spain. She took with her one of the younger sisters, Marie Louise, who continued to live with her there. The two sisters kept a milliner's shop and the younger, Lizette as she was called, became the fiancée of a gifted young Spaniard, Clayico, of whom we shall hear presently from the pen of Beaumarchais himself.

Many years later the elder sister returned to France, a widow without fortune, accompanied by Lizette and two young children. Beaumarchais gave them both a yearly allowance, and at the death of the widow Guilbert, continued to provide for her children whom he gathered under his roof in Paris. Lizette had died some time previously.

Mademoiselle de Boisgarnier married very soon after her brother's return from Spain. She was, however, taken early from her family and friends. She died leaving a daughter who, needless to say, was cared for by her generous uncle, and who later in life owed to him her advantageous settlement and dowry. She seems to have inherited a large share of the family gifts and to have been witty and attractive. In the family circle she went by the name of "the muse of. Orleans," from the city in which she was married and settled.

In estimating the full value of this unusual generosity which, as will be seen, did not show itself in isolated and spasmodic acts, but rather in a constant and inexhaustible stream flowing direct from his heart, it must not be for-gotten that while Beaumarchais was at different periods of his life enormously rich and able to extend his generosity to those outside his family, yet there were other periods when exactly the reverse was the case, when he knew not where to turn for the necessary means of subsistence for himself alone. It was at such times that the true generosity of his nature shone forth in unmistakable clearness; there was never a time in his whole career, no matter what calamity! had befallen him, that he thought of shaking himself loose from the family whose care he had assumed, a burden which indeed he bore very lightly most of the time, but which sometimes became a weight which he could scarcely support. The thought, however, of rising again without every one of those dear to him was so impossible to a nature like his, that it never entered his mind. The very fact that it was difficult, that it was impossible for anyone else was a sufficient spur to his energy. Defeat meant nothing to him, if one thing which he had tried failed, he at once attempted something else, but conquer he must and in the end he almost invariably did.

But to return to Beaumarchais and the family gathered under his roof; as we have seen, his actions speak for themselves and need no interpreters. In a letter to his father written a little later he sums up his experience of the world and his reason for pushing his fortunes so vigorously. He says:

"I wish to walk in the career which I have embraced, and it is above everything else in the desire to share with you in ease and fortune that I follow it so persistently."

That the family of Beaumarchais knew how to appreciate and to return such rare devotion we have incontestible proofs. Especially touching are the outbursts of tenderness which come so spontaneously from the father's heart. Under the date of February 5th, 1763, at the moment of his accepting the home prepared for him by his son the elder Caron writes, "I bless heaven with the deepest gratitude for finding in my old age a son with such an excellent heart, and far from being humiliated by my present situation, my soul rises and warms itself at the touching idea of owing my happiness, after God, to him alone.'

And a little later: "You modestly recommend me to love you a little; that is not possible, my dear friend. A son such as you is not made to be loved a little by a father who feels and thinks as I. The tears of tenderness which fall from my eyes as I write are the proof of this; the qualities of thy excellent heart, the force and grandeur of thy soul, penetrate me with the most tender love. Honor of my gray hairs, my son, my dear 6on, by what have I merited from God the grace with which he overwhelms me, in my dear son? It is, as I feel, the greatest favor which He can accord to an honest and appreciative father, a son such as you."

The sincerity of these lines cannot for a moment be questioned, and we are not surprised to find that the venerable old watchmaker died with a blessing upon his lips. At the age of 77, a few days before his death, he wrote to Beaumarchais, then engaged with his first measures regarding the War of American Independence: "My good friend, my dear son, that name is precious to my heart, I profit by an in- terval in my excessive suffering, or rather in the torment which makes me fall in convulsions, simply to thank you very tenderly for what you sent me yesterday. If you go back to England I beg you to bring me a bottle of salts such as they give people who, like me, fall in fainting fits. Alas! my dear child, perhaps I shall no longer have the need of it when you return. I pray the Lord every day of my life to bless you, to recompense you, and to preserve you from every accident; this will always be the prayer of your good friend and affectionate father,

Caron."

But in 1763, many years of happy relationship between father and son were still before them. It may be of interest to note that the house first bought by Beau-mar-chais, in which the family passed many happy years, is still in existence, possessing much the same external appearance as it did when occupied by him who gave it its historical significance. It bears the number, 26 rue de Condé, in the neighborhood of the Luxembourg. In the iron grating about the windows may still be seen the initials of Beaumarchais.

But while he was laying the foundations of the family happiness in Paris, an event was occurring in the distant capital of Spain the news of which stirred his soul with indignation and caused him to hasten with all speed to the scene of action. True however to the many sided nature so strongly developed within him, he took time thoroughly to prepare himself for the journey.

He received from the patronage of Mesdames important recommendations to the court of Spain, and power to enter into business negotiations at the capital. His faithful friend, Paris du Verney, provided him with letters of credit, destined to place him grandly at Madrid and to enable him to carry on whatever his fertile brain could imagine, or his energy and audacity carry through.

Express trains and automobiles had not been invented in those days, but whatever the century in which he found himself possessed in the way of rapid transit was put to the utmost test in this journey into Spain stopping neither night nor day, and all the while his imagination carrying him still faster, busying itself with the primary cause of his journey and so sure of victory in his overwhelming consciousness of power, that already his indignation was on the brink of turning into pardoning pity, which it was bound to do as soon as his adversary showed any symptom of re-turning to sentiments of honor. Of this rare adventure we must let Beaumarchais tell in his own way.

CHAPTER III

"*Que* dirait *la* Sagesse *si* elle *me* voyait *entre*-mêler *les* occupations *les* phus *graves* dont *un* homme *puisse* s'occu-per, *de soirees* agreables, tantôt *chez* un ambassadeur, tantôt *chez* un *ministre*. . . *Les* contraires *peuvent*-ils *ainsi* aller *dans* une même tête? Oui, *mon* cher père, *je* ressem-*ble* à *feu* Alcibiade, *dont*-il *ne* me manqué *que* la *figure,* la *naissance,* l'esprit et *les* richesses"

Lettre de *Beaumarchais* à *son* père.

Marceline: "Jamais fâché, *toujours* en *belle* humeur; donnant *le* présent à *la* joie, *et* s'inquiétant *de* l'avenir *tout* aussi *peu* que *du* passé, sêmillant généréux généreux"

Bartholo: "Comme **un,** voleur!"
Marceline: "Comme **un** seigneur."
"*Le* Mariage *de* Figaro"—Act I, Scene IV.

Adventure with Clavico—Business Negotiations in Spain— Life of Pleasure at the Spanish Capital—Home Interests and Letters.

FOR several years," wrote Beaumarchais, "I had had the happiness to surround myself with my whole family, The joy of being thus united with them and their gratitude towards me were the continual recompense for the sacrifice which this cost me. Of five sisters which I had, two since their youth had been confided by my father to one of his correspondents in Spain, where they resided, and I had only a faint but sweet memory of them which sometimes had been enlivened by their correspondence.

"In February, 1764, my father received a letter from the elder daughter of which the following is the substance : 'My sister has been outrageously treated by a man as high in public favor as he is dangerous. Twice at the moment of marrying her, he suddenly has broken his word without deigning to give any excuse for his conduct. The offended sensibilities of my sister have thrown her into such a state that from all appearances it is doubtful if we can save her.'

" 'The dishonor with which this event overwhelms us has forced us into seclusion, where I pass the day and night in weeping while endeavoring to offer my sister those consolations which I do not know how to take myself,

" 'All Madrid knows that my sister has nothing with which to reproach herself. If her brother has enough credit to recommend us to the French Ambassador, His Excellency may be induced to protect us from the disgrace which this perfidious man has brought upon us.'

"My father hastened to Versailles to meet me, and weeping gave me the letter of my sister.

" 'See, my son, what you can do for these two unfortunates, they are no less your sisters than the others.'

"I was indeed touched by the account of the distressing situation of my sister, but I said to my father, 'Alas, what can I do? Who knows whether there is not some fault which they hide from us?'

" 'I forgot,' said my father, 'to show you several letters which prove my daughter to be innocent of any fault.'

"I read these letters, they reassured me—then the words, 'She is no less your sister than the others,' went to the depths of my heart.

" 'Do not weep,' I said to my father, 'I have decided on a step which will astonish you, but it seems to me the most certain, the most wise. I will ask to be released from my duties at court, and taking only prudence for a guide I will either revenge my sister or bring them both back to Paris to partake with us of our modest fortune.'

"Further information which I derived from reliable sources which were indicated by my sister, made my blood boil with indignation at the outrage which she had suffered, so without any further delay, I went back to Versailles to notify my august Protectresses, that a sorrowful affair of the highest importance demanded my presence in Madrid, and forced me to suspend my services at court. Astounded at so abrupt a departure, they were kind enough to desire to be informed as to the nature of my trouble. I showed them the letter of my sister.

" 'Go, but act prudently,' was the honorable encouragement which I received from the Princesses; 'that which you undertake is well and you shall have support, if your conduct is reasonable.'

"The warmest recommendations to our ambassador were given me by these august ladies, and became the inestimable price of four years devoted to their amusement.

"At the moment of my departure I received the commission to negotiate a very important affair in Spain for the commerce of France. M. du Verney, touched by the motive of my voyage, embraced me and said, 'Go my son, save your sister. As to the business with which you are charged know that in all you undertake, you have my support. I have promised this publicly to the Royal Family, and I will never go back on my word. Here are my notes for **200,000** francs, which will enable you to draw upon me for that sum.'

"I started and traveled night and day, accompanied by a friend. I arrived at Madrid the 18th of May at eleven o'clock in the morning; I found my sisters expecting me. Scarcely were the first embraces over, than I said to them, 'Don't be surprised if I employ the first moments in learning exactly the nature of your unhappy adventure. To serve you with success I must be informed fully in regard to what happened.' The account they gave me was exact and long. Several of their intimate friends were present who testified to its accuracy. When the story was finished, I kissed my sister and said to her, 'My child, now that I know all, console yourself. I see with pleasure that you no longer love the man; this makes the matter much easier for me. Tell me simply where I can find him.' Everyone present advised me to begin by seeing the ambassador, as our enemy was a man powerfully supported at court.

" 'Very good, my friends,' I said, 'tomorrow I will go and pay my respects to Monsieur the ambassador, but do not be angry if I take certain steps before I see him. The only thing I ask of you is to keep my arrival here absolutely secret.'

"Promptly I had a costume taken from my trunk, and hastily adjusting it, went directly to the house of Joseph Clavico, guard of the archives of the king. He was not at home. I was told where he might be found; I hastened thither and without making myself known I requested an interview at his earliest possible convenience, as I was charged with certain commissions for him from France. He invited me to take my chocolate with him at nine o'clock the next morning; I accepted for myself and my traveling companion.

"The next morning, the 19th of May, I arrived at half-past eight. I found him superbly lodged in the house of a man prominent at court, who is so much his friend, that absent from Madrid he allowed him the use of his home as though it were his own.

" 'I am charged,' I said to him, 'by a society of men of letters, to establish in the cities where I pass a literary cor-respondence with the most learned men of the country. As no other Spaniard writes better than the author of el ***Pen-sador*** to whom I have the honor of speaking, it seems to me that I cannot better serve my friends, than in connecting myself with a man of your merits.'

"I saw that he was enchanted with my proposition, so better to judge the man with whom I had to deal, I allowed him to discourse lengthily upon the advantages which different nations might obtain from similar correspondence. He talked like an angel and simply glowed with pleasure.

"In the midst of his joy, he asked me what was the business which drew me to Spain, saying he would be happy if he might be of any service to me.

" I accept with gratitude your flattering offer,' I replied, 'and I assure you that for you I have no secrets.' Then desiring to mystify him completely so that the end of my discourse alone would explain its import, I presented my friend a second time, saying, 'Monsieur here is not an entire stranger to what I have to say to you, and will not be the least in our way.' This exordium caused him to regard my friend with much curiosity. Then I began:

" A French merchant of limited means had a good many correspondents in Spain. One of the richest of these, nine or ten years ago, in passing through Paris, made him the following proposition: "Give me two of your daughters, I will take them with me to Madrid, they will live with me, who am an old bachelor without family, they will be the happiness of my old days and they shall inherit one of the richest establishments in Spain."

" 'The eldest daughter, already married, and a younger sister were confided to him. In exchange for this favor, the father agreed to supply the Spanish house with whatever merchandise was needed from France.

" 'Two years later the correspondent died,. leaving the sisters without having received any benefit and embarrassed with a commercial house which they were obliged to keep up. (Here I saw Clavico redouble his attention.)

" 'About this time a young man, a native of the Canary Islands, presented himself at the house. (All his gaiety vanished at the words which designated him.) Notwithstanding his small fortune, the ladies, seeing his great ardor to learn the French language and the sciences, aided him by every means in their power.

" 'Full of desire to become celebrated, he formed the project, quite new for the nation, of providing the city of Madrid with a periodical journal in the nature of the English Spectator. He received from his friends encouragement and help of every kind. His enterprise met with great success; then, animated with the hope of making himself a name, he ventured to propose marriage with the younger of the French women. 'Begin by succeeding,' said the elder one, 'if you are able to secure a position which will permit you to live honorably and if she prefers you to other suitors, I shall not refuse my consent.' (Here Clavico began to move about nervously in his chair, but without apparent notice I continued thus:)

" 'The younger, touched by the merits of the man who sought her hand, refused several advantageous alliances, preferring to wait until he had succeeded in obtaining what he desired and encouraged him to issue his first philosophic paper under the imposing title of el ***Pensador***. (Here I saw he looked ready to faint.) The work,' I continued with icy coldness, 'had a prodigious success; the King himself, amused by that charming production, gave the author marks of his satisfaction. He offered him the first honorable posi- tion which should become vacant. At this the young man dispersed all other pretendants to the young woman's hand by publicly announcing his intentions.

" 'The marriage was postponed only by the non-arrival of the desired position. At last, after six years of waiting on one hand, and of assiduous efforts on the other, the position arrived, and at the same moment the young man disappeared. (Here Clavico gave an involuntary sigh and then turned crimson with confusion. I noticed all this without ceasing to speak.)

" 'The affair had made too much noise to permit the ladies to regard this dénoû- ment with indifference. They had taken a house large enough for two families, the bans had been published; the outrage made all their friends indignant. Monsieur the French ambassador interested himself. When the young man in question found that the women were thus protected, fearing to lose his credit, he went and pros- trated himself at the feet of his fiancee. He employed every means in his power to win her back. As the anger of a woman is almost always love disguised, everything was soon adjusted. The preparations for the marriage were recommenced. The bans were published again, and the event was to come off in three days.

" 'The reconciliation had made as much noise as the rupture. . He went to ob- tain leave of the minister to marry, and before going said, "My friends, conserve the wavering heart of my mistress until my return and dispose everything so that I may then conduct her to the altar." (In spite of the horrible state in which my recital put him, Clavico, still uncertain of my motive, looked from time to time from me to my friend, whose sangfroid instructed him as little as my own.) I continued:

"'He returned sure enough two days later, but instead of leading his fiance to the altar he sent her word that he had again changed his mind, and that he would not marry her.

" 'Their friends, infuriated, rushed upon him. The insolent fellow defies them to do their worst, and threatens that if the French women undertake to interfere he has it in his power to ruin them. At this the young woman falls into such a state that her life is in danger. In her utter despair, the elder sister writes to France, recounting the public out-rage they had received. This account touches the heart of a brother who demanded at once permission to come to Spain in order to clear up this affair. He has made but one bound from Paris to Madrid, and this brother am I, who have left everything: country, position, business, family, pleasures, to come here to revenge an innocent and unhappy sister; it is I who come armed with right and firmness to unmask a traitor, and to write his soul in traces of blood upon his face,—and that traitor—*is you!* "

The effect of these words upon the unhappy Clavico, can be imagined better than described. As Beaumarchais finished his long recital he turned and fixed his gaze steadily upon his adversary, who writhed under its spell. As Beaumarchais paused, Clavico began to mutter forth excuses.

To return to the account of Beaumarchais. " 'Do not interrupt me, you have nothing whatever to say, but a great deal to hear. To commence, will you have the goodness to declare before Monsieur here who has come with me from France for this express purpose, whether by breach of faith, frivolity, weakness, or other vice, my sister has merited the double outrage which you have had the cruelty to impose upon her publicly.'

" 'No, Monsieur, I admit that Donna Maria, your sister, is full of spirit, grace and virtue.'

" 'Has she ever given you any subject for complaint?'

" 'Never, never.'

"Then turning to the friend who accompanied me: 'You have heard the justification of my sister, go and publish it, the rest that I have to say to Monsieur does not need witnesses.'

"My friend went out, Clavico rose but I made him sit down.

" 'Now, Monsieur, that we are alone, here is my project which I hope you will approve.'" Beaumarchais then pro-posed either a duel, or a written justification of his sister.

While Clavico rose and paced restlessly up and down the room, Beaumarchais coolly rang for the chocolate to which he helped himself while the unhappy man was going over in his mind what there remained for him to do.

Clavico, though unprincipled in character, was clever enough to recognize the qualities of the man with whom he had to deal. Being possessed of neither physical courage nor training, the first alternative offered by Beaumarchais had no place in his consideration. Obliged to accept the other, he decided to do so with the grace of one having been convinced of his wrong. Beaumarchais, informed of this purpose, summoned several servants of the house whom he stationed in an adjoining gallery as witnesses in case Clavico ever should try to prove that force had been employed. Paper, pen, and ink were brought, Clavico seated himself and meekly wrote, while Beaumarchais walked indifferently to and fro dictating. Again to return to the narrative of Beaumarchais:

"Declaration, of which I have the original:

" 'I the undersigned, Joseph Clavico, guard of the archives of the crown, testify that I have been received with kindness in the house of Madame Guilbert, that I have deceived Mademoiselle Caron her sister by a promise, a thousand times repeated, to marry her, that I have failed in the fulfillment of this promise, without her having committed any fault which could serve as a pretext or excuse for my breach of faith; that, on the contrary, the conduct of that lady, for whom I have the most profound respect, always has been pure and without spot. I testify that by my conduct, by the frivolity of my discourse, and by the interpretation which could be given it, that I have openly outraged this virtuous young lady, of whom I beg pardon by this writing made freely, although I recognize fully that I am unworthy to obtain it, promising her every possible reparation which she could desire, if this does not satisfy her.

"Made at Madrid and entirely written by my hand, in presence of her brother, the 19th of May 1764.

Signed—Joseph Clavico.'

As we have said, Clavico had accepted the role forced upon him with admirable grace. As soon as he had signed the paper and handed it to Beaumarchais, whose anger now was wholly appeased, he began in the most insinuating tones, "Monsieur, I believe that I am speaking to the most offended but most generous of men." He then proceeded to explain how ambition had ruined him; how he had always loved Donna Maria; how his only hope now lay in her forgiveness and in being able to win back her affection; how deeply he realized his unworthiness of this favor and that to obtain it there was only one person to whom he could have recourse and that was the offended brother before him; he therefore implored Beaumarchais to take the paper he had just signed and use it as he wished, but to plead his cause with Donna Maria,

This was a turn in the situation for which the brilliant Frenchman was hardly prepared. The wily Clavico pursued his advantage and before the interview had ended he was already convinced that the man with whom he had to deal was too generous to be really dangerous.

Strong in his position through the written declaration of Clavico, Beaumarchais now hurried back to the home of Madame Guilbert. He found his sisters in the midst of their friends, waiting with indescribable impatience for his return; when he arrived with the paper, when they heard its contents, a scene of the greatest excitement occurred in which amid mutual embraces, with everyone weeping and laughing together, and all talking at once, the whole story little by little at length was brought out.

As can be imagined, the affair made a great stir in Madrid. The influence of the friends of Clavico on the one hand, and on the other, the strong recommendations of the French Ambassador, who took the matter seriously in hand, finally induced the family after several weeks of indecision on their part and of pleading on that of Clavico, to hush the matter by accepting a new alliance. The affair once settled, Beaumarchais, true to his character of doing wholeheartedly whatever he undertook, became at once the warm friend and confidant of Clavico, lent him money, entered heartily into his schemes of advancement, so that the two were constantly seen together. After a short period of this friendship, so sincere on the part of Beaumarchais, imagine his surprise to suddenly find that the cunning Clavico had all along been secretly plotting his ruin and was now on the brink of having him arrested and thrown into prison.

Furious at last, Beaumarchais no longer hesitated in wreaking his vengeance upon his perfidious adversary; he rushed to court, made the whole matter thoroughly known, and the king, having entered into the merits of the case, decided against Clavico whom he discharged from his service and who was obliged to take refuge in a convent out-side of Madrid. From this retreat he addressed a pleading letter to Beaumarchais imploring his commiseration. The latter in speaking of it says, "He was right to count upon it, I hated him no longer, in fact I never in my life hated anyone."

Before going farther, it may be of interest to note that this same Clavico survived Beaumarchais a number of years, dying in Madrid in 1806. He seems to have succeeded in making his way in the world in spite of his temporary loss of favor, and also, to quote Loménie, "after having seen himself immolated during life in the open theater, by Goethe, as a melodramatic scoundrel." He translated Buffon into Spanish and died editor of the **Historical** and **Political** Mercury **and** vice-director of the Cabinet of Natural History of Madrid.

As might be expected the news of Beaumarchais's way of settling the Spanish matter, caused no less joy to the family in France, than to that in Madrid. On June 6th, 1764, his father wrote to him: "How deliciously I feel the honor, my dear Beaumarchais, of having such a son, whose actions crown so gloriously the end of my career. I see at a glance all the good that will result for the honor of my dear Lisette from the generous action which you have performed in her favor. I receive by the same post two letters from the charming Countess (the Countess of Fuen-Clara, one of the patronesses of the père Caron, watchmaker) one to me and the other to Julie, so beautiful and touching, so full of tender expressions for me, and honorable for you, that you will have no less pleasure than I when you read them. You have enchanted her; she never tires of dwelling upon the pleasure it gives her to know you, or the desire she has of being useful to you, or the joy it gives her to see how all the Spanish approve and praise your action with Clavico; she could not be more delighted if you were her own son. Adieu, my dear Beaumarchais, my honor, the joy of my heart; receive a thousand embraces from the kindest of fathers and the best of friends.

Caron."

There is also a letter extant from the abbe de Malespine to the elder Caron. He wrote: "I have read and re-read, Monsieur, the account which has been sent you from Spain. I am overwhelmed with joy at all that it contains. Monsieur your son is a real hero. I see in him the most brilliantly gifted of men and the tenderest of brothers; honor, firmness, everything shines out in his proceedings with Clavico."

When this affair which had occupied him so intensely for almost six weeks was definitely settled, Beaumarchais seems to have given it no further consideration, but to have turned his attention to the business negotiations with which he was charged, and to the life of gaiety and pleasure which his brilliant gifts opened to him. In speaking of this period, Loménie says, "Scarcely arrived at Madrid, we see him ' plunging into the whirlpool of industrial enterprises, pleasures, festivals, gallantries, of music and of song, which was his element. He is in the flower of his age; all his esprit all his imagination, all his gaiety, in a word all his faculties, are at the highest point of their development."

Soon we find him writing to his father, "I follow my affairs with a determination which you know me to possess; but all business between the French and the Spanish is hard to bring to success. I shall have long details to give you when I get back to warm myself at your fire. I work, I write, I confer, I draw up documents, that is my life. I promise you that whether I succeed or not in all that I have undertaken, I will at least bring with me the esteem of all those in this country with whom I have to deal. Take care of your health and believe that my greatest happiness will be to enable you to share whatever good comes to me."

A little later he wrote, "I km now at the flower of my age. It is for me to work and for you to repose yourself. I may perhaps be able to relieve you entirely from all your engagements. To this object I devote all my energy. I will not tell you all now, but understand that I shall not go to sleep over the project which I have always had in my mind to put you on a level with all that is about you. Take care of yourself, my dear father, and live. The moment will come when you will be able to enjoy your old age, free from debts, and satisfied with your children. I have just had your son-in-law appointed paid engineer to the king. If you receive news of me from any inhabitant of Madrid they will say, your son amuses himself like a king; he passes all his evenings at the Russian Ambassador's,—with my lady Rochford; he dines four times a week with the Commander of the engineers, and drives with six mules all about Madrid; then he goes to the *sitio* real to see M. de Grimaldi and other Ministers. He takes one meal a day at the French ambassador's so that his stay is not only charming, but very inexpensive. All this is true as far as amusements go,—but you must not suppose that I neglect my business. I attend to every detail myself. It is in the high society for which I was born that I find the means which I require—and when you see what I have written, you will admit that I have not been walking but running toward my goal."

One of the chief enterprises which Beaumarchais had undertaken was the establishment of a Louisiana Company modeled on that of the British East India Company, which had for its object the securing for France the right to trade in that territory for the next thirty years.

He had a project for the colonization of the Sierra Morena Mountains in Spain, a third for the introduction of a new and more practical method of providing the army with the necessary supplies; then there were innumerable minor schemes for the improvement of agriculture, commerce, industry, and things generally in Spain. Upon all of these subjects, he addresses innumerable memoirs to the Spanish ministers, and, in a word, does his utmost to infuse some of his own energy into that unenterprising nation. Although he almost succeeds in stirring things into a semblance of life, yet it will not be thought surprising when we consider the nation with which he had to deal, that notwithstanding his assiduous efforts, many of his projects failed completely, and others met with but partial success.

There is a lengthy letter given by Loménie addressed by Beaumarchais to his father in which the son goes into minute details about his project for supplying the Spanish army with provisions. It shows, amongst other things, his mastery of calculation on a gigantic scale, and that no enterprise was too vast for his comprehensive intellect.

True to the dictates of his generous soul, here as elsewhere, it is the thought of the ease and comfort which he will be enabled to give to those dear to him that fills his heart with gladness. Still to his father he wrote: "I finish, my dear father, by recommending the care of your health as the most precious thing that I have in this world and I reiterate the tender and respectful attachment with which I have the honor of being, Monsieur and very dear father, your very humble and very obedient servitor and affectionate son, Beaumarchais." . . . (Then in postscript) "I might be able to find ten days that I would employ with a rare satisfaction in procuring you a consultation with M. Tron-chon so as to get at the bottom of your malady. This idea consoles me in advance. It may be that before I go to Lyons, I shall pass by Paris, in which case I will take you with me and the rest will follow of itself. Your health be-comes more and more dear to me, as I feel myself able to augment your satisfaction by my advancement and by the care that I will give to render your old age agreeable in procuring comfort for all those who are dear to you."

But to return to the social life which Beaumarchais was leading at Madrid. We have spoken already of his distaste for card playing. Loménie gives a very characteristic letter of Beaumarchais to his sister Julie, where he paints with rare force and vividness of coloring the scene about a table de jeu in the salon of the Russian Ambassador. The center of the life and movement is naturally himself. With his usual frankness he writes to Julie, "Evenings we have cards or music and then supper, of all of which I seem to be the soul. The society has been increased by all the Ambassadors, who before my arrival lived rather isolated. They say now they have charming evenings because I am there." Then follows a vivid description of the mad playing which ends by Beaumarchais's lending this time, not thirty louis, but two hundred and thirty, besides three hundred and fifty which he had gained at the play, but which were not forthcoming. The debtors in this case were the Russian Ambassador and his wife. As Beaumarchais was now winning he rose and refused to play any longer. The Ambassador and his wife who were excited over their losses, failed in their duties as host and hostess; the matter made a good deal of noise and for ten days coolness reigned in all the social life of Madrid, Beaumarchais vowing that he had played for the last time. During the whole affair he carried himself with so much dignity and showed so much moderation that he won great credit among all the Princes and Ambassadors of that high society. Finally the matter was adjusted, the joyful evenings recommenced, but with grand music instead of cards, and Beaumarchais adds: "Word of honor, let no one ever speak to me of playing again, let us amuse ourselves with other things which do not entail such serious conse-quences." And a little further on, "the friendship is stronger than ever; balls, concerts, but no more cards. I have written some French words to a Spanish air that is very much admired ; I have had two hundred copies made. I will save one to send with the music of the one I sent to my father. Goodnight, I will write Tuesday to my Pauline and her aunt."

But not only the Russian Ambassador rejoiced in the pleasure of the intimate friendship of Beaumarchais, but also—in the words of Loménie: "Lord Rochford dotes upon him, goes to the Prado with him, sups with him, sings duets with him and becomes astonishingly jovial for an English diplomat.

"But this is not all his life at the Capital. In the midst of his industrial enterprises and his aristocratic pleasures, the future author of the Barbier de Seville appears to be continually occupied with his humble family, now displaying a rare tact and without compromising his patrician bearing to force great ladies at Madrid to pay the bills which they had long owed the elder Caron; and with fraternal bonhomie, entering into all the details of the life of his sisters at home, or leaving the salons of the Capital for the modest dwelling of his sisters at Madrid."

That he was not ashamed of their station in life is admirably shown by the following letter addressed to his father. He wrote: "I have seen Drouillet (a French banker established in Madrid). He and his wife called soon after my arrival, but I have not entered into their society although Drouillet is himself an estimable man. The reason I have kept away is the ridiculous airs of his wife, who because she possesses a few more *ecus* than your daughters considers herself above them. She has tried to attract me there by attentions and invitations of every sort but never mentioned my sisters, which made me reply that I was making too short a stay in Madrid to give my time to any but my family. It is the same everywhere, this ridiculous feeling belongs to every country. There are here great and little France. My sisters are too well brought up to belong to the latter and they are not considered rich enough to be admitted to the former, so that the visits of the Drouillets were for me alone; at which Monsieur your son, took the liberty of putting Madame Drouillet in her place; and so she says that I am *malm*. You know what that means, my dear father, and whether there is malice in seeing things clearly and then in saying what one thinks."

In relation to the debtors of the elder Caron at Madrid, allusions frequently occur in the letters. For instance, the father writes, "I see what you have done and what you are doing among my debtors from whom I would never have drawn a farthing but for you." At another time Beaumar-chais writes, "I am in a way to receive payment from all of your grandees—their self esteem is so mixed up with it that I think I shall manage to get all they owe you. My letters to them are polite but proud. The duke and duchess do not seem to want to be under any obligation to me, fearing that I will boast of it and that the length of the credit will be divulged. Let me manage it in my own way."

Here is a sample of his manner of approaching these creditors of his father. "Knowing that a number of idle people do me the honor of disturbing themselves regarding the motives of my stay in Spain, it has seemed to me my duty to tranquilize them by employing my time in soliciting the debts of my house. In consequence I have the honor to demand of your excellency the permission"—here follows a statement of the debt owed to the elder Caron. One of these individuals of quality thus addressed being in no way anxious to pay, revenged herself by trying to show up Beaumarchais as an adventurer. Immediately the latter wrote home and received from his sister Julie by return post, a beautifully printed decree drawn from the "Cabinet rose" by the chimney. There are four great pages containing fifteen articles reinforced by legal terms and extracts of ordinances—the whole surmounted with a beautiful ornament made of acanthus leaves and bearing the following inscription, "Made at the castle of the Louvre by Monsieur Pierre-August Caron de Beaumarchais, Equerry Councilor of the *King,* lieutenant-*general* des *chasses* aux bailliage *et* capitainerie *de* la *varernne* du *Louvre,* grande *vennerie,* fauconnerie *of* France, ***having session in the chamber of council, Tuesday, January 17th, 1764, signed de Vitry, chief registrar." For fear the list was not long enough, knowing well that one can never have too many titles in Spain, his brother-in-law added, "Equerry Councilor, secretary of the king,*** con-trôleur of the house of the king, lieutenant-general, etc."

But it is impossible to touch upon all the details of that correspondence so faithfully sustained on both sides for more than a year, during his stay in Spain. These letters are the chief source from which we have to draw in estimating Beaumarchais the son, brother and friend, as well as the man of the world and the man of business. Fortunately nearly all these letters have been preserved; we shall have occasion to return to them when treating of another phase of the life of Beaumarchais in relation to a connection formed before his sudden departure from Paris. As this incident with its connections takes us away from the outside world and conducts us into the inmost sanctuary of the home established in the rue de Condé, all the letters which touch upon it seem to belong to the next chapter.

It is there we shall see Beaumarchais playing at first the part of the happy and accepted lover of his charming Pauline, but a little later assuming the rather astonishing role of victim, for in the words of Loménie, "In the end he is really the victim, and we shall see that he does his best to be furious. He is here the antithesis of Clavico. It is Pauline who will be Clavico, or rather there will be a Clavico who will carry off Pauline."

CHAPTER IV

"***Figure*** charmante, ***organe*** flexible ***et*** touchant! ***de*** l'âme ***surtout.***"...

"***Les*** deux ***amis***," Act , Scene ***I.***

The Beautiful Creole, Pauline—Beaumarchais the Judge, the Lover, the Friend—Mademoiselle de Boisgarnier Marries Janot de Miron—The Père Caron's Second Marriage.

BEFORE entering into a consideration of the role played by Beaumarchais as lover, a few more touches are neces-sary to represent him as he was before the world. We already have spoken of his various appointments at court, and mentioned the fact that in 1763 he had bought the very honorable charge of ***lieutenant***-général ***des*** chasses ***aux*** bail-***liage*** et ***capitainerie*** de ***la*** varenne ***du*** Louvre.

In order that it may be quite clear to the reader what were the functions assumed in acquiring this office we may explain that the capitameries were territorial circumscriptions in which the right of hunting was reserved exclusively for the king. That known as "la varenne du Louvre" extended for some fifty or sixty miles about Paris. There was a special tribunal called "the tribunal to conserve the pleasures of the king" which tried all cases connected with in-fringements of the regulations belonging to the ***capitaineries.*** The audiences of the particular one in question were held once a week at the Louvre. They were presided over by the duke de la Vallière, whose chief officer Beaumarchais now became.

When the duke was absent, which M. de Loménie assures us was almost invariably the case, Beaumarchais himself presided. Under the latter were many subordinates, some of them noblemen of high rank, so that it is easy to understand the prestige of such an office.

There were innumerable regulations, many of them very trying to private individuals, which it became the duty of the lieutenant-general to enforce. In the territory belonging to the *capitainerie,* no game could be shot, no garden or other wall be constructed without special authorization from the tribunal which presided over these matters. So annoying were these regulations that in 1789 the suppression of the *capitaineries* was one of the most popular measures voted by the Assemblée Constituante. In 1763, however, no one had thought as yet of the possibility of doing without them, so that we shall see Beaumarchais entering with his usual ardor into the exact and circumspect performance of his new duties.

To think of Beaumarchais as he appears later in life, attacking with the audacity which belongs to him alone, the very foundations of feudal despotism in his inimitable ***Mariage* de *Figaro,*** and to see him now in his long judicial robes seated upon the fleur de lis, gravely judging "pale humans" apropos of rabbits, is a contrast which hardly can be met with in any other career, and certainly not in any other century. That he took his functions seriously and that he also knew how to guard such rights as individuals then possessed is clearly shown in the following characteristic anecdote which we quote from Gudin.

"Soon after his return from Spain, Beaumarchais had a quarrel with the Prince of Condé, on the subject of the privileges of the chase, in connection with a certain garden wall which the Prince had torn down and which Beaumarchais as the protector of the rights of the individual had caused to be rebuilt. The Prince was very angry. M. de Beau-marchais mounted on a horse and went to find him while the nobleman was out hunting.

" 'I have come,' said Beaumarchais, 'to give an account of my conduct.

"A discussion at once arose; the Prince had a good deal of *esprit* and what is rarer still in one of his rank, he had liberal ideas.

" 'Certainly, Beaumarchais said to him, 'your Highness can obtain anything you wish. Your rank, your power—'

" 'No, replied the Prince, 'it is as lawyer that I pretend to be in the right.

" 'In that case, said Beaumarchais, 'I demand of your Highness leave to be the lawyer on the opposite side and to plead before you. You shall be the judge.'

"He then proceeded to expose the affair with so much clearness, precision, eloquence, energy, and regard for the Prince that the latter avowed he was in the wrong and from that moment felt for Beaumarchais the greatest affection." And the devoted biographer hastens to add, "It was difficult to see him without loving him; the Dauphin, Mesdames, the Duke de la Vallière, the Duke de Chaulnes and nearly all those with whom he came in contact have experienced the same sentiment."

During Beaumarchais's sojourn in Spain the functions of this office, when not presided over by the Duke in person, were necessarily left to subordinates. Beaumarchais however retained his charge until a period just prior to its final abolishment in 1789.

When in the spring of 1765, Beaumarchais returned from Spain he found the court plunged in mourning, for the Dauphin was very near his end. Concerts for Mesdames were not to be thought of, so very naturally he found him-self drifting farther and farther from the social atmosphere of Court life. We soon shall see him employing his spare moments in literary work but before attempting to study Beaumarchais as an author, let us pause to contemplate him as the lover.

Like most romances connected with the life of this unusual character, the affair which we are now about to consider is not a romance pure and simple, but has also a very prosaic, business-like; matter-of-fact side. It would seem that the story has come down to us only because there was a question of money involved, and of money never repaid to Beaumarchais. In the words of Loménie, "We thank heaven that there was really a matter of business, that is to say, a debt at the end of this love affair, or else it would have met the fate of other episodes of the same nature, the papers relating to which have been destroyed, and so it is in the august character of pièces *justicatives* that some very tender letters of an amiable young lady have been able to traverse the years."

The amiable young lady in question, Pauline, was a charming creole, born on the island of Santo Domingo, then belonging to France. She had lost her parents in early infancy and was brought to Paris, where she was received by an aunt who became a second mother to the young girl. The family estate was estimated to be worth two million francs, but as it was heavily encumbered with debts and in a run-down condition Pauline was no such heiress as at first it would appear.

She was beautiful, however, and is described by those who knew her as tender, delicate, and childlike, with a bewitching voice and good musical ability. The family of Pauline at Paris became intimate with that of the Carons about the time that Beaumarchais made his first acquaintance with Paris du Verney.

From the first, Beaumarchais was much attracted to the beautiful girl, then about eighteen years of age, and as may be imagined had little difficulty in arousing in her a corresponding sentiment. Before demanding her hand in marriage, however, he decided to send a commissioner to Santo Domingo to look carefully into the condition of her affairs and to see what would be best to do for the re-establishment of the estate. An uncle of Beaumarchais, M. Pichon, accepted the commission and set out for Santo Domingo provided with 20,000 francs in money and a cargo of merchandise of which he was to dispose to the best advantage possible. Having taken this step, Beaumarchais wrote the following letter to Pauline in which prudence shows itself quite as clearly as sentiment.

"You thought me sad, my dear and amiable Pauline; I was only preoccupied; I had a thousand things to say to you which seem so serious, so important, that I have thought it wise to put them upon paper so that you can better grasp their import. You could not have doubted, my dear Pauline, that a sincere and lasting attachment was the true cause of all that I have done for you. Although I have been discreet enough not to seek your hand in marriage until I was in a situation to give you your proper station, my whole conduct must have proved to you that I had designs upon your future and that they were honorable. To-day, now that my funds are engaged for the re-establishment of your affairs I am hoping for the sweet fruits of my labors; I even said something to your uncle yesterday, who seemed favorably disposed toward me. I must avow to you that I took the liberty of assuring him that I believed that your consent would not be refused me and I explained clearly to him my intentions. Pardon, my dear Pauline, it was without presumption that I was led to make the avowal to him. It seemed to me that your constant friendship for me was the guarantee of what I advanced. Do you disavow it?

"There is one thing, however, which still deters me, even though, my amiable Pauline, with proper management and a reasonable economy, it is probable that the actual state of my affairs is such that I have enough to make your destiny agreeable, which is the only desire of my heart; yet if through some terrible misfortune all the money which I send to Santo Domingo should be engulfed in the ruinous condition of an affair of which we as yet know nothing but from the testimony of others, these funds deducted from my fortune will no longer permit me to support a condition such as I would have given you; and what would be my sorrow if that were the case!

"This disquietude is the only reason that has forced me to retard the demand for your hand, after which I have sighed for so long a time.

"I do not know what claims you have upon the property of your dear uncle, either in regard to the dowry of your late aunt or for the debts of which I have heard indirectly spoken. It seems very improper for me to broach this subject to you or to him. I revolt at the thought. Nevertheless, my dear Pauline, in order to pass a happy life, one must be without uneasiness as to the future, and no sooner should I have you in my arms than I must begin to tremble lest some misfortune should cause the loss of the funds which I have sent to America; because I have placed no less than 80,000 francs aside for this purpose.

"This then, my dear Pauline, is the cause of my silence which must have seemed strange after all I have done.

"There are two ways out of this difficulty if you accep my proposal; the first is to have patience until the entire success of my plans and the security of my capital permits me to offer you something assured; the ; second is that you engage your aunt to sound your uncle upon what dispositions he intends to make in regard to you. Far, however, from wishing to diminish his comfort in order to augment yours, I am entirely ready to make sacrifices on my part, to render his old age more agreeable if the actual condition of his own affairs holds him in restraint. But if the tenderness which he feels for you leads him to favor your interests, my intentions would never be to permit him to transfer to you anything during his lifetime, but since in case of his death he would be no longer able to enjoy the use of it himself, it does not seem improper to make a similar request of an uncle who takes the place of a father to you, and who has the right to expect your care and your attentions to make his old age agreeable. Assured from this side, we could then conclude our happy marriage, my dear Pauline, and look upon the money sent away as a pierre d'attente, thrown out into the future, to render it more agreeable if it succeeds, but which the future benevolence of your uncle would make good in case of loss.

"Reflect seriously upon what I have written you. Give me your advice in reply. My tenderness for you will always have the ascendency over my prudence. My fate is in your hands; yours is in the hands of your uncle."

This must have seemed a very solemn and business-like letter for a young colonial unused to the minute exactitude of a *French* mcnagère. Her reply shows that the heart had discovered what it most desired to know, but that the mind was confused by the mass of detail on the matter of her fortune which after all must have seemed to her a matter of but secondary importance.

She wrote in reply: "Your letter, Monsieur, my good friend, has thrown me into extreme distress; I did not feel strong enough to reply myself; nor did I feel either that I ought to communicate it to my aunt, her tenderness for me which is her chief merit in regard to me, could not help me in the least. You will no doubt be very much astonished when you learn the intrepid act which I decided upon; the moment was favorable, your letter urgent, my embar-rassment more inspiring than the most prudent counsel. I went and threw myself into the arms of my uncle, I opened to him my heart without reserve, I implored his advice and his tenderness. At last I dared to show him your letter, although without your permission my good friend; all this was done on the impulse but how glad I am that I overcame my timidity, so that he could read into my soul! It seemed to me that my confidence in him augmented his fondness for me. In truth, my good friend, I did well to go to him. I acquired in reasoning with him the certitude of his attachment for me, and what pleases me still more I found him full of esteem for you and he also renders you all the justice which I am sure you merit. I love my uncle a thousand times more because of this. As to the business of your letter, he wishes to confer with you himself. I should manage this too badly to undertake it. He wishes to see you very soon. You have written me that your fate is in my hands, and that mine is in the hands of my uncle; in my turn I give my interests over to you, if you love me as I believe, you will be able to cause a little of your ardor to pass over to my uncle; he complains that he is bound already.

"My good friend, in this conversation, your heart and your mind must work at the same time; nothing resists you when you really set your heart upon it. Give me this proof of your tenderness. I shall regard your success in this as the. most convincing proof of the zeal which you have for what you so sweetly call your happiness and which your Pauline could not read without a fearful beating of the heart. Adieu, my good friend, I hope that your first visit when you come back from Versailles, will be to my uncle. Think of all the respect which you owe him if he is to be yours. I stop, for I feel myself ready to write foolishly. **Bonsoir,** mi-chant!"

Whatever may have taken place at the meeting between Beaumarchais and the uncle, the results were not such as permitted an immediate marriage. It was therefore postponed until the Santo Domingo matter cleared itself. In the meantime, the lovers saw each other frequently and in the intervals letters were exchanged. Those of Beaumar-chais are in every tone; sometimes a lengthy and profound dissertation on the nature of love which accords well with the philosophic side which is by no means the least developed in his surprisingly complex character; others re-veal some touch of a longing for the deeper sentiment of a pure affection which shall be all his own; while others totally at variance with these are in a light jovial vein. The following presents an epistle of this type:

"***Bonjour,*** my aunt; I embrace you, my amiable Pauline; your servitor, my charming Perrette. My little children, love one another; this is the precept of the apostle word for word. May the evil that one of you wishes another fall back upon his own head; this is the malediction of the prophet.. This part of my discourse is not made for tender, feeling souls like yours, I know it, and I never think without an extreme satisfaction how nature, which has made you so amiable, has given you such a portion of sensibility, of equity, and of moderation which permits you to live so happily together and me to be in the midst of so charming a society. This one will love me as a son, that one as a friend and my Pauline, uniting all these sentiments in her good little heart, will inundate me with a deluge of affection, to which I will reply following the power given by Providence to your zealous servitor, your sincere friend, your future ... ***Peste!*** what a serious word I was going to pronounce! It would have passed the limits of the profound respect with which I have the honor to be, Mademoiselle, etc., etc."

Matters were at this pass when Beaumarchais left Paris for Madrid. Soon after his arrival there, news of an alarming nature began to reach France from Santo Domingo. The uncle had met with an unscrupulous relative of Pauline and very soon money and merchandise were lost, and as a crowning misfortune the uncle suddenly died.

The elder Caron, in writing to his son, seems to have intimated a suspicion of foul play, for the son replies from Madrid, after quoting a line from his father's letter, "What do you mean by that? If it is simply that our funds are lost that is a misfortune no doubt, but truly the other thdught is far worse. My heart aches to think of my poor uncle who, having a presentiment of misfortune and death, went to meet his fate with so much good grace; but do not believe that anyone has hastened his end, for we have no proof and the suspicion is the most odious that can enter into the mind of man; the climate alone, even where there are no worries or enfeeblement, carries off two-thirds of the men and it is certainly sufficient calamity for us to feel that we have sent him to a natural death, without gnawing our hearts out by the dreadful idea that we sent him there to be a victim.

"My sisters at Madrid know nothing of my real sorrow. I could have wished that you yourself might have been spared the knowledge of it."

That Beaumarchais conceived the idea of himself going to the West Indies, is proved by a passage in one of his letters to his father in which he speaks of his design to sell his appointment at court and go with Pauline to settle in Santo Domingo.

Through some of the letters of the elder Caron we have a picture of the delightful home life of the family and the gaiety of the sisters of this brilliant brother. On the 22nd of January, the father writes, "Nothing more beautiful than the festival at Beaufort could be imagined. Boisgarnier and Pauline shone with their usual brilliancy. They danced until two, after the concert and the supper; there was nothing wanting but our Beaumarchais."

Julie also wrote to a friend. "We played comedies and we made love, there was a company of forty-five persons and your Julie pleased generally in all her roles. Everyone declared her one of the best actresses. What I say here is not to praise her, because every one knows how modest she is; it is only because of your weakness, and to justify your choice in having made her your friend. We are preparing another more agreeable festival for the return of my brother."

Of Julie's manner of love-making we shall permit her to tell us, a little later, in her own way. For the moment, let it suffice to state the fact, that a certain Chevalier du S, a gifted young man with no fortune, but with a name and a position of honor, had been for some time very assiduous in his attention to the favorite sister of Beaumarchais. He had been well received by the family and had asked her hand in marriage. He was also a native of Santo Domingo, though in no way connected with Pauline, whom he met for the first time at the home of his friends, in rue de Condé.

It does not concern us in the study which we are making to enter very deeply into the merits of this young man since in the end he does not ally himself with the family; we shall, however, be forced to speak of him later, as it is he who turns but to be the other Clavico, who deserts Julie and carries off Pauline. In how far these two are justified for their double desertion, the reader may judge if he has the patience to follow the story to its completion. For the present, let us turn our attention to another pair of lovers, less romantic, perhaps, at least so far as the hero is concerned, —but possessed of more sterling qualities.

It will be remembered that the youngest sister of Beau-marchais, Mademoiselle de Boisgarnier, was rather an at-tractive, though slightly affected, little body. A certain young man, Janot de Miron, had been introduced into the home of the Caron family and had fallen much in love with the rather disdainful young woman in question.

She seems in the beginning to have been but slightly touched by his ardent addresses. She did not find him ele-gant enough for her fastidious taste. But Miron was a tenacious young man whose ardor was only stimulated by the coldness and disdain of her whose heart he never despaired of conquering.

Beaumarchais, unconscious of this and seeing his sister's indifference, had written from Madrid proposing another alliance. Miron, learning of the interference of his friend, promptly grew furious and wrote an indignant letter in which he indulged freely in injurious personalities.

Beaumarchais and the War of American Independence

The reply of Beaumarchais is so characteristic and shows so clearly the crude strength of his nature as well as his sense of justice that we take from it a rather long extract. The affair once settled, true to the instincts of his warm heart, the matter was not only forgiven but also completely forgotten,

Beaumarchais wrote: "It is my turn to reply, my dear Miron, to the very astounding letter which I have just re-ceived from you. ... I want to tell you now, that long ago I was tired of sacrifices and that my one desire has been that everyone around me should be happy; you alone seem to imagine that you have the right to complain of my proceedings. I am not touched by your reproaches, I have done my duty by everyone. I do not need to prove this, that does not concern me now—but to refute the most heavy, awkward, disagreeable jesting which is the tone of your letter, my friend. I am most astonished that those Sapphos of sisters of mine did not prevent your putting such impertinence into the post. It is a fact that you are not made for jesting but for more serious matters. Nothing could be more ridiculous than to see you attempt the lighter vein, which does very well for the little dog of La Fontaine, but which is disgusting in more solid animals. More than this, your ideas are based upon a foundation so false and so equivocally set forth that they fill me with pity. .. As far as my sister is concerned, I shall be very happy if I find her married as her heart dictates when I return; if I find her unmarried, I shall put no obstacle in the way of her happiness. I have two left for whom I will provide according to the turn which my affairs take on. ... I am in no haste for either of them for I have certain ideas about the future which make me feel that the longer they wait the less they will regret not having been in too much of a hurry.

"And now since I do not pretend to give myself airs in disposing of any of my family without their consent, it would have been easy to draw from me an explanation which would have made your letter unnecessary. I am returning the missive to you that you may have the pleasure of regaling yourself thereon if by chance you have not kept a copy.

"For the rest, your desire to marry my sister is an honor to her—I repeat it—

and she is entirely free to choose you if you satisfy her; far from trying to prevent it I give my consent from to-day forth—but always with, the understanding that you never confound the rights which you will acquire over her as her husband, with those which you can never have over me. This is what I wish to tell you once for all in order that nothing of this kind may ever again happen between us.

"I take the liberty of begging you to keep to the only tone which will pass with me—that of friendship. I have need neither of a preceptor who pretends to explore into the motives of my actions, nor of a pedagogue who takes it upon himself to instruct me.

"I do not know why Julie should have communicated to you that which I wrote, and I am still more astonished that she has imagined that your ridiculous letter could affect me. It is my intention never to return to this subject, therefore I beg her by this letter, never again to suffer in her presence that anyone fails in the respect which is due me. I am so indulgent truly, that this need not be denied me.

"You will receive this letter by the way of my father, who sent me yours, so that **All** The *Family* may be the witnesses of the way in which I accept your jesting.

"It is not very agreeable to me to think that my sisters, not wishing to take with me an improper tone, make it their business to pass on to me your words, to relieve themselves of the restraint they have before me.

"After this, jest on as much as you like, you will receive nothing from me to engage a serious quarrel. When you know so little of my life, however, you will spare me your commentaries.

"I am none the less, my dear Miron, your servant and friend

"Beaumarchais."

As he himself has said, "with good hearts, anger is only a pressing need for pardon,' so the matter was not difficult to settle. August 87th, 1764, he writes to Julie, "How is everybody, the christian pedagogue first of all?" and Oct. 86th of the same year, "I have received your letter of the 9th by which you confirm all that has been told me of the moderation of Boisgarnier. I thank her sincerely. Miron has written to me, but while reading, I felt like saying, 'Miron, what do you want of me with this beautiful letter? A month ago my anger was all gone and all this seems to me but tiresome repetition.' "

In spite of her moderation the youngest sister seems to have sided with her brother at her lover's expense, for we soon find the former pleading with her in a letter addressed to his father from Madrid, dated January 14, 1765.

"Monsieur and very dear father:

"I have received your last letter dated December 31st— and that of Boisgarnier. Her reply gave me much pleasure. She is a droll creature, but she has a good deal of intelligence and rectitude of character; now, if I am in any way the cause of the coldness between her and her friend, I say in advance that I have entirely given up my resentment and she will do well to follow my example. For whatever opinion he may have of me, I am determined not to quarrel with him.

"The only thing that can hurt me is that he should speak ill of my heart, I don't care what he says of my mind. The first will always be at his service and the second ready to give him a drubbing if he needs it. . . .

I am indeed sorry if they cannot agree, for Miron is a man who does not lack a single quality which should make an honest woman happy; and if my Boisgarnier is less touched by these qualities than by the defects of a few fri-volous attractions (which for my part I do not deny him) then I should say that she is a child who has not yet ac-quired that experience which prefers happiness to pleasure. To say absolutely what I think, I am convinced that he is right to prefer his qualities to mine, for there are many points where I do not feel that I possess either his virtue or his constancy, and these things are of great price when it is a question of a union for life.

"Therefore I invite my Boisgarnier not to think of our friend except in regard to what there is of him which is infinitely estimable, and soon the matter will adjust itself. I was furious with him for twenty-four hours—nevertheless there is no other man whom I would prefer to be associated with as a brother-in-law.

"I understand all that Boisgarnier would say—yes, he plays on the hurdy-gurdy, that is true, his heels are half an inch too high, he has a nasal twang when he sings—he eats raw apples at night, he is cold and didactic when he talks,—he has a certain awkwardness of manner in everything he does; but still the good people of the rue Condé ought not to be offended at such things;—a wig, a Waist coat, a pair of clogs ought not to drive anyone away when he excels in matters of the heart and his mind is in keeping. Adieu Boisgarnier, here is a long article for thee."

It is interesting to find Beaumarchais candidly acknowledging the lack of certain qualities in himself which at least he knows how to appreciate in others. In his relations with Pauline it will be seen that whatever her real motives may have been, she uses what she considers his inconstancy as a pretext later for her break with him. However, to do him justice, it must be affirmed that there is no evidence that he ever for a moment entertained an idea of abandoning her, or that in his heart he meant to be untrue; yet the fact remains that other women did not lose their charm for him because of her, and while at Madrid he was far from denying himself consolation for being deprived of her society. His letters to her were by no means frequent enough, nor ardent enough to satisfy the longings of a romantic young girl.

Already before his departure for Madrid, he seems to have given ground for complaint, as we find Julie accusing him of levity in a letter to a friend while at the same time she paints in her merriest vein the love-sick condition of the family.

"Our house," she wrote, "is a dovecote where everyone lives on love and hope; I am the one who laughs more than the others, because I am the least in love; Beaumarchais is a perverse being who by his levity teases and grieves Pauline. Boisgarnier and Mir on discuss sentiment till one loses one's breath, and impassion themselves with order up to the point of a sublime disorder. The Chevalier and I are worse than all that; he is as loving as an angel, passionate as a seraph, while I am as gay as a linnet, and malicious as a demon. Love does not make me lon-lan-la like the others, and yet in spite of my madness I could not keep from tasting of it. More's the pity!"

Beaumarchais wrote from Madrid, "I have this afternoon been to the French Ambassador's in the *carosse* of Madame the Marquise de La Croix, who has the goodness to drive me everywhere with her six mules. She is a charming lady who has great credit here by her rank, but still more by reason of her intelligence and the graces which make her dear to all the world. Her society dissipates the dust, the inaction, the ennui, the impatience which seize everyone who remains long in this place. I should die in this dull city if it were not for this delicious company.'

It is quite evident that Beaumarchais is thinking little of Pauline and he will soon find to his chagrin, that she has ceased to think any longer so tenderly of him.

He has not, however, forgotten her interests in Santo Domingo nor his project of going there to settle in case the turn of his affairs should point to that move as the best solution of the difficulties, but in the meantime, he amuses himself in his moments of leisure in the pleasantest way that offers itself.

But not only were the sisters of Beaumarchais living on hope and love, the elder Caron himself was entertaining the same guests as is proved by the following letter written by his son from Madrid.

"Monsieur and very dear father:—

"I am not surprised at your attachment for Madame Henry; she is cheerfulness itself, and has one of the best hearts that I know. I could wish you might have been happy enough to inspire a more lively return of affection. · She would make you happy and you would certainly render agreeable this union founded upon reciprocal affection and an esteem which has lasted twenty-five years. If I were you, I know very well how I should go about it, and if I were she, I know also very well how I should reply; but I am neither the one nor the other and it is not for me to clear up this affair of yours, I have enough of my own."

To which the elder Caron replied, September 19th, 1764, "We supped yesterday with my dear and good friend who laughed heartily when she saw the article in your letter, imagining as she very well could, the way in which you would go about this affair if you were in my place, so that as she says, she only embraces you with all her heart, because you are nine hundred miles away."

But though the amiable Madame Henry was quite ready to laugh at the article in the son's letter she does not ap-pear to have been in any hurry to change the relationship which had so long existed between herself and the elder Caron, for shortly before his return from Madrid we find Beaumarchais writing in relation to the same matter: "A man ought not to be alone. One must hold to something in this life, and the society of your sons and daughters can only be sacrificed to another much sweeter, but which you do not seem on the point of acquiring. I precede my arri-val by a picture of what should be, so that you may have time to determine what you ought to do before my return, which will be soon. What happiness for me, if on reaching there I could on the same day see assured the felicity of my father and my sister."

Unfortunately for us, Beaumarchais returned from Spain in May, 1765, so that the correspondence ceased and with it, our means of following in detail the lives of those in whom we have begun to take so warm an interest. The "felicity" of the father we know, however, to have been consummated, for on January 15, 1766, he was united in marriage with the woman of his choice, Madame Henry, she being then sixty years of age and he sixty-eight. After two years of happy married life, Madame Caron died and we find her husband again returning to the rue Condé to live with his dearly loved son.

In the meantime, Mademoiselle de Boisgarnier had taken the advice of her brother, and we cannot for a moment doubt that she acted wisely; for her lover, Janot de Miron, seems to have been a man of exceptionally fine character. Referring to the letter already quoted in which Beaumarchais pleads with his sister for her friend, M. de Loménie says, "In reading this eulogy of poor Miron, where his moral qualities are exalted rather to the detriment of his brilliant ones, we have need to remember that Beaumarchais previously had declared his friend was not wanting in external accomplishments; and truly he was not. Miron, judging from his letters was rather pedantic, but in no way stupid. The taste for poetry and art, which reigned in the Caron family was no stranger to him. After several years of torment, he succeeded in touching that disdainful little heart and thus his constancy was rewarded. Mademoiselle de Boisgarnier, suitably endowed by her brother, married in 1767 M. de Miron, whom the influence of Beaumarchais later succeeded in having appointed ***Secretaire*** des ***Commandements*** du ***Prince*** de ***Conti.***

In all these matters it will be seen that Beaumarchais did not set himself up to be dictator in his family but was actuated solely by the desire to see consummated the dearest wish of those about him. Pauline he accepted as a settled fact of his existence, treating her as though he were her brother rather than her lover. His taste led him naturally to women more mature in years and experience, and he was far less sentimental than Pauline.

We shall see presently, as we come to treat of Beaumar- chais as an author, that though through flashes of inspiration he may at times attain the heights of the heroic, yet he has in reality small sympathy with it, either in life or literature. At no time, do we find him possessed of one of those absorbing passions which devour all lesser ones and which alone make sacrifice, not only necessary but easy; sacrifice is always distasteful to him. He has an intense desire to be happy and to have all about him happy. We must not expect, in this wise to find him a hero. Beaumarchais is pre-eminently a modern man, and it is no accident that he should have been an instrument to aid in laying the foundations of that modern nation, which more than any other, has brought ease and comfort within the reach of every class and condition of men.

CHAPTER V

"*Les* serments

Des amants

Sont legers *comme* les vents,

Leur air *enchanteur,*

Leur douceur

Sont des piéges *trompeurs*

Caches sous *des* fleurs."

Séguedille *de* Beaumarchats

New study of Beaumarchais by Lintilhac—Beaumarchais's Return from Madrid—The. Lover of Julie Carries off Pauline—the Règlement de compte which Terminated this Romantic Chapter of the Life of Beaumarchais.

AMONG the numerous studies of the life of Beaumarchais which the admirable and scholarly work of M. de Loménie stimulated into being, none takes a higher place than that of Eugène Lintilhac. Fired into enthusiasm by the work of Loménie, and having as he has said, his curiosity rather stimulated than satisfied thereby, he demanded of the descendants of Beaumarchais leave to examine for himself the entire mass of manuscript which had served as the foundation of that great work. He was also actuated, as he tells us, by the sentiment so forcibly expressed by Gu-din, "I soon found that I could not love him moderately when I came to know him in his home," and it was this sentiment which made him desire to refute from direct evidence some unsympathetic writings which had appeared, writings in which the character of Beaumarchais is inverted and all his great and disinterested actions viewed from the standpoint of whatever was ordinary about him, or whatever could be tortured into appearing so, thus making everything seem petty and contemptible, as when a telescope is reversed and all its power directed towards diminishing, the objects upon which it is turned.

Many of the letters which we have already quoted were first published by him, and we shall have occasion, more than once to have recourse to his volume. In the family correspondence M. Lintilhac found several fragments of letters written by friends and especially by one M. de la Chataig-nerie, a man at that time well advanced in years, but devoted to the interests of his friend and who had been left with a certain oversight of the family. He wrote: "The dear sister, who though slightly indisposed, conserves her reason, at least so far as essentials go, begs you to bring everything that you find which is good in all the places where you pass, even the hams of Bayonne. Time presses because the little dog of a Boisgarnier drives me to despair, and beats me— it is true that I deserve no better. Adieu, adieu—deliver me from my guardianship!"

And M. Lintilhac continues: "Nevertheless the care does not rest altogether on him, the main part falls on Julie— who keeps the purse, which is no small matter, for we find that, by the 17th of November she already had given out from 7000 to 8000 francs. We must believe that they were well expended because she no doubt followed the programme traced for her by her brother. 'I recommend to you economy as the mother of comfort,' and he adds without joking, 'modesty as the amiable companion of great success.' He wishes that the family, 'think of him a little in his absence.'

'Men are vain he adds, they like to be flattered."

Beaumarchais, just before leaving Spain, wrote: "So I am putting my whole mind on my business, my Father, while my misfortune causes me to lose. 2000 ecus of income from the provisions of France which dissolve especially to ruin me, the King of Spain and the Ministers cast their eyes on me to be at the head of those in Spain, as my old Du Verney is of those in France. There is talk of joining to this the furnishing in general of all the grain needed for Spain as well as the fabrication of saltpetre and powder, so that I may find myself suddenly at the head of a company for providing provisions, subsistences, munitions and agricultural products.

"Keep this for the family and see that my prospects, honest as they are, are known only by their success."

And Julie replied in her tenderest vein, "My Beaumarchais, my amiable genius, I have seen your letters, your projects, your work and nothing surprises- me, not even your philosophizing over our sad news. When any one ap-preciates you as I do, one has the right to count upon astonishing things. Assuredly we will keep the secret; but when do you return? My heart rebels at your long absence."

M. Lintilhac continues: "We know his grand projects did not receive the aid and sanction of the ministry, but they were dismissed with flattering compliments for him. All his plans, however, had not proved abortive as has so often been said, because on returning to France he writes to his father from Bordeaux, April 2nd, 1765, "I am now at Bordeaux, I don't know whether I shall leave to-morrow or the next day. My Spanish business requires certain information which I can obtain only here, or in some other seaport, I received a letter from Durand at Madrid very satisfactory in regard to the obliging regrets of the honest people of Madrid as well as for the affairs to which I have there attached him. I am absolutely alone, my valet de chambre stayed at Bayonne with a groom and three beautiful horses, which at Paris ought to pay the price of their journey as well as my own."

No record has come down to us of the meeting of Beau-marchais and his family after their long separation, but now that we know them all so intimately it is not difficult to reconstruct the scene, the venerable father pressing his son to his bosom, the tears of tenderness welling to his eyes, the sisters rushing to embrace him, the friends and domestics even, eager to clasp his hand, and all radiant with the thought of having him in their midst. Then this outburst of affection over, what gaiety and mirth follow, and all that human expansiveness which comes so spontaneously from the heart!

But though the family tie remained as strong as ever, a decided change had come already into the situation between him and Pauline. Nevertheless, matters were smoothed over and the marriage was definitely decided upon. Misunderstandings, however, continued from time to time, and in the midst of these troubles, a rumor reached the ears of Beau-marchais, that the Chevalier du S. had intentions upon Pauline. Beaumarchais, furious, wrote a letter to the Chevalier who in turn defended himself in a letter which is as follows: "It seems to me, Monsieur, that a counterfeit story ought to find less credit in your eyes than in those of others, since you have been all your life the butt of such reports. For the rest, I beg you to believe that I do not write to obtain grace, but because I owe to Mile, de L. B.— to make known the truth upon a point which compromises her, and because it would be hard and very hard for me to lose your esteem."

Pauline replied to the same charge with an indifference which shows a great change of sentiment on her part.

"As I was ignorant of the project of M. le Chevalier before I received your letter, and as I know nothing of the matter, you will permit me to inform myself before I reply. As to the reproach which you make in regard to Julie, I do not feel that I merit it, if I have not sent to know how she is, it is because I have been assured that she was very much better and had been seen at her window, which made me think that it was true. If my aunt were not ill, which prevents my leaving, I would assuredly go to see her. I embrace her with all my heart."

M. de Loménie says: "The two were perhaps innocent at that moment, if I can judge from a letter of a cousin of Pauline's and a friend of Beaumarchais, very badly treated by the latter in regard to this affair, 'When you have a more tranquil mind so that you will do me justice,' says the cousin, 'I will speak openly with you and prove to you that you, who condemn others so easily, are more culpable than those you believe to be dissimulating and perfidious. Nothing is so pure as the heart of the dear Pauline, nothing nobler than that of the Chevalier, or more sincere than my own, and you look upon all three as though we were monsters.' "

The above letter of November 8, 1765, is all we have to fix the date of the previous one. During the interval which follows, it is impossible to determine exactly what happened, but true it is that by February 11th, 1766, the definite rupture had taken place and even the cousin undertakes no longer to shield the "dear Pauline." As to the Chevalier, who a year before had written of Julie, "She is the unique object of my tenderest desires," it may be that Julie herself had much to do with his estrangement, for in a letter already quoted we have her own authority for believing that she was never very deeply in love, and her "maliciousness," may have helped to cool the ardor of the Chevalier. Certain it is, that Julie with all her warmth and expansiveness was not by nature any more formed for absorbing passions than was her brother. A letter belonging to a very much earlier period, proves that love was at no time a very serious matter with her, while it paints to the life the gaiety of her character. She writes, "You must know, my dear Lhénon upon what terms of folly I am with your brother. His air of interest for me, of which I wrote a month ago, has developed singularly and beautified itself since our friends have gone to the country. He comes nearly every evening to supper and stays till midnight or one o'clock. Ah my dear Lhénon, you should hear him recounting to me, and me retorting in the same tone with that air of *folie* that you have always known me to possess; but in the midst of all these pleasantries I have sometimes found a happy way of expressing myself, so as to persuade him seriously that I do not love him, and I believe him convinced, although I have never said half as many sweet things to him as I do now, because of an agreement which we have to love each other two days of the week, he has chosen Monday and Saturday, and I took Thursday and Sunday. On those days we say very tender things, although it is agreed that there shall always be one farouche when the other loves."

This to be sure was a girlish fancy, but the character of Julie retained to the end much of the *folie* of which she here speaks, without, however, in the least impairing its real seriousness. But whatever the cause, the fact remains that the

Chevalier du S. declared himself to Pauline, who in turn disengaged herself from Beaumarchais. The corre-spondence ended with two long letters from the latter and one short, dry note from Pauline. M. de Loménie in speaking of the letters of Beaumarchais observes, "In novels each impulse of the human heart is ordinarily painted separately with vivid colors, well marked and without blending. In reality, things seldom pass that way; when one impulse is not strong enough to stifle all the others, which generally is the case, the human heart presents a confused medley where the most diverse sentiments, often directly opposite, speak at the same time." It is thus that in the letters which are given, one can discern in the heart of Beaumarchais, to quote Loménie, "a remnant of love reawakening, excited by jealousy and restricted in its expression by vanity, scruples of delicacy and honor, the fears of what they will say, the need to prove that he has no reproach to make to himself, the determination to wed, and yet perhaps a certain fear of being taken at his word, because, although these letters contain a very formal offer of marriage, they also contain certain passages sufficiently mortifying, so that the pride of Pauline would reply by a refusal. Again it is evident that Beaumarchais fears a refusal and whether from love or self esteem he wishes to triumph."

"You have renounced me," he wrote to Pauline, "and what time have you chosen to do it? The very moment which I had announced to your friends and mine, would be that of our union. I have seen the perfidy which has caused everything to turn against me, even to my offers. I have seen you, you who have so often sighed at the injustice which others have done me, join yourself to them to create wrongs of which I never thought. If I had not had the intention of marrying you, would I have put so little form into the services which I rendered you? Would I have assembled your friends and mine two months before your refusal, to announce to them my resolution ? Everything has turned against me. The conduct of a friend, two-faced and perfidious, in giving me a cruel lesson, has taught me that there is no woman so honest and so tender who cannot be seduced and made to change. Also the contempt of all those who have seen him act, is his just recompense. Let us come back to you. It is not without regret that I have turned my thoughts from you, since the first heat of my resentment has passed, and when I insisted that you should write formally that you refused my offer of marriage, there was mixed with my chagrin, an obscure curiosity to see whether you would take this last step with me; to-day I must know absolutely how I stand. I have received very advantageous propositions of marriage, on the point of accepting I felt myself suddenly arrested; I do not know what scruple of honor, what return toward the past, made me hesitate. I have every reason to feel myself free and disengaged from you after all that has passed; nevertheless, I am far from tranquil, your letters do not say formally enough what is most important for me to know. Reply truly, I beg of you. Have you so completely renounced me that I am free to contract with another woman? Consult your heart upon this point, while my delicacy questions you. If you totally have cut the knot which should unite us, don't fear to tell me so. In order that your ***amour*** proper be completely at ease upon the demand which I make, I add this, that in writing to you I have put back everything to where it was before all these storms. My demand would not be just if, setting a trap for you, I did not give you the liberty of choice in your reply. Let your heart answer alone. If you do not give me back my liberty, write me that you are the same Pauline, sweet and tender for life, whom I used to know, and that you believe yourself happy to belong to me, instantly I break with everything that is not you. If your heart is turned to another, and invincibly estranged from me, do me the justice of admitting that I have been honest with you. Give to the bearer of this, the declaration which frees me and I shall feel that I have accomplished my duty and shall have no reproach to make myself. Adieu, I am, up to the moment of your reply, under whatever title it shall please you to choose, Mademoiselle, your very humble servant, etc.

De Beaumarchais.

"A few hours later followed a second letter: "I send you back the package of your letters, if you keep them, join mine to your reply. The reading of your letters has moved me deeply, I do not wish again to experience that pain, but before replying examine well what is the best for you, as well for your fortune as for your happiness. My intent is that, forgetting everything, we pass our days in tranquillity and happiness. Do not let the fear of living with the members of my family who do not please you arrest your sensibility, if another passion has not extinguished it. My home is so arranged that whether it be you, or whether it be another, my wife shall be the peaceful and happy mistress there. Your uncle laughed in my face when I reproached him with having opposed me. He told me that his opinion was that I need not fear a refusal or else that his niece's head had been turned. It is true that at the moment of renouncing you forever, I felt an emotion which showed me that I held more strongly to you than I thought. What I write therefore is from the sincerest faith in the world. Don't flatter yourself ever to give me the chagrin to see you the wife of a certain man. He must be very daring to think of raising his eyes before the public if he proposes to accomplish this double perfidy. Pardon me if I grow warm! Never has that thought entered my mind that all my blood has not boiled in my veins.

"But whatever your resolution, don't keep me waiting, because I have suspended all my business to give myself over once more to you. Your uncle tried to convince me that this marriage with you was not all to my advantage, but I am very far from occupying myself with these considerations. I wish to possess you only for yourself, and that it be for life. ... I admit that it would be sweet to me, if while the enemies slept, peace should be concluded between us. Re-read your letters and you will understand that I found again in the depths of my heart all the sentiments that they had there called into being."

Loménie remarks: "The reply of Pauline is much more laconic and much more direct. With her there is no con-flict of sentiments: she does not love Beaumarchais any more; that is very simple and very clear.

" I can only repeat, Monsieur, what I said to Mademoiselle your sister, that my stand is taken not to return, there-fore I thank you for your offers, and I desire with my whole heart that you may marry the person who will make you happy; I assured Mademoiselle your sister of this. My aunt and I feel it our duty to tell you how unhappy we are that you should fail in respect to us in treating so badly a man whom we consider as our friend. I know better than anyone else that you have no right to call him perfidious. I said once more this morning to Mademoiselle your sister, that a demoiselle who used to live with my aunt was the cause of what happens to-day. You have still several of my letters which I ask you to return. I will beg one of our friends to arrange with you about everything which remains to be adjusted. I am, very perfectly, Monsieur, your very humble and obedient servant,

L. B.

Still quoting Loménie: "Pauline who used to sign herself, I am for life thy faithful Pauline now signs politely her family name, and so this correspondence ends like so many others of the same nature, by, I have the honor to be,' or I am very perfectly' which succeed the protestations of an eternal love."

And now follows a second letter from the cousin in relation to this unhappy affair, "All is said, my dear Beaumar-chais, and without hope of return. I have notified Madame G. (the aunt of Pauline) and Mlle. Le B of your dispositions, they ask nothing better than to come to an honorable arrangement in this rupture. It remains now to regulate the account between Mlle. Le B and you, and to take measures to secure for you the sum which is due. These ladies beg you to give back all the papers which you have concerning the affairs of Mlle. Le B. You cannot tell how unhappy I am not to have been able to unite two hearts which for so long have seemed to me made for each other, but man proposes and God disposes. I flatter myself that on both sides the justice which I feel belongs to me, will be rendered. I have let you read in my heart, and you must have seen that I know neither disguisement nor artifice. Adieu, my friend, I will go to see you as soon as I can; in the meantime write to me. I embrace you, I am as always,

"Your sincere friend P

"February 11th, 1766—"

In the words of Loménie, "Let us accord this worthy cousin, whose sentences are more consoling than new, the justice which he claims, and acknowledge that he is a stranger to the perfidy of the Chevalier. If we were writing a romance we would stop here, or else end with the death of Beaumarchais, he killing himself in despair, or by the death of the Chevalier, immolated by the fury of his rival; but as we are writing a history we are obliged above all else to be exact and instead of stating that the adventure ends by a suicide or a duel we are forced to state that it terminates much more prosaically, by a règlement *de* comptes **where the future author of the** Mariage *de* Figaro makes an amusing enough figure in his role of betrayed lover and uneasy creditor."

There is, we must admit, an indefinable humor in the idea of the brilliant genius Beaumarchais, deserted by his Pauline, seating himself, *le* coeur *gros,* the tears of anger and mortification welling to his eyes, intent upon regulating, with the same minute exactitude that he showed in making the watch to be set as a jewel in a lady's ring, the account existing between him and Pauline.

As a matter of fact, he had been far less prudent in his generous advances of money than in the expression of his sentiments as a lover, for not only had he risked large sums on the Santo Domingo property, but he had been in the habit of advancing money both to Pauline and to her aunt without keeping any special count. To return to the account of Lomènie, "He groups the capital with the interest and presents a bill of the most scrupulous rectitude. The Cheva- Her, who has no time to bother with such vile details, and who has gone to pass his honeymoon I don't know where, sends to Beaumarchais his older brother, the abbe du S, respectable, but a little quick tempered, who not only quibbles over the bill, but permits himself sometimes to deepen a bleeding wound by opposing the lover to the creditor. From that come stormy discussions, of which the following letter of Beaumarchais to the abbe will serve as illustration.

" 'Monsieur l'abbé,

" 'I beg you to notice that I never have been lacking in politeness towards you, but that I owe nothing but con-tempt for him whom you represent, as I have had the honor of saying to you twenty times, and as I strongly would have desired to say to him if he had been as exact in showing himself as he has been clever in taking my place. The proof that Mlle. Le B wished well of me, of my affection, of my counsels, of my money, is that without your brother she would still make use of all my gifts which I lavished upon her as long as they were agreeable and useful to her. It is true that she bought my services very dear, since she owes to our affection for your brother the happiness of having married him, which she would not have done, if he had remained without knowing us in the place where he then vegetated. I do not understand the secret of the phrase about the apology, so I am dispensed with replying to it. I regret that he is absent, only because I would have the greatest pleasure to testify to him in person, what he can now only know through proxy. I shall not cease to prepare myself for atrocities and injustices by benevolent acts. It always has agreed with me very well to do good in the expectation of evil, and your counsel adds nothing to my disposition in that regard.

" 'Since you admit that you have lost your temper with me, it would be out of place for me to reproach you with it. It is sufficient that you accuse yourself, for me not to hold any resentment.

" 'I do not know why you have underlined the words, "your sister," in recalling to me that I said that it was in this way that I loved Mlle. Le B. Does this irony fall back on her, on me, or on your brother? Just as you please, for that matter. Although the fate of Mlle. Le B interests me no longer, it would be out of place for me, in speaking of her, to use other terms than those which I have employed. It is not her that I blame; she is as you have said, young and without experience and although she has very little fortune, your brother has used well his experience and has made a good affair in marrying her.

" 'Remember, I beg you, Monsieur l'abbé, that all which is addressed to him has nothing to do with you. It would be too humiliating for a man of your station to be suspected of having had any part in the perfidy of your brother in my regard; let him bear the blame, and do not take up those things which do not deserve to have a defender as honest as yourself.

" 'I have the honor to be, etc.

" 'Beaumarchais.' "

The matter finally was adjusted and the account reduced to 24,441 livres, 4 sous, 4 deniers.

One would almost think that after making such important reductions the sum might have been rounded off by the omission of the 4 sous, 4 deniers. Not so Beaumarchais—the whole debt might go unpaid for he was not a man to make much trouble about that, but in any case, the matter must stand in its absolute exactitude. M. de Loménie terminates this interesting chapter of the life of Beaumarchais in the following manner: "And now I demand pardon of the shade of the charming Pauline, but it seems certain that this debt, recognized and accepted by her, was never paid. Not only do I find it amongst papers of a later date classed as almost hopeless debts, but the touching solicitude of the cashier Gudin, after the death of his master, for the least letter of Pauline, is sufficient to demonstrate that this too must be ranged amongst those debts recognized but not dissolved, where so many amiable women, poets, and great lords have left their traces in the papers of Beaumarchais. It is true that Pauline was left a widow a year after her marriage, and this misfortune no doubt spoiled the arrangement of her affairs—and I conclude that if the young and beautiful Creole left her debt unpaid, it must have been because the habitation of Santo Domingo was seized by the other creditors, or plundered by the blacks or swallowed up by an earthquake."

> For our part let us hasten to add that we are very grateful to the Chevalier du for carrying off Pauline.

Charming as she was, she did not possess those sterling qualities which alone could have enabled her to be a real helpmeet to him in the terrible trials, which were preparing for him. Overwhelmed as we shall presently see him, a nature like hers would have been as a millstone about his neck, and he inevitably must have succumbed. As we shall see, the woman who eventually comes to share his life was of a very different mould. Misfortune and all the terrors of the Revolution only served to bring into more striking relief the vigor of a character already pronounced in its strength and womanliness.

Our gratitude to the Chevalier du S is no less great, in that by abstracting Pauline, he left to Beaumarchais the truest support of his life, the woman who better than any one else understood the inmost recesses of his nature, and who at no moment of his career failed in giving him the affection, the encouragement, which he needed, and that served as the solid basis upon which he could build. In leaving to Beaumarchais the undisputed possession of his

sister Julie, the Chevalier du S has won our undying gratitude, and so in all sincerity we say, ***requiescat in pace.***

CHAPTER VI

*"**Je** laisserai **sans** réponse **tout** ce **qu'on** a **dit** contre Vou-**vrage**, persuade **que** le **plus** grand **honneur** qu **on ait** pu **lui** faire, **aprcs** celui **de** s'en **amuser** au **theatre, a** été **de** ne **pas** le **juger** indigne **de** toute **critique"***

***Beaumarchais** in **"Essai sur** le **genre** dramatique sérieux," prefixed **to** the **edition** of "Eugenie"*

"Eugénie"—"Les ***deux*** Amis'—Second *Marriage* of ***Beau***marchais—*The* Forest *of* Chinon—***Death*** of ***Madame*** de ***Beaumarchais.***

THE immediate effect of Pauline's desertion of Beaumar-chais was to turn his thoughts from the gay world in which he was so brilliant and so striking a figure, to the more sober realms of literature. His talent as an author already had manifested itself by several farces and charades written for his colleague, M. Lenormant d'Étioles, the husband of Madame de Pompadour, at whose château d'Étioles they were produced.

The very spicy charade, *"**John** Bête à **la** Foire," was written in 1762 for a special festival given at this chateau in the forest of Senart. On this occasion and* *on all similar occasions the farces of Beaumarchais found no more spirited interpreters than his own sisters. Fournier says, "The youngest played comedies with a surprising* verve *de* gaillardise, *and it would seem, was not frightened by the most highly seasoned of her brother's productions. She and the Countess of Turpin played the leading parts. Comedies and charades were also played enchantingly by Julie who frequently arranged them in her own style; several scenes and not the least spicy, according to family tradition, passing as her own production."*

But this vein of true Gallic wit which was later to carry its possessor to almost unprecedented heights of fame was not in keeping with the spirit in which Beaumarchais found himself during the winter of 1766.

The entire family as we have seen possessed in an unusual degree a warm life blood which burst spontaneously into joyful expression, but it showed itself also in sentimental sallies. The English novelist, Richardson, was a favorite with them all and we find Julie writing in her diary, about this time, "I see in Beaumarchais a second Grandison; it is his genius, his goodness, his noble and superior soul, equally sweet and honest. Never a bitter sentiment for his enemies arises in his heart. He is the friend of man. Grandison is the glory of all who surround him, and Beaumarchais is their honor."

The father writing to his son during an illness said: "In the intervals when I suffer less I read Grandison and in how many things I have found a just and noble resemblance between him and my son. Father of thy sisters, friend and benefactor of thy father, 'if England,' I said to myself, 'has her Grandison; France has her Beaumarchais; with this difference, that the English Grandison is the fiction of an amiable writer, while the French Beaumarchais really exists to be the consolation of my days.'"

It was, therefore, Beaumarchais, as Grandison, whom we now find seriously occupying himself with the thought of literature. Nor shall we be surprised later to find those of the literary profession preparing to meet him in very much the same spirit as did in the beginning M. Lepaute, watchmaker, and a little later, *Mes-*

sieurs les *Courtisans* at *Versailles.* So long as his literary ambition limited itself to charades, farces, and comic songs the antagonism of men of letters was not aroused; but that he who had received no regular training in the schools should presume, *de* se méler, with serious literary productions was quite another matter.

Lintilhac says: "But our immature author, shaking his tête carrée braved this danger like all the rest, arming him-self with patience and esprit; let us see him at his work.

"A literary instinct had from the beginning led him straight to those Gallic writers whose race he was destined to continue. We find him studying Montaigne; he extracts notes and imitates Marot, translates in verse and sets to music one of the hundred and twenty romances of the Cid going against the Moors in the eleventh century.

"But his taste for the ancestor of the *esprit* français is not exclusive; he is happy to find it among their direct descendants: Regnier, whom he quotes abundantly, La Fontaine, of whom he is a disciple, Molière and Pascal, who furnish the models of his chefs-d'oeuvre. More than that, he goes back to their antique masters. The rudiments of Latin which he learned at school serve to help him to read Lu-crece, Catulle, Tibulle, Horace, Ovid, and Seneca, and to take from them that salt of citation with which he heightens so effectively the sallies of his Gallic wit."

Among the manuscripts of the Comédie Française are a number of pages covered with Latin citations, elegantly translated, which Beaumarchais adapted to the circumstances of his life and works, with a precision which could not have been the result of chance.

"This is. the serious side of hia education, but it was not all; the unfolding and development of his talents must have been deeply influenced by that society of which he was the *bout*-en-*train,* and where the Prince de Conti and the Countess de *Boufflers,* la *divine* Comtesse, *restored the ancient traditions of epicurean esprit. What did he not owe to conversation, often free, always piquant, of the aristocratic and bourgeois salons, to the foyers of the theaters and cafes which he frequented, and in which he was past-master, fencing with such skilled champions as Chamfort, as Sophie Arnould, those little kings* de *l'*esprit! We must therefore give to. these brilliant contemporaries of our author the honor of having shaped his genius." (M. de Lomçnie.)

We have spoken already of Beaumarchais's natural aversion to the heroic in literature, all his instincts led him to-ward the new dramatic school which was then appearing in France, and whose master was Diderot. In this school the old heroic tragedy was replaced by a domestic tragedy in which the ordinary events of daily life formed the theme. By the side of this, there was to be a serious comedy, not clearly defined from the tragic element, but which was to take the place of the "gay comedy" of the past,

More than a century of democratic ideas has so far removed the present generation from the ideas of the past, that it is difficult for us to appreciate the magnitude of the innovation made by this new style of literature when it first appeared in France. It was, however, but the natural outgrowth of that new order of things which was year by year becoming more pronounced, in which the bourgeoisie of France rises to a state of self consciousness which demands expression. The splendor of the monarchy as upheld by Louis XIV had faded from men's minds. The people were beginning to realize that they themselves, with their joys and sorrows, their loves and hates, belonged to the realm of art.

Beaumarchais forcibly expresses the new ideas when in his essay "*Sur* le *Genre* Sériewx," he says, "If our heart enters into the interest taken in tragic personages, it is less because they are heroes and kings than because they are human beings and miserable. Is it the Queen of Messina that touches me in Méropé? No, it is the mother of Égite. Nature alone has right over our hearts.—The true relation of the heart is, therefore, always from man to man, and never from man to king. The brilliancy of rank far from augmenting the interest which we feel in a tragic personage, on the contrary destroys it. The nearer to mine the condition of him who suffers, the more touched am I by his woes. It belongs to the essence of the serious drama to offer a more pressing interest, a more direct morality than that of the heroic tragedy, and there should be something more serious than mere gay comedy." After developing this theme for a considerable length he terminates thus, "The morality of comedy is nil, the reverse of what should be in the theater."

Beaumarchais, a few years later, yielding with his usual suppleness to the inevitable, when he found the public re-fusing to be interested in his serious mediocrities, abandoned the *genre* sérieux, which in the beginning he so warmly defended. He did not leave it, however, without a last thrust at his critics.

In his preface to the "***Barbier* de *Seville*,**" which he published eight years later, he thus alludes to these earlier productions: "I had the weakness, Monsieur, to present to you at different times two poor dramas, monstrous productions as is very well known, because between tragedy and comedy no one is any longer ignorant that nothing exists, that is a point settled ... As for myself, I am so completely convinced of the truth of this that if I wished again to bring on the scene, a mother in tears, a betrayed wife, a forlorn sister, a son disinherited, in order to present them decently to the public, I should begin by placing them in a beautiful kingdom where they had done their best to reign, and I " should situate it near one of the archipelagoes, or in some remote corner of the world. . . . The spectacle of men of medium condition, crushed and suffering, how absurd! Ridiculous citizens and unhappy kings, there is nothing else the theatre will permit."

For those of Beaumarchais's admirers who consider the creation of Figaro as his highest title to fame, it is no matter of regret that after imperfect success with his first drama, and almost failure with his second, he should have made the transition to gay comedy. Figaro, however, as we shall see, did not come before the public simply for its amusement, he came as the announcement of that complete change which already was taking place in the social institutions of modern Europe, first breaking out in France, so that his apparition, therefore, was no mere accident, but a momentous event.

At the present moment in 1766, no one could be farther than Beaumarchais from the possibility of such a creation, for although he had brought with him from Spain the crude outline of the *"Barbier,"* he lacked as yet all that experience which was to give political significance to the play, and which was destined to enable him to voice for all time the right of the individual to be heard in his own cause. In 1766 he not only imagined himself to be, but was, one of the most loyal, one of the most respectful subjects of the king. His life of adventure apparently was over. He asked for nothing better than the fortune and position he had acquired already. At heart he was sbove everything else domestic and was therefore warmly attracted toward the new literary school. Loménie says, "He precipitated himself with his ordinary fervor into the *drame* domestique *et* bourgeois, which seemed to him an unknown world of which Diderot was the Christopher Columbus, and of which he hoped to be the Vespucius."

In speaking of Beaumarchais's attraction for this school Gudin says: "Struck with the new beauties which the French stage displayed from day to day, drawn on by his own talent he descended into the arena, to mix with the combatants who disputed the palms of the scenic plays.

"Never before had been seen such an assemblage of excellent actors, the theater was not simply a place of amusement, it was a course in public instruction; here were displayed the customs of all nations and the principal events. of history; all the interests of humanity were there developed with that truth which convinces, and arouses thought in every mind.

"Diderot proposed to paint upon the scene the different duties of the social condition, the father of the family, the magistrate, the merchant, in order to show the virtues which each requires. It was certainly a new point of view which he offered to the public. Beaumarchais felt his heart deeply touched, and yielding to the impulse which he felt, he composed, almost in spite of himself, his touching *Eugenie*,

"This is the picture of a virtuous girl infamously seduced by a great lord. No piece ever offered a more severe morality, or more direct instruction to fathers of vain women, who allow themselves to be blinded by titles and great names. It is the duty of every author to attack the vices of his own century. This duty the Greeks first understood. But in France a thousand voices were raised against the innovation, Beaumarchais, whom nothing intimidated, dared in his first play to attack the vice so common among great lords, especially under Louis XV.

"Certainly this ought to have made him applauded by every friend of virtue. The opposite occurred. The friends kept silence. Those who were guilty of similar vice cried out against the play, their flatterers cried still louder, jour-nalists and the envious authors hissed and cried out that it was detestable, scandalous, badly conceived and executed, immoral. Not one applauded the energetic audacity of the author who dared to raise his voice against the luxurious vice permitted by the monarchy and even by the magistrates. Beaumarchais, however, had the public on his side, the piece remained upon the stage and was constantly applauded."

Although the fastidious French taste, apart from all the enmity aroused by the many-sided success of its author, found much to criticise in the production, Eugénie, *or* la *Vertu* malheurewse**, the piece retains its place upon the repertoire of the** Théâtre *Frangais* and is still occasionally given.

Outside France it met with a much warmer reception. The German writer, Bettleheim, assures us that it was at once translated into most of the Kultur-Sprachen of Europe and was produced in the principal theatres everywhere. In England, through the support of Garrick, then director of the Drury Lane theater, and in Austria, through that of Sonnenfels, it met with an astounding success.

In Germany the translation was very soon followed by an imitation called "***Aurelie,*** oder *Trkumph* der *Tugend.*"

Of the English play Garrick writes to Beaumarchais: "The School for Rakes, which is rather an imitation than a translation of your Eugénie, has been written by a lady to whom I recommended your drama, which has given me the greatest pleasure and from which I thought she could make a play which would singularly please an English audience; I have not been deceived, because with my help, as stated in the advertisement, which precedes the piece, our Eugénie has received the continual applause of the most numerous audiences."

In Italy the success of ***Eugenie*** was scarcely less pronounced. It was first produced in Venice in 1767, and in the criticism which follows the publication of the translation we read: "The whole city was in great expectancy when it was known that this drama was to appear upon the scene. The impressions made upon the hearts of the spectators corresponded with the fame which had preceded it and instead of diminishing this constantly continued to increase in such a manner that the whole of Italy, although rich in her own productions, has not grown weary of praising the piece."

But for Beaumarchais the important thing was to win recognition from his own country. This was no easy mat-ter; he, however, did not despair, and set about it with his usual tenacity of purpose, infinitude of resource and ver-satility of genius.

M. de Lomenie says: "Beaumarchais worked with all his energy to prepare a success for his play; we are indeed, far from 1784, at which time the author of the ***Mariage*** de ***Figaro*** only had to hold back the feverish impatience of a public that awaited the performance of the piece as one of the most extraordinary events. We are in 1767, Beaumarchais is completely unknown as an author. He is a man of business, a man of pleasure who has been able to push himself somewhat at court, about whom people talk very differently, and whom men of letters are disposed to consider, as did the courtiers, an intruder. From this arose the necessity for him to push ahead, ,to arouse curiosity and to secure from all ranks supporters for his play. This is what he does with that aptitude which distinguishes him.

"When, for instance, it is a question of obtaining the privilege of reading his drama before Mesdames, he poses as a courtier who has condescended to occupy himself with literature in the interest of virtue and good manners. He assumes a celebrity which he has not yet acquired and on the whole seems endowed with a rare presumption; here is the letter:

" 'Mesdames:

" 'The comedians of the Comédie Francaise are going to present in a few days, a drama of a new kind which all Paris is awaiting with lively impatience. The orders which I gave to the comedians in making them a present of the work, that they should guard the secret of the name of the author, have not been obeyed. In their unfortunate enthusiasm, they believed that they rendered me a service in transgressing my wishes. As this work, child of my sensibility, breathes the love of virtue, and tends to purify our theater and make it a school of good manners, I have felt that I owe a special homage to my illustrious protectresses. I come, therefore, Mesdames, to beg you to listen to a reading of my play. After that, if the public at the representation carries me to the skies, the most beautiful success of my drama will be to have been honored by your tears, as the author has always been by your benefits.'

"With the duke of Noailles, to whom he had read the piece, and who had shown an interest, Beaumarchais poses as a statesman who has missed his calling. The letter to the Duke of Noailles is as follows:

" 'It is only in odd moments, Monsieur le duc, that I dare give way to my taste for literature. When I cease for one moment to turn the earth and cultivate the garden of my advancement, instantly what I have cleared is cov-ered with brambles so that I must recommence unceasingly. Another of the follies from which I have been forced to tear myself is the study of politics, a subject thorny and repulsive for most men, but quite as attractive as useless for me. I loved it to madness, and I have done everything to develop it, the rights of respective powers, the pretentions of princes, by which the mass of mankind always is kept in commotion, the action and reaction of governments, all these are interests made for my soul. Perhaps there is no one who has felt so much the disadvantage of being able to see things **en grand**, being at the same time the smallest of men. Sometimes I have gone so far as to murmur in my unjust humor that fate did not place me more advantageously in regard to those things for which I believed myself suited, especially when I consider that the missions which kings and ministers give to their agents, have the power to confer the grace of the ancient apostleship, which instantly made sublime and intelligent men of the most insignificant brains.' "

To the duke of Nivernais, Beaumarchais was indebted for a useful criticism of the weak side of his play. It probably may be due to that nobleman's observations that he made the important change of transporting the scene to England, and giving the characters English names. As the play now stands, after decided modifications made immediately following the first representations, the story is this:

Eugénie, the daughter of a Welsh gentleman, supposes herself the wife of Lord Clarendon, nephew of the Minister of War. Clarendon, however, basely has deceived her by a false marriage in which his steward plays the role of chap- lain, and he prepares to marry a wealthy heiress the very day that his victim arrives in London.

The weakness of the play consists in this, that while the character of Eugenie in its delicate, sweet womanliness, enlists our entire sympathy and admiration, we are not sufficiently prepared at the end of the fifth act to see the man who has so deceived her, pardoned and reacepted on his giving up his intended marriage along with the ambitious schemes of his powerful uncle, even though the old baron utters the sublime truth that "he who has sincerely repented is farther from evil than he who has never known it."

In the words of the Duke of Nivernais, "In the first act Clarendon is a scoundrel who has deceived a young girl of good family by a false marriage, he prepares to wed another, and this is the man, who in the end finds grace in the eyes of Eugenie, a being who interests us. It requires a great deal of preparation to arrive at this conclusion." This was the whole difficulty, and though Beaumarchais retouched as best he could the character of Clarendon, making as much as possible of the extenuating circumstances, and emphasizing his hesitation and remorse, the play remains weak in this respect.

The English imitation before spoken of, rectifies this difficulty by altering the role of Clarendon. In the advertise-ment, the author says, however, "I have not dared to deviate from the gentle, interesting Eugénie of Beaumarchais."

The play finally was given for the first time, January 29th, 1767. In the "***Annie** Littéraire" **of that year this passage occurs:*** "Engérde, played for the first time January the 29th of this year, was badly received by the public and its reception had all the appearance of a failure; it has raised itself since with brilliancy, through omissions and corrections; it occupied the public for a long time and this success greatly honors the comedians."

"The changes made by Beaumarchais between the first and second representations were sufficient," says Loménie, "to bring into relief the first three acts, which contain many beautiful parts, and which announced already a rare talent of ***mise*** en ***scene*** and of dialogue. The refined, distinguished acting of an amiable young actress, Mlle. Do-ligny, who represented Eugenie, contributed not a little to save the drama and make it triumph brilliantly over the danger that threatened its first representation."

Beaumarchais had gained the public ear, but not the critics. As Lintilhac says: "The enterprise did not proceed without scandal, for at the second representation instead of hissing, the public weeps. The critic enraged at the success of the piece cried, 'It is all the fault of the women— talk to them of ***Eugenie***; it is they who have perverted the taste of our dear young people.' Nevertheless the piece endures in the face of censures and cabals.—He managed his dramatic affairs quite as cleverly as the others. Abuse goes along with success, ***tant*** mieux! So much the better, it gives him the opportunity of lashing criticism with witty replies, which he prints with his play in a long preface of justification."

"Into what a wasps nest you have put your head," said Diderot to him.

Gudin observes, "He was not one to be frightened at their buzzing, or to stop on his way to kill flies. He was busying himself with a new drama."

That this first production, "This child of my sensibility," as he called it, was always dear to his heart is proved by the fact that years afterwards Beaumarchais gave the name of Eugenie to his only daughter, of whom we shall have much to say later on.

But in the meantime, an event occurred which for period of two years had an important bearing on his life. To quote Gudin: "It was about this time that Madam B., celebrated for her beauty, came one day to find the sister of Beaumarchais and asked her what her brother was doing as she had not seen him for a long time.

" 'I do not know if he is at home, but I believe he is working on his drama.'

" 'I have something to say to him.'

"He was called. He appeared looking like a hermit, his hair in disorder, his beard long, his face illumined by medi-tation.

" 'Well, my friend, what are you busying yourself with when an amiable woman, recently a widow, sought already by several pretendants, might prefer you? I am to ride with her to-morrow in that secluded avenue of the Champs Élysées, which is called *l'allee* des *Veuves;* mount on horseback, we will meet you there as if by chance; you will speak to me, and then you shall both see whether or not you are suited to one another.

"The next day Beaumarchais, followed by a domestic, appeared mounted on a superb horse which he managed with grace. He was seen from the coach in which the ladies were riding long before he joined them. The beauty of the steed, the bearing of the cavalier worked in his favor; when he came near, Madam B. said she knew the horseman. Beaumarchais came up and was presented to the lady.

"This meeting produced a very vivid impression; the veil, the crèpe, the mourning costume served to bring into re-lief the fairness of the complexion and the beauty of the young widow. Beaumarchais soon left his horse for the carriage, and as no author dialogued better for the stage so no man ever brought more art into his conversation. If at first it was simply sallies of wit, it became by degrees more interesting and finished by being attractive. Beau-marchais finally proposed that the ladies should come and dine at his home. Madam B. persuaded the young woman to consent, although she refused several times. He sent back his horse by his domestic which was the signal arranged with his sister in order that she might prepare to receive the ladies, one of whom was an entire stranger.

"It is very different seeing a man out riding and seeing him in his own home. It is there that one must follow him in order to judge him rightly and so it was on entering that unpretentious, though elegant and convenient home, seeing Beaumarchais surrounded by his old domestics, seated between his father and sister, the latter a young woman of much intelligence and proud of such a brother, the young woman could not but realize that it would be an honor to have him for her husband. The table disposes to confidence, the heart opens and discloses itself; they had not left it before each was sure of the other and they had but one desire, never to separate. They were married in April, 1768. His fortune was increased by that of his wife, and his happiness by the possession of a woman who loved him passionately."

His wife's name was Madame Lèvêque, née Genevieve Madeleine Watebled. She was possessed of an ample fortune which added to that of Beaumarchais made their position in every way desirable. The world at last seemed ready to smile upon him and he quite content to settle down to peaceful enjoyment of all the blessings with which his life was now crowned.

Gudin says, "Happy in love and in his friends, he amused himself in painting the effects of these passions in a drama, *'Les* Deux *Amis.*" The following year a son was born to him, the happiness of being a father was the only happiness which had hitherto been denied him.

The new drama, "*Les* Deux *Amis*" although he himself says of it, "It is the most powerfully composed of all my works," was not a success before the Parisian public. In the provinces and in the most of Europe it met with a very different reception, long retaining its favor with the public there.

It is the story of two friends who live in the same house, Malac père, *collector of rents for a Parisian company, and Aurelly, merchant of Lyons, where the scene is laid. Aurelly is expecting from Paris certain sums to enable him to meet a payment which must be made in a few days. Malac* père *learns that the money from Paris will not arrive and to save his friend turns into the latter's case all which he has in his possession as collector of rents, allowing his friend to think that the money from Paris has arrived. At this moment the agent-general of the Paris company appears demanding the rents. During two acts Malac* père allows himself to be suspected of having appropriated the money, meekly accepting the disdain of the friend whose credit he has saved.

The real situation discloses itself at last and through the heroism of Pauline, the niece of Aurelly, and the curi-osity of the agent-general, St. Alban, the threatened ruin is averted.

In connection with the main action, Beaumarchais has joined a charming episode of the loves of Pauline and Malac *fils*. The play opens with a pleasing scene, where the young girl is seated at the piano playing a sonata while the young man accompanies her with the violin; the scene and the conversation which follows are a touching souvenir of the early days of Beaumarchais's attachment for the beautiful creole, Pauline.

The piece was produced January 13, 1770, and was given ten times. Loménie says, in explaining the reason for the short duration of the play: "Each one of us suffers, loves and hates in virtue of an impulse of the heart, but very few have a clear idea of what is felt by one exposed to bankruptcy or supposed guilty of misappropriating money. These situations are too exceptional to work upon the soul, too vulgar to excite the imagination, they may well concur in forming the interest of a drama, but only on condition that they figure as accessories. Vainly did Beaumarchais blend the loves of Pauline and Malac fils, trying to sweeten the aridity of the subject. Several spiritual or pathetic scenes could not save the too commercial drama of 'Les *Deux* Amis: "

The author having, as he said, the advantage over his sad brothers of the pen in that he could go to the theater in his own *carosse*, and making perhaps a little too much of this advantage, the effect of the failure of his drama was to call out many witticisms. It is said that at the end of the first representation a wag of the parterre cried out, "It is question here of bankruptcy; I am in it for twenty sous."

Several days afterward Beaumarchais remarked to Sophie Arnould, apropos of an opera *Zoroaster* which did not succeed, "In a week's time you will not have a person, or at least very few."

The witty actress replied, "*Vos* Amis will send them to us."
Finally the capital fault of the play is very well drawn up in the quatrain of the time,

"*I* have *seen* Beaumarchais*'s* ridiculous *drama*
, *And* in *a* single *word* I *will* say *what* it *is;*
It is *an* exchange *where* money *circulates*,
Without producing *any* interest"

Lintilhac remarks, "He gave in this crisis a double proof of his genius; in the first place, he allowed his piece to fall without comment, and in the second he did not despair of his dramatic vocation."

Already Beaumarchais was meditating his Barbier de Seville but in the meantime he was seriously occupied with a new and extensive business transaction. The fortune of his wife had enabled him to enter into a partnership with old Du Verney in the acquisition of the vast forest of Chinon, which they bought from the government. A letter to his wife, dated July 15, 1769, shows him at his work.

"De Rivarennes.
"You invite me to write, my good friend, and I wish to with all my heart, it is

an agreeable relaxation from the fatigues of my stay in this village. Misunderstandings among the heads of departments to be reconciled, complaints, and demands of clerks to be listened to, an account of more than 100,000 ecus, in sums of from 20 to 30 sous to regulate, and of which it was necessary to discharge the regular cashier, the different posts to be visited, two hundred workmen of the forest whose work must be examined, two hundred and eighty acres of wood cut down whose preparation and transportation must be looked after, new roads to be constructed into the forest and to the river, the old roads to be mended, three or four hundred tons of hay to be stacked, provisions of oats for thirty dray horses to be arranged for, thirty other horses to be brought for the transport of all the wood for the navy before winter, gates and sluices to be constructed in the river Indre in order to give us water all the year at the place where the wood is discharged, fifty vessels which wait to be loaded for Tours, Saumur, Angers and Nantes, the leases of seven or eight farms to sign, beside the provision for housing thirty per-sons ; the general inventory of our receipts and expenses for the last two years to regulate, voilà**, my dear wife, briefly the sum of my occupations of which part is terminated and the rest** en ***bon*** tram."

After two more pages of details Beaumarchais terminates his letter thus: "You see, my dear friend, that one sleeps less here than at Pantin, but the forced activity of this work does not displease me, since I have arrived in this retreat inaccessible to vanity, I have seen only simple people with unpretentious manners, such as I often desire myself to be. I lodge in my office which is a good peasant farm, between barnyard and kitchen garden, surrounded with a green hedge. My room with its four white-washed walls has for furniture an uncomfortable bed where I sleep like a top, four rush-bottomed chairs, an oaken table and a great fireplace without ornament or shelf; but I see from my window on writing you, the whole of the Varennes or prairies of the valley which I inhabit, full of robust, sunburned men who cut and cart hay with yokes of oxen, a multitude of women and girls each with a rake on the shoulder or in the hand, all singing songs whose shrill notes reach me as I write. Across the trees in the distance I see the tortuous course of the Indre and an ancient castle flanked by towers which belongs to my neighbor Madame de Roncée. The whole is crowned with wooded summits which multiply as far as the eye can see, the highest crests of which surround us on all sides in such a manner that they form a great spherical frame to the horizon, which they bound on every side. This picture is not without charm. Good coarse bread, the most modest nourishment with execrable wine composes my repasts. In truth, if I dared wish you the evil of lacking everything in a desolate country I should deeply regret not having you by my side. Adieu, my friend. If you think that these details might in-terest our relatives and friends you are free to read my letters to them. Embrace them all for me and good night —it seems hard to me sometimes not to have you near— and my son, my son! how is he? I laugh when I think that it is for him that I work."

In January, 1770, Beaumarchais could easily afford the ill success of his drama, for he was one of the best placed men in France. As we see him at this moment nothing seems lacking to complete his happiness. All his ambitions either are satisfied, or submerged. Of fierce trials, overwhelming calamities, of revolutions, and ignominy worse than death, he had as yet no idea. In 1767, he had written in his preface to his ***Eugenie***, "What does it matter to me, peaceful subject of a monarchial state of the eighteenth century, the revolution of Athens and Rome ? Why does the story of the earthquake which has engulfed the city of Lima with all its inhabitants, three thousand miles away, fill me with sorrow, while the judicial murder of Charles committed at the Tower only makes me indignant? It is because the volcano opened in Peru might explode in Paris and bury me in its ruins, while on the other hand I can never apprehend anything in the least similar to the unheard of misfortune which befell the king of England." This from the pen of Beaumarchais! Beaumarchais, who in 1784 was to produce his famous ***Moriage*** de ***Figaro,*** of which Napoleon said it was, "The Revolution in action." Yes the Revolution, but not at all like the Revolution in England whose results were only political, but one which went down to the very foundation of the human soul changing the psychology of every individual man, woman and child in the fair land of France and from thence spreading its influence over the entire civilized world! Here again we have a startling proof of what already has been advanced, namely that the great actions in the life of Beaumarchais do not come from his own willing or contriving. In the sublime naivete of his genius he became the instrument of those mysterious forces, so gigantic, which first manifested themselves in France, and whose revolutionary power continues to be felt over the whole world to-day. For the moment, however, his thoughts and interests were all for the restricted circle of his family and friends. He laughed when he thought of the son for whom he was working. But alas, as no happiness had been denied, so no human calamity was to escape him, he must drink his cup of grief and abasement to the dregs.

Already the wife whom he cherished was attacked by a fatal malady which only could end in the grave, the son for whom he worked so gaily was soon to follow her; his property was to be seized, his aged father and dearly loved sister were to be turned adrift. Deprived of his liberty, entangled in the meshes of a criminal lawsuit and under circumstances so desperate that no lawyer could be found bold enough to plead his cause, it was then that the true force and grandeur of his soul were to be made manifest; it was then that he found himself caught on the crest of that giant wave of public opinion now forming itself in France, his petty personal affair was to become the affair of the nation. It was not to be himself as a private individual who opposed his wrongs against despotic power, but the people of France found through him a voice crying aloud for vengeance.

But the time was not yet ripe. Beaumarchais, happy in the bosom of his family, thought only of sweetening the remainder of that life which was perishing in his arms.

"Before his second marriage, Madam Beaumarchais realizing to the full how difficult it was to see him without loving him," says Gudin, "and knowing how much he cherished women in general, said to him, 'You are a man of honor, promise me that you will never give me cause for jealousy and I will believe you.' He promised her and kept his word." Gudin further says, "When she was stricken with a fatal and contagious disease, he was even more assiduous than before in his devotion. Reading in her eyes the fears that devoured her, he sought to dissipate them by his care and that host of little attentions which have so great a price for the hearts which understand each other. She received them with all the more gratitude in that she could not fail to realize that she had lost those charms which had made her attractive, leaving only the memory of what she had been, joined to the sentiments of a pure soul already on the point of escaping from a frail body.

"Father, sisters, all the relatives of Beaumarchais, alarmed at his attachment, trembled lest he too should contract the malady and follow her to the tomb. She died on the 21st of November, 1770, leaving him the one son before mentioned. Her fortune, which had consisted almost entirely of a life income, was cut off with her death."

Paris du Verney had died the same year. The moment had arrived when the storm so long gathering was about to break. The first part of the career of Beaumarchais was over, the dream of a quiet, peaceful life vanished forever, while stern and unending conflict entered to take its place.

CHAPTER VII

"*La calomnie, Monsieur*! *vous* ne *savez* guère *ce* que vous dédaignez; *j'ai* vu *des* plus honnétes *gens* prêts *d'en* être accablès. *Croyez* qu'il *n'y* a *pas de* plate méchancete, *pas* d'horreurs, *pas* de *conte* absurde, *qu'on* ne *fosse* adopter *aux* oisifs *d'une* grande *ville* en *s'y* prenant *bien*.... *D'abord* un *bruit* leger *rasant* le *sol comme* hirondelle *avant* l'orage, *pianissimo* murmure *et file*, et *seme* en *courant* le *trait* empoisonné. *Telle bouche* le *recueille*, et *piano*, piano, *vous* le *glisse* en l'oreille *adroitement*. Le *mat* est *fait;* il *germe*, il *rampe*, il *chemine* et *rinforzando* de *bouche* en *bouche* il *va* le diable; *puis* tout *a* coup *on* ne *sait* comment, *vous* voyez *la* calomnie *se* dresser, *siffler,* s'enfler, *grandir a vue* d'oeil. *Elle* s'*elance,* étend *son* vol, *tourbSlonne,* en-veloppe, *arrache*, entrame, éclate *et* tone*, et* devient, grace *au* ciel, *un* cri *general*, un *crescendo* public, *un* cho-rus *uni*-versel *de* home *et* de *proscription.* Qui *diable* y résisterait?" "Le *Barbier* de *Seville,*" Act II, Scene VII.

The Death of Paris Du Verney—The Lawsuit La Blache— Judgment Rendered in Favor of Beaumarchais—The Comte de La Blache—Appeals to the New Parliament— Private Life of Beaumarchais at This Period.

AS will be remembered, it was in 1760 that Beaumarchais entered into relationship with Paris du Verney. During the ten years which followed there had been considerable movement of capital between the two, very many business transactions more or less sustained by the old financier, numerous loans of money, and finally the partnership in the forest of Chinon, without their ever having arrived at a definite settlement.

Beaumarchais, always minutely careful in matters where money was concerned, realizing the advanced age of du Ver-ney often had urged upon his friend the necessity of such a settlement. Finally in April, 1770, after several years of correspondence, an act was drawn up in duplicate by Beaumarchais, dated, signed, and sealed by du Verney.

By this act, after a long and detailed enumeration of the rights on both sides, Beaumarchais gave back to his old friend 160,000 francs of the latter's notes and consented to the dissolution of the partnership in the Forest of Chinon.

Du Verney, on his side, declared Beaumarchais absolved from all debts against him, recognized that he owed the latter 15,000 francs and obliged himself to loan 75,000 francs without interest, for eight years.

Du Verney died before the last two clauses had been executed, so that it was to his heir, the Comte de la Blache, that Beaumarchais presented the act demanding its execution.

This was the moment for which the count had been so long waiting. Already for years he had been saying of Beaumarchais, "I hate that man as a lover loves his mistress."

M. de Loménie, after giving reasons natural enough for the hatred of an heir presumptive for a person constantly receiving benefits from an old man whose fortune he was to inherit, has said, "The Comte de la Blache had very particular motives for hating Beaumarchais. This latter was closely united with another nephew of du Verney's, M. Paris de Meyzieu, a man distinguished in every way, who had powerfully aided his uncle in the founding of. the École Militaire, but being very much less skillful in the difficult and painful matter for a man of heart, to secure to himself a succession to the property—had withdrawn from the contest allowing himself to be sacrificed to a more distant relative."

Beaumarchais, finding this sacrifice unjust, had not ceased to combat the weakness of his old friend du Verney, and to plead for M. de Meyzieu with a frankness and a vivacity proved by his letters, of which I will only cite a fragment, but which has relation precisely to the settlement in question.

"I cannot endure," he wrote to du Verney on the date of March 9, 1770, "that in case of death you place me vis-à-vis with M. le Comte de la Blache, whom I honor with all my heart but who, since I have seen him familiarly at the house of Madame d'Hauteville, never has given me the honor of a salutation. You make him your heir, I have nothing to say to that, but if I must, in case of the greatest misfortune which I could imagine, be his debtor, I am your servant for the arrangement. I will not dissolve our partnership. But place me vis-à-vis with my friend Meyzieu, who is a gallant man, and to whom you owe, my good friend, reparation for debts of long standing. It is not apologies which an uncle owes to a nephew, but kindness and above all some benevolent act, when he knows that he has done him wrong. I never have hidden my opinion in this matter from you. Put me visà-vis with him. This is my last word; you, or in your absence Meyzieu, or else no dissolution. I have other motives in relation to this last point, which I will reserve till the time when I can give them by word of mouth. When do you wish to see me? Because I notify you that from now until then, things shall remain as they are."

It is evident from this and similar letters that Beaumar- chais had no illusions as to the difficulties of his situation. With the increasing failure of the old man's faculties, his cunning nephew so exercised his ascendency that it was with the greatest difficulty that Beaumarchais could obtain an interview with his old friend. Du Verney, it would seem, hid, so far as possible, all connection which he had with his nephew. This state of affairs, M. de Loménie assures us, accounted for the absence of the duplicate acts and all letters in relation to the matter, which alone could make a lawsuit possible.

When after du Verney's death, Beaumarchais presented the act, demanding its execution, the Comte de la Blache coolly replied that he did not recognize his uncle's signature and that he believed it false.

The matter was taken to law. Not daring, however, directly to accuse Beaumarchais of forgery, he demanded that the act be annulled, declaring that it contained in itself proofs of fraud. Again to quote Loménie, "Thus Beaumarchais found himself caught in the meshes of an odious snare, because while not daring to attack him openly for forgery, the Comte de la Blache did not cease to plead indirectly this possibility and after an infamous discussion he had the audacity to take advantage of this very act which he declared false and turned it against his adversary.

"Thus refusing to pay the 15,000 francs recognized by the act signed by du Verney, he demanded of Beaumarchais payment of 139,000 francs from which the act discharged him."

"In this way," said Master Caillard, a very ingenious lawyer chosen by the Comte de la Blache, "justice will be avenged, and honest citizens will see with satisfaction a similar adversary taken in the snares which he has himself set."

Not to enter too deeply into the tedious details of this suit, we will content ourselves with a few pages taken from the account of M. de Loménie as giving a sufficiently clear idea of its nature as a whole.

He says, "Let us suppose that Beaumarchais had wished to fabricate a false act, would he have given it the form of this one? It is a great sheet of double paper, very complicated details of the settlement written by the hand of Beaumarchais fill the first two pages, at the end of the second page it is signed on the right by Beaumarchais, and on the left dated and signed by the hand of du Verney, the third page contains a résumé of the same settlement. What did the lawyer of the Comte de la Blache say of this? He discussed it with the facility of a lawyer. At times he insinuated that the signature of du Verney was false, then when summoned to plead the falsity of the act he declared that if it was true, that it belonged to a date earlier than 1770, 'at which time,' he said, 'the old du Verney had a trembling hand, while the one at the foot of the act is a bold writing from a hand firm and light.'

"Here the lawyer pretended not to see that just above the signature was written in the same hand these words, 'At Paris, the 1st of April, 1770,' that is to say that du Verney had not only signed, but dated the act in question, which obliged one to suppose that the old financier had amused himself in his youth or in mature years in signing and dating in advance, blank signatures for the period of his old age. Repelled on this side the lawyer insinuates that the paper must be a blank signature signed and dated by du Verney in 1770, secured and filled by Beaumarchais."

Feeling the weakness of his arguments, the lawyer came back to the clauses which were complicated, diffuse, and mixed with observations foreign to the settlement in question; this was true, but in favor of Beaumarchais, because had he been fabricating an act, it would have been brief, methodical, and clear, while in regulating a long account with an old man of eighty-seven this act must necessarily correspond to the prolixity, or the fantasies of, this advanced age.

But one will say, why, when he had only to contend against such feeble arguments, was it possible for Beaumar-chais, after gaining his suit in the first instance to lose it in the second, as we shall presently see him do?

The story is long and involved, and many pictures are needed to convey the scene in all its intensity and intricacy.

A sentence dated February 22, 1772, rejects the demand of the Comte de la Blache, and a second dated March 4th, 1772, orders the execution of the act. Upon this the adversary appeals to the grand chamber of Parliament.

Although victorious in his struggle, Beaumarchais was vilified by the crafty Caillard to the extent of the latter's power. The credit and influence of the Comte de la Blache excited against him a swarm of writers, and the gazettes, especially the foreign periodicals, made the most of all the atrocious calumnies which had been set going regarding his character. The sudden death of his two wives served as a pretext for the most infamous accusations. All the confusing details of this disastrous lawsuit have been fully investigated and the whole matter clearly exposed by M. de Loménie and we know that the final decision rendered at Aix in 1778 exonerated Beaumarchais from every semblance of fault or dishonorable action. That which concerns us at this time is to learn what effect all these infamous machinations had upon a character which we have recognized already as strong, elevated, and free.

From the bitterness of the attacks of his enemies, let us turn to the refreshing and faithful picture which his de- voted friend Gudin makes of him at this time.

He writes: "It was in the winter of 1771 that I met Madame de Miron, sister of Beaumarchais, at the home of a woman of my acquaintance. She had been invited to a reading of one of my poems. In the beginning she showed no interest, but as I read, her face became animated and at the end she was as prodigal of her praise, as at first she had been indifferent. She spoke to me of her brother. She found me without prejudice for his dramas, but naturally biased in regard to his character of which I had heard much adverse criticism.

"Satisfied with my discourse, she resolved to conquer me for her brother and accordingly invited me to dine with her at a time when the abbé Délille was to read some verses still unknown to the public.

"Given to study and retirement, rather reserved in my friendships, and not desiring to make new ones, I refused at first; she urged my acceptance with so much grace, however, that I could not persist in my refusal.

"I went to her home, I found the abbé, I applauded his verses as all Paris has since done, but I did not see the brother of the mistress of the house. . . .

"At last one evening, while I was visiting Madame de Miron, he came in. She presented him to me and begged me to recite some verses of the poem which had made her wish to interest me in him.

"He showed the same indifference as his sister had done at the beginning, but glowed with even finer interest as I proceeded. He wished to take me at once to sup with him with Madame le Comtesse de Mir. ... I refused abso-lutely, and did not yield to any of his solicitations although they were very ardent. I did not wish that my first step should give him the idea of a frivolous man who could be disposed of lightly.

"The next morning he called on me and brought me an invitation from Madame le Comtesse de Mir . . . and in the evening he came for me. Two days later he invited me to his house, presented me to his father, to the one sister who lived with him, and whom I had never met.

"I saw him as simple in his domestic circle as he was brilliant in a salon. I was very soon certain that he was a good son, good brother, good master, and good father because he had still a little son, a young child whose infantile words were often repeated to us, which charmed me all the more because it betrayed his paternal tenderness and showed how much more powerful were his sentiments than his ***esprit.***

"We soon learned to esteem each other from a similar foundation of severe principles, hidden in his case under an exterior of lightness and gaiety, by a vivid and constant love of the good, the beautiful, the honest, by an equal disdain for prejudice, and for all opinions ill-founded.

"We became intimate friends through the similarities and differences of our characters, and the congeniality of our interests.

"The taste for letters, for the theatre, for the arts, the same indulgence for the weaknesses of the human heart, strengthened our union. We passed many evenings together, now in the midst of a great number, now in more restricted circles. Poetry, music, new scientific discoveries, all were subjects of our discourse. I heard him blend witticisms, graceful stories, the best pleasantries, all the charm of an esprit free, abundant, and varied with the effusions of a sensible, active, generous heart.

"He never criticised any work, on the contrary he always brought out beauties which others had not noticed, extolled talent, repelled scandal; he defended all those whose merit he heard depreciated, and never listened to slander. 'I am, he used to say, 'an advocate of the absent.'

"I noticed that he never spoke evil of his enemies, even of those whom he knew to be the most intent on ruining him. One day when I had learned some most injurious details in regard to the conduct of the man who had brought suit against him, I expressed my astonishment that I had not learned these facts from him, but rather from a relative of the man himself.

" 'Eh, my friend,' he replied, 'should I lose the time which I pass with you in recalling the things which would only afflict your spirit and mine. I try to forget the folly of those about me, and to think only of what is good and useful ; we have so many things to say to each other, that such topics should never find a place in our conversation.'

"And in fact there scarcely passed a day when we did not express our pity for the sterility of spirit and the dryness of heart of the many people who have nothing to say unless they talk scandal.

"Beaumarchais was at this time secretary to the king, lieutenant-general of the preserves of the king and enjoyed an income of from 15 to 20 thousand francs a year. He thought of nothing but to make use of his own talents, to cultivate his friends, music, and the theater. I see by a letter to the Duchess de that he was already forming a project for enlarging the range of the drama, so as to give to the French scene more variety and interest. These objects alone occupied him when I made his acquaintance.

"The suit in which he was engaged in the first place, gave him no disquietude, he believed that he could not lose it, but this suit was to be the stumbling block which was to destroy his happiness, to tear from him the possibility of disposing of himself according to his own will, or to live as his taste dictated.

"It precipitated him into a succession of events which never permitted him for a moment to enter into the tranquil career which he had proposed for himself. His life so fitted for pleasure and the beaux-arts became a combat which never ceased. It is thus that events often dispose of men in spite of themselves.

"During the delay accorded by law and which circumstances required, Beaumarchais composed a comic opera, which he ornamented with couplets to the Spanish and Italian airs which he had brought back with him from Madrid. He read the piece to the Comedians of the so-called It aliens, who were in possession of the right to play this kind of production. That evening, supping with Mademoiselle M, *femme* d'esprit, whom we shall see later, in an assembly of several men of rank, Beaumarchais told us that his piece had been refused by the theater of Souz.

"We congratulated him, we knew his piece, we assured him the comedians of the Théâtre Français would be more sensible, that he would only lose the couplets, and that the **Barbier** de **Seville** would have more success at the theater of Molière than at the Harlequin.

"Marmontel and Sedaine, who were of the company, knowing very well all of the Comédiens **des** It **aliens**, reveiled to us the secret of the disgrace of the Barbier. They told us that the principal actor, before showing himself on the stage, had figured, razor in hand in the shops of the wig-makers, and now he did not wish to produce anything which would recall his origin. We laughed, we moralized and it was decided that Beaumarchais should carry his work to the Théâtre-Français."

Beaumarchais and the War of American Independence 125

It is this many-sided, this complex character of Beaumarchais which makes him so difficult to understand. Immersed in financial difficulties which would have overwhelmed an ordinary man, we find him composing an immortal dramatic production. Still deeper plunged in distresses, and caught in a net of harassing circumstances almost unbelievable, we find him attacking single-handed one of the greatest wrongs of the nation and pulling himself out of a quicksand to be borne in triumph on the shoulders of the people of France.

In 1772, two years before the time of the lawsuit brought by the Comte de la Blache against Beaumarchais, by an arbitrary act of the Chancellor Maupeou under the sanction of the old king Louis XV, the ancient parliaments of the realm had been dissolved and in their place a new one had been set up, called the Parliament Maupeou. From the beginning it met with very bitter opposition. To quote Loménie, "The nation had bowed itself under the glorious scepter of Louis XIV, but that scepter fallen into the hands of Louis XV no longer inspired respect. The spirit of resistance to arbitrary power was general. In the absence of every other guarantee, the parliaments presented themselves as the one barrier which could be opposed to the caprices of a disorderly power, and whatever were the particular vices of those bodies, judicial and political, every time that they resisted the royal will they had with them the sympathy of the public.

"Supported by this, the parliaments saw themselves growing stronger day by day. Closely united the one to the other, they declared themselves 'the members of a single and individual body, inherent in the monarchy, an organ of the nation, essential depository of its liberty, of its interests and of its rights.'

"Every one of their combats with royalty terminated by a victory, until at last a man issuing from their ranks, an audacious and obstinate character, undertook to command or crush them. This man was the Chancellor Maupeou.

"Sustained by Madame du Barry, who dominated the King, the Chancellor issued the edict of December 7th, 1770, which changed the entire organization of the parliaments. The one of Paris protested and repelled the edict. The Chancellor instead of following the ordinary methods dissolved this parliament, confiscated the charges of the magistrates, exiled them and installed a new parliament composed for the most part of members of the Grand Council. The eleven Parliaments of the provinces addressed the most vehement remonstrances; the one in Normandy went so far as to send a decree, declaring the new magistrates intruders, perjurers, traitors, and all the acts null that emanated from that bastard tribunal. All the princes of the blood except one refused to recognize the judges installed by Maupeou; thirteen peers adhered to the protestation. The *cour* des *aides* protested equally by the eloquent voice of Malesherbes. The Chancellor resisted the storm, he prevented the dissenting princes from being admitted to court; he broke the *cour* des *aides* dissolved in turn all the parliaments of the provinces and replaced them in the midst of an unheard of fermentation. 'It is not a man,' wrote Madame du Deffand, 'it is a devil; everything here is in a disorder of which it is im-possible to predict the end; it is chaos, it is the end of the world.'

"To dissolve these ancient and formidable bodies whose existence seemed inseparable from the monarchy and whose suppression delivered France to the regime of Turkey or Russia, was truly a very hazardous enterprise.

"The chancellor took care to sweeten and color the act by blending some very important reforms, long desired by the people. Thus the mass of the people little understanding the gravity of the plan of Maupeou showed themselves indifferent, but the enlightened classes of society refused to purchase a few needed reforms at the price of an ignominious servitude and sided unitedly with the destroyed parliaments.

"Very soon followed a deluge of sarcastic pamphlets against the king, against his mistress, against the chancellor, and the new parliament. This last, hastily formed of heterogeneous elements, into which several men but lightly esteemed had been introduced, had not in the beginning found either lawyers, attorneys, or litigants who wished to appear before it. Nevertheless, Maupeou counting upon the mobilité française, opposed perseverance to the clamor, and at the end of a year most of the lawyers were tired of keeping silence; under the influence of the celebrated Gerbier and that of the same Caillard whom we have seen so violent against Beaumarchais, they had taken up their functions.

"The dissenting princes demanded to be taken back into favor, the dispossessed magistrates of the dissolved parliaments consented to the liquidation of the charges against them, the pamphlets diminished, and things came back to their ordinary course. Maupeou held himself assured of triumph and vaunted that he had saved the crown from the registrar.

"But he had deceived himself. When any large part of a nation, honest and intelligent, feels itself wounded in its dignity, though the wound may close in appearance, it does not heal; that which was in the beginning a flame became a smouldering fire, which hidden under the ashes of an apparent non-resistance was in reality but waiting an opportunity to break forth into a devouring element.

"It was reserved for Beaumarchais to fan this into a flame with a suit for fifteen louis, and to destroy both Mau-peou and his parliament."

It was then to this parliament and Maupeou that the Comte de la Blache made his appeal. The institution was the more to his liking, since at its head presided a certain counsellor by the name of Goëzman who seemed especially made for his purpose.

We shall have much to say of this same Goëzman in a succeeding chapter when it comes to the question of the famous lawsuit concerning the fifteen louis. At this time, however, Beaumarchais's case was very strong and none of his friends seriously supposed that the count would be able to turn the suit against him.

It was at this crisis that a circumstance, one of the most bizarre of all the strange happenings in the life of Beaumar-chais, suddenly placed him at the mercy of his bitterest enemy.

For a minutely detailed account of this incident we have Beaumarchais's own account as rendered to the lieutenant of police after the matter had been taken up by the authorities. While Gudin on his side, who, as we shall see, had his own part to play in this singular drama, gives a no less circumstantial account of the whole proceeding.

When in 1855, M. de Loménie published his important work, the incident about to be related was wholly unknown to the public although as he tells us, "The author of the *Barbier* de *Seville* had collected with care all the documents relating to this strange affair. Upon the back of the bundle of papers was written with his own hand, 'Material for the memoirs of my life. "

As M. de Sartine, at that time lieutenant general of police, later became a warm friend of Beaumarchais, the latter was able to obtain all the letters deposited by each one of the actors of this tragi-comique scene.

We can do no better than follow the account of M. de Loménie with occasional touches from Gudin.

CHAPTER VIII

La Jeunesse—"*Y*-a-*t*-il *de* la *justice*?"

Bartholo—"De *la* justice? C'est **bon** pour **les** autres misérabies, *la* justice. *Je* suis maître, *moi,* pour *avoir toujours* raison."

Le Barbier *de* Séville**, *Act II,*** Scene VII.
Beaumarchais and the Due de Chaulnes—Attempt Upon the Life of Beaumarchais—Same Evening Gives the Promised Reading of the *Barbier* de Séville—Victim of a *Lettre* de *Cachet.*

IT will be remembered that Gudin in his history of Beau-marchais speaks of a meeting of literary men at the table of a certain Mademoiselle Menard, *femme* d'esprit where the subject of the comic opera lately composed by Beaumarchais was discussed. It was this same Mademoiselle Menard who in the words of Loménie was "the cause of an Homeric combat between Beaumarchais, prudent and dexterous as Ulysses, and a duke and peer, robust and ferocious as Ajax."

Mademoiselle Menard was a young and pretty actress, who in June, 1770, had made her debut with success at the Comédie Italienne. In his **Correspondence** littéraire, of June, 1770, Baron von Grimme, the great critic of the time, says of her after a rather cold analysis: "Mademoiselle Menard must be given a trial; she seems capable of great application. It is said that her first occupation was that of a flower girl on the boulevards, but wishing to withdraw from that estate which has degenerated a little from the first nobility of its origin, since Glysère sold bouquets at the doors of the temple of Athens, she bought a grammar and applied herself to a study of the language and its pronounciation, after which she tried playing comedies. During her first attempts, she has addressed herself to all the authors, musicians, and poets, asking their counsels with a zeal and docility which has had for recompense the applause which she has obtained in her different roles. M. de Pequigny, to-day the due de Chaulnes, protector of her charms, has had her portrait painted by Greuze; so if we do not retain her in the theater we shall at least see her at the next salon."

Acting on the wishes of her protector, Mademoiselle Menard had renounced the theater and was in the habit of receiving at her house poets, musicians, and great lords, Beau-marchais among the rest.

"The due de Chaulnes," says Loménie, "was a man notorious for the violence and extravagance of his character. The history of Beaumarchais by Gudin contains details about him in every way confirming the testimony of other contemporaries."

"His character," wrote Gudin, "was a peculiar mixture of contradictory qualities; ***esprit*** without judgment, pride, with such a lack of discernment as to rob him of dignity before superiors, equals or inferiors, a vast but disorderly memory, a great desire to improve himself, a still greater taste for dissipation, a prodigious strength of body, a violence of disposition which rendered him extremely unreasonable and robbed him of the power to think clearly, frequent fits of rage which made of him a savage beast incapable of being controlled.

"At one time banished from his country for five years, he spent the time of his exile in making a scientific expedition. He visited the pyramids, lived with the Bedouins and brought home many objects of natural history."

To this portrait by Gudin, Loménie adds the following: "In the midst of his disorderly and extravagant life, he had conserved something of the taste of his father, a distinguished mechanician, physicist, and natural historian who died an honorary member of the Academy of Natural Sciences. The son loved chemistry passionately and made several discoveries. Nevertheless even here he displayed many eccentricities. Thus, to verify the efficacy of a preparation he had invented against asphyxiation, he shut himself up in a glass cabinet and asphyxiated himself, leaving to his valet de chambre the care to come to his aid at the proper moment to try his remedy. Happily his servant was punctual and no harm was done.

"The peculiar character of the duke rendered his liaison with Mademoiselle Ménard very stormy. At the same time brutal, jealous, and unfaithful, he inspired in her little sentiment other than fear. Suddenly becoming infatuated with Beaumarchais, he introduced him to the young woman in question."

Gudin says, "ne of the greatest wrongs that I have known in Beaumarchais was to appear so amiable to women that he was always preferred, which made him as many enemies as there were aspirants to please him."

The due de Chaulnes, perceiving very soon that Mademoiselle Menard found Beaumarchais very agreeable, his friendship turned to fury.

"Frightened by his violence," says Loménie, "she begged Beaumarchais to cease his visits. Out of regard for her, he consented, but the bad treatment of the duke continuing, she decided to take the desperate step of shutting herself up in a convent. When she believed that the danger was over and that she would be safe in her own home, she returned and invited her friends, Beaumarchais among them, to come to see her."

The duke during his intimacy with Beaumarchais had received many favors from him, notably important sums of money which, of course, he never repaid. It was at the moment of the return of Mademoiselle Menard to her home that Beaumarchais wrote the following letter to the duke.

"Monsieur le Due,

"Mademoiselle Menard has notified me that she has returned to her home and has invited me to come to see her along with all her other friends, when I can make it convenient. I judge that the reasons which forced her to the retreat now have ceased. She tells me she is free and I congratulate both of you sincerely. I expect to see her sometime to-morrow. The force of circumstances has then done for you what my representations were unable to accomplish. I have known by what pecuniary efforts you have tried again to bring her to be your dependent, and with what nobility she has refused your money.

"Pardon me if I make certain reflections, they are not foreign to the end which I have in view in writing this. In speaking to you of Mademoiselle Menard I forget my personal injuries. I forget that after making it clear to you that my attachment for you alone inspired the sacrifices which I made, and that after having said to me very disad-vantageous things about her, you have changed and said things a hundred times worse to her about me. I pass also in silence the scene, horrible for her—and disgusting to me, where you so far forgot yourself as to reproach me with being the son of a watchmaker. I, who honor myself in my parents in the face of those even, who imagine they have the right to outrage their own. You must feel, Monsieur le due, how much more advantageous my position is at this moment than your own, and except for the anger which makes you unreasonable, you would certainly appreciate the moderation with which I repelled the outrage against him whom I have always made profession of loving and honoring with all my heart. But if my respectful regards for you have not gone so far as to make me fear you, then it is because it is not in my power to fear any man. Believe me, Monsieur le duc, I have never tried to diminish the attachment of this generous woman for you. She would have despised me if I had attempted to do so. You have had, therefore, no enemy but yourself. Recall all that I have had the honor to say in regard to this subject and give back your friendship to him whom you have not been able to deprive of his esteem for you. If this letter does not appeal to you, I shall feel that I have done my duty to the friend whom I have never offended, whose injuries I have forgotten, and to whom I come now for the last time. . . ."

The duke did not reply to this letter and matters remained at a standstill until one morning the infatuated duke took it into his head to kill Beaumarchais.

"Fatality," says Gudin, "was the cause that I who never left my study in the morning unless it was to go and turn over the pages of the books or ancient manuscripts in the Bibliotèque du Roi, had gone out that morning by request of my mother, it being the 11th of February, 1773. My commission for her finished and finding myself near the lodging of Mademoiselle Menard whom I had not seen for a long time, I mounted to her apartments.

" 'It is a great while since I have seen you,' she said, 'I feared you no longer had any friendship for me.' I assured her of my regard and seated myself in an armchair. Soon she burst into tears as if her heart could not contain its grief, and began to recount the violences of the duke and spoke of a very insulting remark which he had made about Beau-marchais. At that moment the duke entered the room, I rose and gave him my place.

" 'I weep,' she said, 'and I beg M. Gudin to induce Beau-marchais to justify himself for the ridiculous accusation you have made against him.'

" 'What need is there for a scoundrel like Beaumarchais to justify himself?

" 'He is a very honest man,' she said, shedding more tears.

" 'You love him,' cried the "duke. 'You humiliate me. I declare to you that I *wiil* kill *him!*

"The duke sprang up and rushed from the room. We all rose and cried out. I ran to prevent his escape, but he evaded me. I turned back into the room, I cried to the women that I would warn Beaumarchais and prevent the combat.

"I was beside myself, I left and ran to his house. I met his carriage in the Rue Dauphine. I threw myself in front of the horses, stopped them, mounted on the steps of his car-rosse, and told him that the due de Chàulnes was hunting for him and wished to kill him.

" 'Come home with me, I will tell you the rest.'

" 'I cannot,' he answered, 'the hour calls me to the tribunal of the varenne du Louvre, where I must preside, I will come to you as soon as the audience is finished.'

"His carriage started and I went back home. Just as I was mounting the steps of the Pont-Neuf I felt myself violently pulled by the skirts of my coat, I fell backward and found myself in the arms of the due de Chaulnes who, using his gigantic strength, picked me up like a bird, threw me into a fiacre, cried to the coachman, 'Rue de Condé,' and said to me with horrible oaths that I should find for him the man he sought to kill.

" 'By what right,' I said, 'Monsieur le due, you who are always crying for liberty, do you take mine from me?'

" 'By the right of the strongest. You will find for me— Beaumarchais or—

" 'Monsieur le duc, I have no arms, you will perhaps wish also to assassinate me?'

" 'No—I will only kill that Beaumarchais.'

" 'I do not know where he is and if I did, I would not tell you while you are in the fury of your present rage.'

" 'If you resist, I will give you a blow.'

" 'And I will return it.'

" 'What, you would strike a duke!' With that he threw himself upon me and tried to seize my hair. As I wore a wig it remained in his hand, which made the scene very amusing as I perceived from the laughter of the populace outside the fiàcre, all the doors of which were open. The duke who saw nothing, seized me by the neck and wounded me on my throat, my ear, and my cheek. I stopped his blows as best I could and called the guard with all my might. The duke grew calmer and we arrived at the home of Beaumarchais.

"The duke jumped from the carriage and pounded on the door. I sprang from the other side of the carriage and knowing that my friend would not be found, I escaped to my own home by the side streets, there to await the coming of Beaumarchais.

"I waited in impatience,—he did not come, I grew uneasy, fear seized me, I gave orders that he should await me, I ran to his home. Here is what happened and which is to be found in his petition to the marshals of France." "Exact recital of what passed Thursday, the 11th of February, 1773, between M. le duc de Chaulnes and myself, Beaumarchais.

"I had opened the audience of the *capitamerie,* when I saw M. le duc de

Chaulnes arrive with the most bewildered air that could be imagined and he said aloud that he had something very pressing to communicate to me and that I must come out at once. I cannot, Monsieur le duc, the service of the public forces me to terminate decently what I have begun.' I had a seat brought for him; he insisted; everyone was astonished at his air and tone. I began to fear that his object would be suspected and I suspended the audience for a moment and passed with him into a cabinet. There he told me with all the force of the language *des* holies, that he wished to kill me at once and to drink my blood, for which he was thirsty.

" 'Oh, is it only that, Monsieur le duc? Permit then, that business go before pleasure. I wished to return; he stopped me, saying that he would tear out my eyes before all the world if I did not instantly go out with him.

" 'You will be lost, Monsieur if you are rash enough to attack me publicly.'

"I re-entered the audience chamber assuming a cold manner.

"Surrounded as I was by the officers and guards of the ***capitaimerie,*** after seating le duc de Chaulnes, I opposed during the two hours of the audience, a perfect ***sang-froid*** to the petulant and insane perturbation with which he walked about troubling the audience and asking of all, 'Will this last much longer?'

"Finally the audience was over and I put on my street costume. In descending, I asked M. de Chaulnes, what could be his grievance against a man whom he had not seen for six months.

" 'No explanation, he said to me, let us go instantly and fight it out.'

" 'At least,' I said, 'you will permit me to go home and get a sword? I have only a mourning sword with me in the carriage.'

" 'We are passing the house of M. le Comte de Turpin, who will lend you one and who will serve as witness.'

"He sprang into my carriage. I got in after him, while his equipage followed ours. He did me the honor of assuring me that this time I would not escape him, ornamenting his sentences with those superb imprecations which are so familiar in his speech. The coolness of my replies augmented his rage.

"We arrived as M. de Turpin was leaving his home. He mounted on the box of my carriage.

" 'M. le duc,' I said, 'is carrying me off. I do not know why he wants us to cut one another's throats, but in this strange adventure he hopes that you will wish to serve as witness of our conduct.'

"M. de Turpin replied that a pressing matter forced him to go at once to the Luxembourg and would detain him there until four o'clock in the afternoon. I perceived that M. de Turpin had for his object to allow time for the rage of Monsieur le duc to calm itself. He left us. M. de Chaulnes wished to take me to his home. 'No, thank you,' I replied, and ordered my coachman to drive to mine.

" 'If you descend I will poniard you at your own door.'

" 'You will have the pleasure then, because it is exactly where I am going.' Then I asked him to dine with me.

"The carriage arrived at my door, I descended, and he followed me. I gave my orders coldly, the postman handed me a letter, the duke seized it from me before my father and all the domestics. I tried to turn the matter into a joke, but the duke began to swear. My father became alarmed, I reassured him and ordered dinner to be served in my study."

At this point we return to the account by Gudin which is much less detailed than Beaumarchais's recital.

"The duke followed him, and on entering the study though wearing a sword of his own, he seized one of Beaumarchais's which was lying on the table and attempted to stab him, but found himself seized and enveloped before he had time completely to draw the sword from its case. The men struggled together like two athletes, Beaumarchais less strong, but more master of himself, pushed the duke toward the chimney and seized the bell cord. The domestics came running in and seeing their master assailed, his hair torn and his face bleeding, they attacked the duke. The cook arming himself with a stick of wood was ready to break the skull of the madman. Beaumarchais forbade them to strike, but ordered that they take away the sword which the duke held in his hands. They so far disarmed him but did not dare to take the sword which he still wore at his side. In the struggle, they had pushed and pulled each other from the study to the steps, here the duke fell and dragged Beaumarchais with him. At this moment I knocked at the street door. The duke immediately disengaged himself and threw open the door. My surprise can be imagined.

" 'Enter,' cried the duke, seizing me, 'here is another who will not go out of here,' his mania seemed to be that no one should leave the house until he had killed Beaumarchais.

"I joined my friend and tried to make him enter the study with me; the duke opposed himself to us with violence and drew his own sword. Beaumarchais seized him by the throat and pressed him so closely that he could not strike. Eight of us came instantly to his aid and disarmed the duke. A lackey had his head cut, the coachman his nose injured and the cook was wounded in the hand. We pushed the duke into the dining-room which was very near the street door and Beaumarchais went up stairs.

"As soon as the duke ceased to see his enemy he sat down by himself at the table and ate with a furious appetite."

Here Beaumarchais shall continue with the account: "The duke again heard a knocking at the door and rushed to open it. He found M. the commissioner Chenu, who, surprised at the disorder in which he found the establishment, and at my appearance as I descended to greet him, inquired the cause of the confusion. I told him in a few words. . At my explanation the duke threw himself once more upon me striking me with his fists, unarmed I defended myself as best I could before the assembly who soon separated us. M. Chenu begged me to remain in the salon while he took charge of the duke, who had begun to break glass and tear his own hair in rage at not having killed me. M. Chenu at last persuaded him to go home and he had the impertinence to have my lackey whom he had wounded, dress his hair. I went to my room to have myself attended to and the duke throwing himself into my carriage rode away.

"I have stated these facts simply, without indulging in any comments, employing as far as possible the expressions used, and endeavoring to state the exact truth in recounting one of the strangest and most disgusting adventures which could come to a reasonable man."

Gudin ends his account with a very characteristic picture of Beaumarchais.

"Anyone else, after an equally violent scene, would have been overwhelmed with anxiety and fatigue, would have sought repose, and would have been anxious in regard to precautions against the repeated violence of a great lord, but Beaumarchais, as cheerful and assured as if he had passed the most tranquil day, was not willing to deny himself a moment of pleasure. That very evening, at the risk of encountering the duke, he went to the home of one of his old friends, M. Lopes, where he was expected to give a reading of his **Barbier** de Séville.

"Upon his arrival he recounted to them the adventures of the day. Everyone supposed that after such an exciting experience, there would be no feeling on his part for comedy. But Beaumarchais assured the ladies that the scandalous conduct of a madman should not spoil their evening's pleasure and he read his play with as much composure as if nothing had happened. He was as calm, as gay, and as brilliant during supper as usual, and passed a part of the night playing on the harp and singing the Spanish seguedillas or the charming scenes he had set to music which he accompanied with so much grace upon the instrument which he had perfected.

"It was thus that in every circumstance of his life he gave himself entirely to the thing which occupied him without any thought of what had passed or was to follow, so sure was he of all his faculties and his presence of mind. He never needed preparation upon any point, his intelligence was always ready, and his principles of action faultless."

As might be expected, the scandalous adventure made a great deal of noise. It was taken up by the marshals of France, judges in such cases between gentlemen, and a guard was sent to the home of each one of the adversaries. Lo-ménie says, "In the interval the duke de la Vrillière, minister of the house of the king, ordered Beaumarchais to go into the country for some days, and as the latter protested energetically against such an order the execution of which, under the circumstances, would have compromised his honor, the minister had directed him to stay at his home until the matter had been taken before the king.

"The marshals then successively called each combatant in turn to appear before them. Beaumarchais had no trouble in proving that his only wrong consisted in being permitted the friendship of a pretty woman, and the result of the investigation having been unfavorable to the due de Chaulnes, he was sent on the 19th of February by a *lettre* de *cachet* to the château of Vincennes. The Marshals of France then sent for Beaumarchais a second time and declared him free.

"All this was just, but Beaumarchais, not over confident in human justice, went to the duke de la Vrillière to assure himself that he was free. Not finding the nobleman at home he addressed a note to Sartine, lieutenant-general of police, to ask the same question. This latter replied that he was perfectly at liberty, then for the first time Beaumarchais ventured to stir abroad. But he counted even then prematurely on the justice of the court. The very small mind of the due de la Vrillière was offended that the tribunal of the marshals of France should discharge arrests given by him and so to teach the tribunal a lesson and to show his authority, on the 24th of February he sent Beaumarchais to For-l'Eveque."

As may be imagined, this was a terrible blow to a man of his active temperament and especially at this time when his enemy the Comte de la Blache was capable of using the advantage thus acquired to complete his ruin. Nevertheless his first letter from prison shows his usual serenity of mind. He wrote to Gudin: "In virtue of a *lettre* sans cachet called *lettre* de *cachet* signed Louis and below Philippeaux, recommended—Sartine, executed—Buchot, and submitted Beaumarchais, I am lodged, my friend, since this morning at For-1'Eveque, in an unfurnished room at 2160 livres rent where I am led to hope that, except what is necessary I shall lack nothing. Is it the family of the duke whom I have saved a criminal suit who have imprisoned me? Is it the ministry whose orders I have constantly followed or anticipated? Is it the dukes and peers of the realm with whom I am in no way connected? This is what I do not know, but the sacred name of 'King' is so beautiful a thing that one cannot multiply it or employ it too frequently àpropos. It is thus that in every country which is governed by police they tor-ment by authority those whom they cannot inculpate with justice. Wherever mankind is to be found, odious things happen and the great wrong of being in the right is always a crime in the eyes of power, which wishes to punish unceasingly, but never to judge."

The two rivals were thus very securely lodged for the present and Mademoiselle Menard, the unwilling pretext of all the trouble, was quite safe from her tormentor. Before the rendering of the sentence, however, which confined the due de Chaulnes to the prison of Vincennes, in the fear which the violence of his character inspired, this "beautiful Helen," says Loménie, "went and threw herself at the feet of M. de Sartine, imploring his protection." The next day she wrote a letter communicating her fixed resolve to retire to a convent. Other letters follow and four days after the terrible scene which has been described, Mademoiselle Menard entered the *convent* des Cordelières, *faubourg* Saint-*Marceau,* Paris.

M. de Sartine had entrusted the very delicate, not to say hazardous mission of seeing the young woman in question safely lodged in a convent, to a worthy priest, l'abbé Dugué. This very respectable, very good and very *naif* abbe, wrote the same evening a lengthy letter to the lieutenant general of police in which he showed himself very anxious not to compromise his own dignity as well as not to incur the enmity of a great duke still at liberty, whose character was universally known.

After explaining the difficulties he had encountered, and his just uneasiness in finding himself entangled in what to him was a very embarrassing affair, he humbly begged that the duke be prevented from disturbing the young woman, the circumstances of whose history he has been forced to hide from the good sisters of the Cordèlieres. If the interference of the duke could be prevented, he hoped that the repose, joined to the sweetness of the appearance and character of this "affligée *recluse*" would work in her favor in this home of order and prevent his passing for a liar, or even worse, as though being in fault for irregular conduct.

"I left the ladies," he continues, "well disposed for their new pensionaire, but I repeat, what disgrace for me, if jealousy or love, equally out of place, find her out and penetrate even to her parlor there to exhale their scandalous or their unedifying sighs."

The good abbe's fears in regard to the young woman were, however, groundless, for as we have seen, by the 19th of February the due de Chaulnes was safe in the fortress of Vincennes.

Loménie continues: "This affligée *recluse,* as the good abbe Dugué said, was not at all made for the life of a convent, she had scarcely enjoyed the existence within its protecting walls a fortnight before she felt the need to vary her impressions, and she abruptly returned to the world, tranquilized by the knowledge of the solidity of the walls of the chateau de Vincennes which separated her from the due de Chaulnes."

Beaumarchais, inactive at For-l'Eveque, having heard of Mademoiselle Menard's return to the world wrote her a most characteristic letter full of brotherly advice in which is shown his tendency to regulate the affairs of those in whom he feels an interest, as well as a certain chagrin perhaps, that the young woman in question should enjoy her liberty when he, Beaumarchais, is forced to remain inactive at For-l'Evêque.

He wrote: "It is not proper that anyone should attempt to curtail the liberty of others, but the counsels of friend-ship ought to have some weight because of their disinterestedness. I learn that you, Mademoiselle, have left the convent as suddenly as you entered it. What can be your motives for an action which seems imprudent ? Are you afraid that some abuse of authority will force you to remain there? Reflect, I beg you, and see if you are more sheltered in your own home, should some powerful enemy think himself strong-enough to keep you there? In the painful condition of your affairs having no doubt exhausted your purse by paying your pension quarter in advance, and furnishing an apartment in the convent, ought you to triple your expense without necessity? The voluntary retreat where sorrow and fear conducted you, is it not a hundred times more suited to you than those lodgings from which your feelings should wish to separate you by great distance? They tell me that you weep. Why do you do so? Are you the cause of the misfortunes of M. de Chaulnes or of mine? You are only the pretext, and if in this execrable adventure anyone can be thankful, it ought to be you who have no cause to reproach yourself and who have recovered your liberty from one of the most unjust tyrants and madmen who ever took upon themselves the right of invading your presence.

"I must also take into account what you owe the good and worthy abbe Dugué, who to serve you, has been obliged to dissimulate your name and your trouble in the convent, where you were sheltered on his word. Your leaving, which seems like a freak, does it not compromise him with the su-periors of the convent, in giving him the appearance of being connected with a black intrigue, he who put so much zeal and compassion into what he did for you? You are honest and good, but so many violent emotions may have thrown your judgment into some confusion. You need a wise counsellor who will make it his duty to show you your situation just as it is, not happy, but bearable.

"Believe me, my dear friend, return to the convent where I am told you have made yourself loved. While you are there, discontinue the useless establishment which you keep up against all reason. The project which it is supposed that you have of returning to the stage is absurd. You should think of nothing but tranquilizing your mind and regaining your health. In a word, whatever your plans for the future, they cannot and ought not to be indifferent to me. I should be informed, for I dare say that I am the only man whose help you should accept without blushing. In remaining in the convent it will be proved that there is no intimate connection between us, and I shall have the right to declare myself your friend, your protector, your brother, and your counselor.

Beaumarchais."

But all these remonstrances were in vain. Mademoiselle Ménard persisted in remaining in the world. Beaumarchais resigned himself as she became very useful in soliciting his release. Her name, however, very soon disappears from the papers of Beaumarchais. His own affairs take on so black an aspect that he had little time to busy himself with those ' of others. As for the duc de Chaulnes before leaving prison he addressed a humble letter to M. de Sartine in which he promised never again to torment Mademoiselle Ménard nor to interfere with Beaumarchais, asking only that the latter keep himself at a distance.

Thus ends the famous quarrel whose consequence had so profound an effect upon the career of Beaumarchais as we shall see in the next chapter.

CHAPTER IX

"*La* Jeunesse—*Mais* quand *une* chose *est* vraie. . . . *Bartholo—Quand* une *chose* est *vraie*! *Si* je *ne* veux pas *qu'elle* soit *vraie*, je *pretends* qu'ette *ne* soit *pas Ovraie*. Il *n'y* aurait *qu'*a *permettre* à *tons* ces *faquins*-là *d'avoir* raison*, vous* verrez bientôt *ce* que deviendrait l'autorité."

"*Le* Barbier *de* Séville;' Act II, Scene VII.
Beaumarchais at For-l'Evêque—Letter to his Little Friend —Second Trial in the

Suit Instituted Against Him by the Count de la Blache—Efforts to Secure an Audience with the Reporter Goezman—Second Judgment Rendered Against Beaumarchais—He Obtains his Liberty—Loudly Demands the Return of his Fifteen Louis.

ALTHOUGH Beaumarchais's first letter froim For Eveque sounded philosophical, his situation was cruel in the extreme. Loménie says: "This imprisonment which fell in the midst of his suit against the Comte de la Blache did him frightful harm; his adversary profiting by the circumstance, worked without relaxation to blacken his character before the judges, multiplying his measures, his recommendations, his solicitations; and ardently pressing the de-cision of his suit, while the unhappy prisoner whose fortune and honor were engaged in this affair, could not even obtain permission to go out for a few hours to visit the judges in his turn.

"M. de Sartine showed him the greatest good-will but he was unable to do more than mitigate his situation, his liberty depending on the minister.

"Beaumarchais had begun by pleading his cause before the Duke de la Vrillière, as a citizen unjustly imprisoned. He sent him memoir after memoir proving ably that he had done no wrong; he demanded to know why he had been detained, and when M. de Sartine warned him in a friendly way that this tone would lead to nothing, he replied with dignity, 'The only satisfaction of a persecuted man is to render testimony that he is unjustly dealt with.' "

While he was consuming himself in vain protestations, the day for the judgment of his suit approached. To the demands of M. de Sartine soliciting permission for Beaumarchais to go out for a few hours each day the due de la Vrillière replied always, "That man is too insolent, let him follow his affair through his attorney!" and Beaumarchais, indignant and heart-broken, wrote to M. de Sartine:

"It is completely proved to me that they desire that I shall lose my suit, if it is possible for me to lose it, but I admit that I was not prepared for the derisive answer of the due de la Vrilliere to solicit my affair through my attorney, he who knows as well as I, that it is forbidden to attorneys. Ah, great heavens! cannot an innocent man be lost without laughing in his face! Thus, Monsieur, have I been grievously insulted, justice has been denied me because my adversary is a man of quality, I have been put in prison, I am kept there, because I have been insulted by a man of quality. They even go so far as to blame me for enlightening the police as to the false impressions they have received, while the immodest gazettes Les Deux-Ponto and Hollande unworthily dishonor me to please my adversary. A little more and they would say that it was very insolent in me to have been out- raged in every way by a man of quality, because what is the meaning of that phrase, 'He has put too much boasting into this affair?' Could I do less than demand justice and prove by the conduct of my adversary that I was in no way wrong? What a pretext for ruining an offended man, that of saying, 'He has talked too much about his affair.' As if it were possible to talk of anything else! Receive my sincere thanks, Monsieur, for having notified me of this refusal and this observation of M. the due de la Vrillière, and for the happiness of the country may your power one day equal your sagacity and your integrity! My gratitude equals the profound respect with which I am, etc.,

"Beaumarchais. This March 11th, 1773"

But the correspondence of Beaumarchais with M. de Sar-tine did not advance matters in the least. What M. the due de la Vrillière exacted before everything else was that he cease to be insolent, that is to demand justice, and that he ask for pardon.

Beaumarchais resisted this for about a month, when on the 20th of March he received a letter without signature, written by a man who seemed to interest himself in the situation and who endeavored to make Beaumarchais understand that under an absolute government, when anyone has incurred disgrace at the hands of a minister, and that minister keeps one in prison when one has the greatest possible interest to be free, it is not the thing to do to plead one's cause as an oppressed citizen but to bow to the law of force and speak like a suppliant.

What would Beaumarchais do? He was on the brink of losing a suit most important for his fortune and his honor, his liberty was in the hands of a man unworthy of esteem, because the duc de la Vrillière was one of the ministers the most justly disdained by history, but the situation was such that this man disposed at will of his destiny. Beau-marchais resigned himself at last, humiliated himself. See him in the part of suppliant.

"Monseigneur,

"The frightful affair of M. the duc de Chaulnes has become for me a succession of misfortunes without end, and the greatest of all is that I have incurred your displeasure in spite of the purity of my intentions. Despair has broken me and driven me to measures which have displeased you, I disavow them Monseigneur, at your feet, and beg of you a generous pardon, or if it seems to you that I merit a longer imprisonment, permit me to go during a few days to instruct my judges in the most important affair for my fortune and my honor, and I submit after the judgment to whatever pain you may impose. All my family weeping join their prayers to mine. Everyone speaks, Monseigneur, of your indulgence and goodness of heart. Shall I be the only one who implores you in vain. You can with a single word fill with joy a host of honest people whose gratitude will equal the very profound respect with which we are all, and I in particular, Monseigneur, your, etc.,

"Beaumarchais."

From For-l'Eveque, March 21, 1773."

The duc de la Vrillière was satisfied in his petty vanity, so a reply was soon forthcoming. The next day, March 22nd, the minister sent to M. de Sartine the authorization to allow the prisoner to go out during the day, under the conduct of an agent of police, but obliging him to eat and sleep at For-l'Evêque.

In the meantime, however, another disgrace was threatening him. Some enemy had taken advantage of his absence to attack his rights as **lieutenant**-general **des** chasses, "From the depths of his prison," wrote Loménie, "he reclaimed them immediately in a letter to the duc de La Val-lière where he appeared proud and imposing as a baron of the middle ages."

"Monsieur le duc,

"Pierre-Augustin Caron de Beaumarchais, lieutenant-general at the court of justice of your *capitainerie*, has the honor of representing to you that his detention by order of the king has not destroyed his civil estate. He has been very much surprised to learn that in violation of the regulation of the *capitainerie* of May 17th which says that every officer who does not bring valid excuse for not being present at the reception of a new officer will be deprived of his *droit* de *bougies,* etc., etc. The exactitude and zeal with which the suppliant has always fulfilled the functions of his charge to the present day makes him hope, Monsieur le duc, that you will be so good as to maintain him in all the rights of the said charge against every kind of enterprise or infringement. When M. de Schomberg was in the Bastille the king permitted him to do his work for *les* Suisses which he had the honor to command. The same thing happened to the M. the duc du Maine.

"The suppliant is perhaps the least worthy of the officers of your *capitainerie* but he has the honor of being its lieu-tenant-général and you will certainly not disapprove, Monsieur le duc, that he prevents the first office of that *capitainerie* to grow less under his hands or that any other officer takes upon himself the functions to its prejudice.

Caron de Beaumarchais."

In striking contrast to this picture of Beaumarchais defending so proudly his rights before, a great noble, is an-other, also drawn by his own hand, in a letter to a child of six years in which all the warmth and goodness of his heart, as well as the delicacy of his sentiments, manifest themselves.

We already have mentioned the fact that as secretary to the king, Beaumarchais was the colleague of M. Lenormant d'Étioles, the husband of Madame de Pompadour. After the death of his first wife in 1764, he had married a second time and he now had a charming little son, six and a half years old. Beaumarchais, intimate with the family, completely had won the heart of this little boy whose pretty ways were a constant reminder of the child he had lost. Learning that his friend was in prison, the child spontaneously wrote the following letter:

"Neuilly, March 2nd, 1773.
"Monsieur,

"I send you my purse, because in prison one is always unhappy. I am very sorry that you are in prison. Every morning and every evening I say an Ave Maria for you. I have the honor to be, Monsieur, your very humble and very obedient servitor

Constant." Beaumarchais instantly replied:

"My good little friend Constant, I have received with much gratitude your letter and the purse which you joined to it. I have made a just division of what it contained among the prisoners, my companions, according to their different needs, while I have kept for your friend Beaumarchais the best part, I mean the prayers, the Ave Marias, of which I certainly have need, and so have distributed to the poor people who suffer imprisonment all that the purse contained. Thus intending to oblige only a single man you have acquired the gratitude of many. This is the ordinary fruit of such good actions as yours.

"Bonjour, my little friend Constant,
Beaumarchais."

And to the child's mother he wrote at the same time: "I thank you very sincerely, Madame, for having sent me the letter and the purse of my little friend Constant. These are the first outbursts of the sensibility of a young soul which promise excellent things. Do not give him back his purse, in order that he may not think that such sacrifices bring a similar recompense, but later you may give it to him that he may have a reminder of the tenderness of his generous heart. Recompense him now in a way that will give him a just idea of his action without allowing him to pride himself upon it. But what am I thinking of to join my observations to the pains that have caused to germinate and to develop so great a quality as benevolence at an age when the only morality is to report everything to oneself. Receive my thanks and my compliments. Permit that M. l'abbé Leroux participate in them. He has not satisfied himself with teaching his pupils to decline the word virtue, he inculcates the love of it. He is a man full of merit and more fitted than anyone to second your views. This letter and the purse have caused me the joy of a child. Happy parents! You have a son capable at the age of six of this action. And I also had a son, I have him no more, and yours gives you already such happiness. I partake in it with all my heart, and I beg you to continue to love him a little who is the cause of this charming outburst of our little Constant. One cannot add anything to the respectful attachment of him who honors himself, Madame, etc.

Beaumarchais." From For-l'Eveque, March 4, 1773"

"And this," says Loménie, "is the man whom the Comte de la Blache charitably calls a finished monster, a venomous species of which society should be purged, and at the moment when the count says this, it is the opinion almost universally adopted. It is in vain that Beaumarchais follows his guard and returns every evening to his prison, passing his day in hastening from one to another of his judges, the discredit attached to his name followed him everywhere.

"Under the influence of this discredit, and upon the report of the Counsellor Goëzman, the parliament decided at last between him and M. de la Blache, and gave, April 5th, 1773, a strange judgment from a legal point of view. This judgment, declared nul and of no effect the act made between the two majors, saying that there was no need of ***let***-tres ***de*** récision, that is to say, that the question of fraud, surprise or error being set aside, Beaumarchais found himself indirectly declared a forger although there was against him no inscription of forgery."

In the words of Bonnefon, "Precisely the counsellor designated as ***rapporteur*** in the affair of Beaumarchais by la Blache was one of the least scrupulous members of that strange parliament. A learned legist, he had begun his career as judge of the superior council of Alsace, and the chancellor Maupeou, in quest of magistrates who could be bought, had raised him to his new functions.

"Valentine Goëzman was not overly scrupulous in regard to the means of conviction employed and if he kept his doors well closed to all litigants it was only to make them open all the wider by the money of those who solicited his audiences.

"Needy himself he had married a second wife, young and coquettish, even less delicate than her husband as to the choice of means. 'It would be impossible, she was heard to say, 'it would be impossible for us to live from what is given us, but we know how to pick the chicken without making it cry out.'"

It was a certain publisher, who according to Loménie, "hearing that Beaumarchais was in despair at not being able to find access to his reporter, sent him word that the only means of obtaining the audience and assuring the equity of the judge was to make a present to his wife, who demanded two hundred louis."

But of this strange proceeding, let us allow the victim to step forward and speak for himself. In the exposition made in the first of those famous memoirs of which we shall soon speak, Beaumarchais wrote: "A few days before the one appointed for the judgment of my suit, I had obtained from the minister permission to solicit my judges under the express and rigorous conditions of going accompanied by a guard, the sieur Santerre, named for this purpose, and of going only to the judges, returning to the prison for all my meals and to sleep, which exceedingly embarrassed my movements and shortened the time accorded for my solicitations.

"In this short interval I presented myself at least ten times at the office of Monsieur Goëzman without being able to see him. I was not very much affected by this. M. Goëzman was of the number of my judges but there was no pressing interest between us. On the first of April however when he was charged with the office of reporter of my suit he became essential to me.

"Three times that afternoon I presented myself at his door always with the written formula, 'Beaumarchais prays Monsieur to be so good as to accord him the favor of an audience, and to leave orders with the door keeper setting the hour and day.' It was in vain. The next morning I was told that Monsieur Goëzman would see no one, and that it was useless to present myself again. I returned in the afternoon; the same reply.

"If one reflects that of the four days which were left me before the decision, one and a half had already been spent in vain solicitations and that twice a friend of Monsieur Goëzman had been to him and vainly pleaded for an audience for me, one can conceive of my disquietude.

"Not knowing what to do, on returning I entered the home of one of my sisters to take council and to calm my mind. It was then that the sieur Dairolles, lodging at my sister's, spoke of a certain publisher, Le-Jay, who perhaps might procure for me the audience which I desired. He saw the man and was assured that by means of a sacrifice of money an audience would be promptly given."

At this point let us break the narrative of Beaumarchais while we listen for a moment to Gudin. "I was with him when he was told that if he wished to give money to the wife of the reporter he could obtain the audiences he desired, and that this was only too necessary in our miserable manner of gaining justice. I remember very well the anger which seized him at this proposition and the pride with which he rejected it.

"But his friends and family as well as myself, alarmed at what his enemies were doing to ruin him, united our solicitations and tore from him rather than obtained his consent."

And Beaumarchais, after giving in great detail the above scene, continues, "To cut the matter short, one of the friends present ran home and brought two rolls of fifty louis each, which I did not possess, and gave them to my sister, and these were finally delivered to Madame Goëzman while I returned to prison."

The details which follow are too numerous to be given here. It is sufficient to say that though the reporter promised an audience for nine o'clock that same evening, Beau-marchais on arriving found that he was not expected. He was, however, this time not to be rejected and finally succeeded in forcing admittance. It was the moment when Madame and Monsieur Goëzman were preparing to seat themselves at table. A few moments' conversation con-vinced Beaumarchais that the judge's mind was made up and he returned to his prison, more alarmed than ever. His desire for a satisfactory audience was augmented rather than diminished. It was the fourth of April, the following day the final decision was to be given. Through the sieur Dairolles and Le-Jay Madame Goëzman demanded a second hundred louis and promised this time to secure the audience. Beaumarchais did not possess the money but offered a watch set with diamonds which was of equal value. She accepted the watch, but demanded fifteen louis extra as a gratification for her husband's secretary. Beaumarchais, desperate, gave them, although as he told us, with a very bad grace. The audience was promised for seven o'clock.

Beaumarchais presented himself, but in vain. This time he was unable to force an entrance and returned without seeing the judge.

He continues: "The reader, tired at last of hearing so many vain promises, so many useless steps, will judge how beside myself I was to receive the one and to take the other. I went back to prison, rage in my heart. Now came a new course of intermediaries, this time the curious reply which was brought to me cannot be omitted. 'It is not the fault of the lady if you have not been received. You may present yourself to-morrow. But she is so honest that if you cannot obtain an audience before the judgment she assures you that you shall receive again all that she has received of you.'

"I argued evil from this new announcement. Why did the lady engage herself to return the money? I had not asked for it. I made the most of the melancholy reflections on this subject. But although the tone and the proceeding seemed absolutely changed, I was none the less resolved to make a last effort to see my reporter the next morning; the only instant of which I could profit before the judgment."

An interested friend had succeeded in penetrating to the presence of Goëzman the night before and the judge promised to see Beaumarchais the next morning. The latter says: "If ever an audience seemed sure, this one certainly did, promised on the one hand by the reporter while his wife received the price on the other. Nevertheless, in spite of the assurances of all, we were no happier than on former occasions. . . . Santerre and I remained for an hour and a half, but the orders were positive, we were not allowed to cross the threshold.

"But I had lost my suit, the evil was consummated. The same evening, sieur Dairolles returned to my sister the two rolls of fifty louis each and the watch. As for the fifteen louis, he said since they were required by the secretary of M. Goëzman, Madame Goëzman believed herself discharged from returning them.

"This conduct of the secretary was an enigma to me, I wished to fathom it. In the beginning he had modestly re-fused ten louis voluntarily offered him. I begged the friend who finally had induced the secretary to accept the ten Louis to inquire if he had received the fifteen louis given to Madame Goëzman for him. He replied that they had never been offered to him and if they had been, he would not have accepted them. . . .

"Stung by the dishonest means employed to retain the fifteen louis, believing even that the sieur Le-Jay whom I did not know at all perhaps had wished to keep them, I demanded of him through the sieur Dairolles what had be-come of them.

"He affirmed that Madame Goëzman had refused to give them back, and assured him that it had been arranged that in any case they were lost to me. He could not endure that it should be supposed that he had kept them, the lady herself was not to be seen, but I might write to her.

"The 21st of April, that is, seventeen days after the judgment, I wrote her the following letter.

" 'I have not the honor, Madame, of being personally known to you and I should be very far from importuning you, if after losing my suit, when you were good enough to return to me the two rolls of louis and my watch, you had at the same time returned the fifteen louis, which the common friend who negotiated between us left you in supererogation.

" I have been so horribly treated in the report of Monsieur, your husband, and my defence has been so trampled under foot before him that it is not just that to the immense loss which this report has cost me should be added that of fifteen louis which it is impossible should have strayed in your hands. If injustice must be paid for, it should not be paid by him who has so cruelly suffered.

" 'I hope you will be so good as to respect my demand,. and that you will add to the justice, of returning me these fifteen louis that of believing me, with the respectful consideration which is due to you Madam, your, etc."

Bonnefon says: "To this demand the wife of the counsellor grew indignant and cried aloud. Beaumarchais was not to be intimidated and maintained his demand. It was then that the counsellor intervened and complained first to Monsieur the due de la Vrillière and then to M. de Sartine; badly instructed perhaps and feeling sure of an easy triumph over an enemy already half-vanquished, he brought a suit for calumny before the parliament.

"Beaumarchais did not draw back. The counsellor accused him of attempt at corruption; his presence of mind did not desert him. He replied to everything with a vivacity and an apropos truly remarkable. Listen to him.

". . . 'It is time that I speak. Let me wash myself from the reproach of corruption by a calculation and some very simple reflections.

" 'It cost me a hundred louis to obtain an audience of M. Goëzman. Be so good as to follow the trace of that money and then judge, if from the distance where I remained from the reporter it was possible that I had formed the mad project of corrupting him.

" 'In ceding to the necessity of sacrificing one hundred louis which I (one person) did not possess; a friend (two persons) offered them to me, my sister (three) received them from his hands, she confided them to sieur Dairolles (four) ; who gave them to the sieur Le-Jay (five) to be given to Madame Goëzman (six) who kept them, and finally Monsieur Goëzman (seven), whom I could see only at that price and who knew nothing about the whole affair. See then from M. Goëzman to me a chain of seven persons of which he says I hold the first link as corrupter, while he holds the last as incorruptible. Very good. But if he is judged incorruptible how will he prove that I am corrupter?' . . ."

Monsieur Loménie, entering into more detail, says of Goëz-raan: "He must have been convinced that his wife had seriously compromised herself. Compromised himself through her, he had to choose between several different measures; all of them, in presence of a litigant discontented and fearless, offered great disadvantage for his reputation; the one which he adopted was incontestably the most daring, but also the most dishonorable.

"Starting from the idea that Beaumarchais had not the force to resist him, he imagined that in taking the initia-tive and attacking him while maneuvering in such a way that the truth might not be made known, he might be able to ruin him who had given the fifteen louis, and save her who had received them. It will be seen that the stratagem of Goezman was baffled and his crime cruelly punished."

But to return to the decision given by the parliament on the report of Goezman April 5th. Lomenie says: "At the same time that this decree dishonored Beaumarchais it was a rude blow to his fortune. The Parliament had not dared award to the Comte de la Blache as he had demanded, the passing of the act of settlement declared by it nul; the iniquity would have been too glaring; but it condemned his adversary to pay fifty-six thousand livres of debt annulled by the act of settleiqent, the interests of the debt and the costs of the suit.

"It was enough to crush him for at the same time the Comte de la Blache seized all his goods and revenues, other pretending creditors with equally false pretentions, united their persecutions with those of the Comte de la Blache, and the man thus attacked demanded in vain, with loud cries that the doors of his prison be opened.

" I am at the end of my courage,' he wrote April 9, 1773, to M. de Sartine. 'The opinion of the public is that I am entirely sacrificed, my credit has fallen, my business is ruined, my family of which I am the father and the support is in despair. Monsieur, I have done good all my life without ostentation and I have never ceased to be torn to pieces by those evilly disposed.

" 'If my home were known to you, you would see me in the midst of its members, a good son, a good brother, a good husband, and a useful citizen; I have assembled only benedictions about me, while my enemies calumniate me at a distance.

" 'Whatever vengeance one may wish to take of me for that miserable affair of Chaulnes, will it then have no limits? It is well proved that my imprisonment makes me lose a hundred thousand francs. The form, the ground, everything makes one shudder in that iniquitous sentence, and it is impossible for me to rise above it so long as I am kept in this horrible prison. I have courage to support my own misfortunes; but I have none against the tears of my respectable father, seventy-five years of age, who is grieving himself to death for the abject state to which I have fallen. I have none against the anguish of my sisters, of my nieces, who already feel the horror of my detention and know of the disorder which has come to my affairs because of it. All the activity of my being is again turned inward, my situation kills me, I am struggling against an acute malady of which I feel an agonizing premonition, through loss of sleep and disgust with food. The air of my prison destroys me.'

"It was in this state of deep depression and misery when the soul of Beaumarchais seemed overwhelmed and all his manhood slipping from him, that the petty detail of the fifteen louis came to stir his mind once more to action, and while his sisters wept and his father prayed, his proud and unconquerable spirit rose triumphant out of the abyss into which for a moment it hall fallen, and with fresh courage gleaming in his eyes he began pacing the floor of his prison, already 'meditating his memoirs.'

"The minister de la Vrillière allowed himself at last to be touched, and on the 8th of May, 1778, after two months and a half of detention without cause, he gave the prisoner his liberty.

"It is here that out of this lost process sprang suddenly another more terrible still, which should complete the ruin of Beaumarchais, but which saved him and made him pass in a few months from the state of abjection and of misery where to use his own expression, 'He was an object of disgust and pity to himself, to a state where he is acclaimed the vanquisher of the hated parliament and the favorite of the nation.' "

"He was," says Grimm, "the horror of Paris a year ago; everyone upon the word of his neighbor, believed him ca-pable of the greatest crimes; all the world dotes on him to-day." It remains for us now to explain how this change of opinion came about.

CHAPTER X

"*Mais* que *dira*-t-*on* quand *on* apprendra *que* ce Beaumarchais*, qui* jusqu'a *present*'est *connu* que *par* son maltéra-*ble* gaité*, son* imperturbable *philosophie,* qui *compose* à *la* fois *un* air *gracieux,* un *malin* vaudeville*,* une comédie *folle,* un *drame* touchant*, brave* les *ptdssants*, rit des *sots* et s*'amuse* aux dépens *de* to ut *le monde?*"
Marsolier—"*Beaumarchais* à *Madrid*" Act IV, Scene V
The Goëzman Lawsuit—The Famous Memoirs of Beaumarchais.

WE have come at last to the turn of the tide in the career of Beaumarchais, which in his case is no ordinary tide but a tidal wave so gigantic in force that he is carried by it to such a height of popularity as fixes upon him for the time the attention of Europe.

"The degree of talent which he displayed," says La Harpe, "belongs to the situation. It came from his perfect accord with the time in which he lived and the circumstances in which he found himself. The secret of all great success lies in the power of the man to see with a comprehensive glance what he can do with himself and with others."

Already we have had occasion to note that in this harmony between Beaumarchais and the circumstances of his life lies the secret of his genius. He is no moralizer, but he sees things clearly and in just proportion and he knows how to take advantage of his own position as well as of the weakness of his adversaries.

In relation to the lawsuit of which we now write, La Harpe further says, "What would have disconcerted or ren-dered furious an ordinary person did not move the spirit of Beaumarchais. Master of his own indignation and strong with that of the public, he called upon it to witness the fraud which has been employed against him." At first many cry out that it is ridiculous to make such a fuss about fifteen louis; his family, his friends, Gudin among the number, implore him to desist; wiser than they, he instinctively feels that in the very pettiness, the absurdity of the charge, lies its gigantic force.

Again quoting La Harpe, "It was a master stroke, this suit about the fifteen louis; and what joy for the public, which in reading Beaumarchais saw in his different memoirs which rapidly succeeded one another, only the hand which took upon itself to revenge the people's wrongs. The facts did not speak, they cried!"

When Beaumarchais found himself actually charged with a criminal accusation capable of sending him to the public infamy of the pillory or the galleys, unable to find a lawyer willing to plead his cause, it was then that the whole power of his genius was revealed to him. Instantly he realized that he was to be his own lawyer, and that from the magistracy before him, it was to the people that he must appeal, "that judge of judges," and we see him flinging forth one factum after another, while all the force of his soul, the gaiety of his character, the brilliancy of his wit, returned to him in overabundant measure. The family and friends, lately so depressed, rose with the rising of his courage, lent to him the whole force of their beings and formed the constant inspiration of his ever-increasing success. . In a few weeks his first memoir had attracted the attention of all France, while in less than three days after the publication of the fourth, more than six thousand copies had been sold. At the ball or the opera, people tore them from one another's hands, and in the cafe's and foyers of the theaters they were read out loud to enthusiastically admiring crowds.

What could be more surprising? Judicial factums or memoirs universally recognized as being the dryest and most uninteresting of writings come to be preferred to all others?

It was, as Voltaire said, after reading the fourth memoir, "No comedy was ever more amusing, no tragedy more touching," and Lintilhac taking up this judgment and applying it to the memoirs has made perhaps the most brilliant of the many criticisms which this subject has called forth.

"The judgment of Voltaire," he says, "reveals to us the most original of their merits, that of being a tragi-comedy in five acts. The unity of the subject is placed in evidence by this question which is so often raised. Who is culpable of the crime of corruption—the judge whose surroundings put his justice at auction, or the litigant thus constrained to scatter gold about the judge?

"The five memoirs mark the phases of the debate. The first is a perfect exposition of the subject destined to soothe the judges. After having made, a resume of the preceding incidents, and taken his position, Beaumarchais engages the offensive and orders his intrigue by light skirmishes in the form of episodes. Then he opens a dramatic perspective upon the sudden changes of the contest.

"From the first to the second memoir during the entre-act the action has advanced. A rain of ridiculous and arrogant factums, of false testimonies and infamous calumnies has poured down upon the victim of the piece. The black intrigue is knotted, the scenes press varied and picturesque. At first it is that of the registrar, then Madame Goëzman comes before us with insults but ends with artful pretty faces. After this comic prelude, the two principal characters engage in the background, in a dramatic contest.

"'Give me your hand,' cries Beaumarchais, and illuminating the scene, he ousts his crafty adversary, seizes him, drags him frightened like a thief in the night to the nearest lamp post, that is to say, the crude illumination of the foot lights, crying in his face the invective: 'And you are a magistrate ! To what have we come, great heavens !

"Similar to the third act of a strongly intrigued play, the third memoir throws the adversaries on the scene and en-gages them in a furious fray. We have just seen the judge imprudent enough to descend from the tribunal to the arena, he lies there panting under the grip of his adversary, it is then that fly to his aid 'that swarm of hornets.' The image is piquant, the scene, does it not renew the ***parabase*** des Guêpes? 'Six memoirs at once against me ! cries the valiant athlete in an outburst of manly gaiety. He takes up the glove, salutes them all around with an ironic politeness, and then sends all of them, Marin, Bertrand, Arnaud, Baculard, even to Falcoz, who in vain tries to turn in a whirligig upon an absurdity, to bite the dust by the side of Goëzman. It is the moment to bring up the reserves, They arrive in serried ranks. Here comes a president and a whole host of counsellors. 'My, what a world of people occupied to support you, Monsieur !

"A daring offensive alone can disengage Beaumarchais. He instantly makes it, and following his favorite tactics, he wears it as an ornament, an accusation of forgery well directed against Goëzman changes the roles; this is the grand counter movement of the piece.

"A sudden stupor has broken up the allies, their adversary knows how to profit

Beaumarchais and the War of American Independence

by their confusion, and throws out his petition of mitigation. It is the fourth act. He prepares briefly and wisely the fifth. Beaumarchais with an affected and deadly moderation, sums up the facts, fortifies himself in the conquered position and prepares the supreme assault.

"At last in the fourth memoir he gives out the fifth act of the peace.

"Without ceding in the least to the third memoir in point of composition, the fourth in spite of an occasional 'abuse of force,' according to La Harpe, surpasses it by its heat and brilliancy.

"There reigns above everything else an ease that Beaumarchais announces from the beginning. 'This memoir,' he says, 'is less an examination of a dry and bloodless question, than a succession of reflections upon my estate as accused.'

"It is the best of his dramas, a ***melange*** of mirth and pathos, where are centered and dissolved with an authoritative cleverness, all the elements of interest and of action which he draws from the heart of his subject and which are multiplied by his fancy and his fears. In the beginning, an invocation, the prelude of a héraique-*comique* drama, then thanking a host of honest people who applaud and whose aid he skilfully declines, the hero springs with one bound into the fray.

"He directs his finishing blows to each one of his adversaries, and making a trophy of their calumnies, he awards himself an eloquent apology which he modestly entitles, 'Fragments of my voyage in Spain.' The episode of Cla-vico, thanks to the touching interest which it excites, crowns the memoir like the recitals which unravel the plot in classic plays, and whose discreet eloquence leads the soul of the auditor to a sort of final appeasement.

"If the action is dramatic, the characters are no less so. First Madame Goëzman advances, a scowl upon her face, but at a gracefully turned compliment from her adversary, 'at once a sweet smile gives back to her mouth its agreeable form.' "

And so with the rest. "But the most vivid of all his portraits is that of the principal personage, the author himself, this propagandist always en scene, who is never weary, whom one sees or whom one divines everywhere, animating everything with his presence, the center of all action and interest. He is endowed with such a beautiful sang-froid, which acts under all circumstances, and such vivid sensibility that everything paints itself in his memory, everything fixes itself under his pen. So that he appears to us in the most various attitudes; here the soul of gallantry, advancing to offer his hand to Madame Goëzman; there of modesty lowering his eyes for her, or again, hat in hand very humbly inclining before the passage of some mettlesome president."

But as Gudin assures us, "The courage of Beaumarchais was not insensibility. The tone of his memoirs showed his superiority but he was none the less deeply affected. I have seen him shed tears, but I have never seen him cast down. His tears seemed like the dew which revivifies. The hour of combat gave him back his courage. He advanced, dauntless, against his enemies; he felled them to the ground and caused to react upon them the outrages with which they attacked him. In their despair they published that he was not the author of his memoirs. 'We know,' they cried, 'where they are composed and who composes them.

"It was this accusation which gave to Beaumarchais the opportunity for one of his wittiest retorts. 'Stupid people, why don't you get your own written there?'"

Gudin was even accused of writing them,—faithful Gudin, whose history of France in thirty-five volumes never found a publisher, and "whose prose," says Loménie, "resembled that of Beaumarchais about as the gait of a laboring ox resembles that of a light and spirited horse."

Rousseau when he heard the accusation cried out, "I do not know whether Beaumarchais writes them or not, but I know this, no one writes such memoirs for another."

Voltaire in the depths of his retreat read the memoirs with eager interest. Personal reasons had made him in the beginning a supporter of the parliament Maupeou. Little by little, he changed his opinion; "I am afraid," he wrote, "that after all that brilliant, hare-brained fellow is in the right against the whole world." And a little later, "What a man! He unites everything; jesting, gravity, gaiety, pathos,—every species of eloquence without seeking after any; he confounds his adversaries; he gives lessons to his judges. His naïveté enchants me."

As to the most atrocious calumnies circulated against him, La Harpe who knew him well, although never intimately, has said: "I have not forgotten how many times I heard repeated by persons who did not believe in the least that they were doing wrong, that a certain M. de Beaumarchais who was much talked about had enriched himself by getting rid successively of two wives who had fortunes. Surely this is enough to make one shudder, if one stops to reflect that this is what is called scandal (something scarcely thought sinful) and that there was not the slightest ground for such a horrible defamation. He had, it is true, married two widows with fortunes, which is surely very permissible for a young man with none. He received nothing from the one, because in his grief he forgot to register the contract of marriage duly, and this alone which rendered the crime useless was sufficient to prove his innocence.

"He inherited something from the second who was a very charming woman, whom he adored. She left him a son, whom he lost soon after his wife's death. I do not know why no one ever accused him of poisoning the child, that crime was necessary to complete the other. It is evident, even if he had not loved his wife, that in keeping her alive he had everything to gain, as her fortune was in the main hers only during life.

"These are public facts of which I am sure, but hatred does not look for the truth, and it knows that it will not be required.of it by the thoughtless. Where are we, great Heavens, if a man cannot have the misfortune to inherit from his wife without having poisoned her? . . ."

When Voltaire, who had heard the calumny, read the memoirs of Beaumarchais, he said, "This man is not a poisoner, he is too gay."

La Harpe adds, "Voltaire could not know as I do, that he was also too good, too sensible, too open, too benevolent to commit any bad act, although he knew very well how to write very amusing and very malicious things against those who blackened him."

Compelled to defend himself and to prove himself innocent of a crime so horrible that its name could scarcely be forced to pass his lips, he replies with a gentleness, but a power of eloquence which confounds his adversaries. "Cowardly enemies, have you then no resource but base insult? Calumny machinated in secret and struck out in the darkness? Show yourselves then, but once, if for nothing more than to tell me to my face that it is out of place for any man to defend himself. But all honest people know very well that your fury has placed me in an absolutely privi- leged class. They will excuse me for taking this occasion to confound you, where forced to defend a moment of my life I am about to spread a luminous daylight over the rest. Dare then to contradict me. Here is my life in a few words.

"For the last fifteen years I honor myself with being the father and the sole support of a numerous family, and far from being offended at this avowal which is torn from me, my relatives take pleasure in publishing that I have always shared my modest fortune with them without ostentation and without reproach.

"O you who calumniate me without knowing me, come and hear the concert of benedictions which fall upon me from a crowd of good hearts and you will go away undeceived.

"As to my wives, from having neglected to register the contract of marriage, the death of the first left me destitute in the rigor of the term, overwhelmed with debts and with pretentions which I was unwilling to follow, not wishing to go to law with the relatives, of whom, up to that moment, I had no reason to complain. My second wife in dying carried with her more than three-fourths of her fortune, so that my son, had he lived, would have found himself richer from the side of his father than that of his mother....

"And you who have known me, you who have followed me without ceasing, O my friends, say, have you ever known in me anything but a man constantly gay, loving with an equal passion study and pleasure, inclined to raillery but without bitterness, welcoming it against himself when it was well seasoned, supporting perhaps with too much ardor his own opinion when he believed it to be just, but honoring highly and without envy everyone whom he recognized as superior, confident about his interests to the point of neglecting them, active when he is goaded, indolent and *sta.g*-nant after the tempest, careless in happiness but carrying constancy and serenity into misfortune to the point of astonishing his most intimate friends . . .

"How is it that, with a life and intentions the most honorable, a citizen sees himself so violently torn to pieces? That a man so gay and sociable away from home, so solid and benevolent in his family, should find himself the butt of a thousand venomous calumnies ? This is the problem of my life. I search in vain for its solution."

It was by such outbursts of feeling that Beaumarchais won the hearts of all except those who for personal reasons were bent upon his ruin. But as the admiration of the one side increased, the fury of the other was proportionally augmented. Under the able guidance of M. de Lomenie, let us examine a few of the adversaries who presented themselves, and from the few, the reader may judge of the rest.

First of all is Madame Goëzman, "who," says Loménie, "wrote under the dictates of her husband and threw at the head of Beaumarchais a quarto of seventy-four pages, bristling with terms of law and Latin quotations.

"Beaumarchais sums up in a most *spirituelle* manner the profound stupidity of the factum when he cries out, 'An ingenuous woman is announced to me and I am presented with a German publicist.'

"But if the memoir of Madame Goëzman is ridiculous in form, it is in matter of an extreme violence. 'My soul,' it is thus that Madame Goëzman begins, 'has been divided between astonishment, surprise, and horror in reading the libel of sieur Caron. The audacity of the author astonishes me, the number and atrocity of his impostures excite surprise, the idea he gives of himself fills me with horror.' When we remember that the honest lady who speaks has in her drawer the fifteen louis, whose reclamation excites the astonishment, surprise, and horror, one is inclined to excuse Beaumarchais for having permitted himself certain liberties of language. It is very well known with what mixture of ironic politeness and pressing argumentation he refutes, irritates, embarrasses, compliments, and confounds Madam Goëzman.

"Who has not burst into laughter on reading that excellent comic scene where he paints himself dialoguing with her before the registrar? The scene is so amusing that one would be tempted to take it for a picture drawn at fancy. This is not the case however." . . .

A few extracts from this comic scene will give the reader an idea of *la* force *de* tête of the pretty woman attempting to face so subtle an adversary as Beaumarchais.

"Confrontation of myself with Madame Goezman.

"No one could imagine the difficulty we had to meet one another, Madame Goëzman and I. Whether she was really indisposed as many times as she sent word to the registrar, or whether she felt the need of preparation to sustain the shock of a meeting so serious as that with me, nevertheless we at last found ourselves facing each other.

"Madame Goëzman, summoned to state her reproaches if she has any to formulate against me, replied, 'Write that I reproach and recuse monsieur because he is my capital enemy and because he has an atrocious soul, known for such in Paris, etc. The phrase seemed a little masculine for a lady, but on seeing her fortify herself, leave her natural character, inflate her voice to utter these first injuries, I decided that she felt the need of beginning her attack by a vigorous period and so I did not mind her bad temper.

"Her reply was written verbatim and I was questioned in my turn. Here is my answer: 'I have no reproach to make against madame, not even for her little bad humor which dominates her at this moment; but many regrets to offer for the necessity of a criminal process in order to present to her my homage. As to the atrocity of my soul I hope to prove to her by the moderation of my replies and by my respectful conduct that her counsel has evilly informed her in my regard.'

"And it was written down. This is the general tone that prevailed during the eight hours that we passed together the twice that we met."

After several pages of this interrogation, Beaumarchais gives us, "The Confrontation of Madame Goëzman With Me." From which we give the following extracts:

"I took the liberty of saying, 'To-day, Madame, it is I who hold the attack, we shall first take up your interroga-tions.'

"I took the papers to run them over.

" 'What? This Monsieur here, has he the liberty to read all that I have been made to write?'

" 'It is a right, Madame, which I shall use with all possible deference. In your first interrogation, for instance, to the sixteen consecutive questions upon the same subject, that is, to know whether you received one hundred louis from Le-Jay to procure an audience for le sieur Beaumarchais I see to the great honor of your discretion that the sixteen replies are not charged with any superfluous ornaments.

" 'Questioned as to whether you have received one hundred louis in two rolls?'

"You reply, 'That is false.'

"'If you put them in a case ornamented with flowers?'

" 'That is not true.'

" 'If you kept them until the day after the suit?'

" 'Atrocious lie.'

" 'If you did not promise an audience to Le-Jay for the same evening?'

" 'Abominable calumny.'

" 'If you had not said to Le-Jay, money is not necessary, your word is sufficient?'

" 'Diabolical invention,' etc., etc. Sixteen negations following one another in relation to the same subject.

"And yet you admit freely at the second interrogation that 'It is true that Le-Jay presented one hundred louis, that I put them away in an *armoire* and kept them a day and a night, but simply to accommodate that poor Le-Jay, because he was a good man and did not realize the consequences, and because the money might make him tired in carrying it about.' (What goodness, the sums were in gold!)

" 'As these replies are absolutely contrary to the first, I beg you madame to be so good as to tell us which of the two interrogations you decide to hold to in this important matter?'

" 'Neither to the one nor to the other, Monsieur, all that I said there means nothing, and I shall only hold to my verification which is the only thing that is true.' All this was written down.

" 'It must be admitted, Madame,' I said to her, 'that the method of recusing this your own testimony after having recused that of every one else would be the most convenient of all if it could only succeed. In waiting for the parlia-ment to adopt it let us see what is said of the one hundred louis in your verification.'

"Madame Goëzman here assured us that she begged Le-Jay to take away the money with him and that when he was gone she was astonished to find it in a case decorated with flowers which was on the mantel piece. She sent three times during the day to that poor Le-Jay begging him to come and get his money, which he did not do until the day after.

" 'Observe, Madame, that in the first instance of all, you have rejected the one hundred louis with indignation, then put them aside with complaisance, while in the last case it is without your knowledge that they remained with you. Here are three narrations of the same act, what is the true version I beg you?'

" 'I have said to you, Monsieur, that I shall hold to my verification,' etc., etc., etc."

Then comes the question of the fifteen louis: "I begged her to be so good as to tell us clearly and without equivocation whether she had not required fifteen louis of Le-Jay for the secretary, and if she had not put them in the bureau when Le-Jay gave her the money.

" 'I replied clearly and without equivocation that Le-Jay never spoke to me of the fifteen louis, neither did he give them to me.'

" 'Observe, Madame, that there would be more merit in saying, 'I refused them,' than in maintaining that you know nothing about them.'

" 'I maintain, Monsieur, that no one ever spoke to me of them. Would there have been any sense of offering fifteen louis to a woman of my quality, after having refused a hundred the day before?'

" 'The day before what, Madame?'

" 'Eh, monsieur, the day before the day (she stopped suddenly and bit her lip.)

" 'The day before the day,' I said to her, 'on which no one ever spoke to you about the fifteen louis, *n'est*-ce-pas?

" 'Stop this,' she said, rising furious to her feet, 'or I will give you a box on the ears. I've had enough of those fifteen louis! With all your despicable little ***tournures*** de ***phrases*** you try to confuse me and make me blunder, but I tell you in truth that I shall not answer you another word.' And her fan assuaged by redoubled strokes the fire which had mounted to hex face . . . She was like a lioness feeling that she had just escaped being taken.

"After Madame Goëzman came Bertrand who began with this epigram taken from the Psalms '***Judica*** me, ***Deus,*** et dis-***cerne*** cansam ***meam*** de ***gente*** non ***sancta,*** et ***ab homine*** iniquo ***et*** doloso ***erue*** me."

Beaumarchais avenged himself on *le* grand Bertrand by inflicting upon him the celebrity of ridicule. Here, as elsewhere, the shade of the physiognomies is perfectly grasped. It is in vain that Bertrand attempted to deal terrible blows, in vain that he committed to writing such phrases as, "cynic orator; buffoon; brazen-faced sophist; unfaithful painter who draws from his own soul the filth with which he tarnishes the robe of innocence; evil, from necessity and from taste; his heart hard, implacable, vindictive; light-headed from his passing triumph; and smothering without remorse human sensibility . . ." instead of paying back anger for anger, Beaumarchais contented himself with painting his enemy. He painted him talkative, shrewd for gain, undecided, timid, hot-headed, but more stupid than bad, in a word exactly as he showed himself in the four grotesque memoirs with which he has enriched this famous suit.

The fourth champion who precipitated himself upon Beaumarchais, the head lowered to pierce him through by the first blow, was a novelist of the time, amusing enough in a melancholy way, who prided himself as he said, upon having *l'embonpoint* du *sentiment*. It is d'Arnaud-Baculard, who, to be agreeable to the judge Goëzman, wrote a letter containing a false statement and who, after being very politely set right in the first memoir of Beaumarchais, replied in this style:

"Yes, I was on foot and I encountered in the rue de Condé, the sieur Caron *en* carrosse—*dans* son *carrosse*," and as Beaumarchais had said that d'Arnaud had a somber air, he grew indignant and cried, 'I had an air, not somber but penetrating. The somber air goes only with those who ruminate crime, who work to stifle remorse and to do evil— There are hearts in which I tremble to read, where I measure all the somber depths of hell. It is then that I cry out, 'thou sleepest, Jupiter! for what purpose then hast thou thy thunderbolts?'"

"One sees," said Loménie, "that if d'Arnaud on his side was not méchant, *it was not from lack of will. The reply of Beaumarchais perhaps will be found interesting; there it will be seen with what justice he gave to each one his deserts, and what attractive serenity he brought into the combat. He began by reproducing the phrase of d'Arnaud about the* carrosse.

" '*Dans* son *carrosse,* you repeat with great point of admiration, who would not believe after that sad, 'yes I was on foot' and that great point of admiration which runs after my *carrosse,* that you were envy itself personified. But I, who know you to be a good man, I know that the phrase *dans* son *carrosse,* does not signify that you were sorry to see me in my *carrosse,* but only that you were sorry that I did not see you in yours.'

" 'But console yourself, Monsieur, the *carrosse* in which I rode was already no more mine when you saw me in it. The Comte de la Blache already had seized it with all my other goods. Men called à hawtes *armes,* with uniforms, bandoliers and menacing guns guarded it, as well as all my furniture; and to cause you, in spite of myself, the sorrow of seeing me in my *carrosse* it was necessary that same day that I had that of demanding, my hat in one hand and a ***gros*** ecu ***in the other, the permission to use it, of that company of officers, which I did, ne*** vous déplaise, every morning, and while I speak with such tranquillity the same distress reigns in my household.

"'How unjust we are! We are jealous of and we hate such and such a one whom we believe happy, who would often give something over, to be in the place of the pedestrian who detests him because of his *carrosse*. I, for ex-ample; could anything be worse than my actual situation? But I am something like the cousin of Heloise, I have done my best to cry; the laugh has to escape from some corner. This is what makes me gentle with you. My philosophy is, to be, if I can, contented with myself and to let the rest go as it pleases God.

"And at the end, after the honey comes the sting. 'Pardon, Monsieur, if I have not replied by an express writing to you alone, to answer all the injuries of your memoir, pardon, if, seeing you measure in my heart the somber depths of hell, and, hearing you cry, "***Tu*** dors, ***Jupiter***; quoi ***te*** sert ***donc*** ta ***foudre***?" I have replied lightly to so much bombast. Pardon, you were a school boy, no doubt, and you re-member that the best blown up balloon needs only the stick of a pin.' "

But it is impossible without becoming wearisome to draw forth all the charac-ters and to allow them to pass in re-view. Let us turn our attention for a few mo-ments to the sublime invocation of the fourth memoir, and with it a few observa-tions of M. de Sainte-Beuve, taken from his admirable criticism of the memoirs of Beaumarchais in his famous "***Causeries*** de ***Lundi.***"

In this invocation the orator supposes himself to be speaking with God, "that Beneficent Being who watches over all." The Supreme Being deigns to speak even to him, saying, "I am He who is all. Without me thou didst not exist. I gave thee thy body, healthy and strong, I placed in it the most active of souls. Thou knowest the profusion with which I have poured sensibility into thy heart, and gaiety into thy character; but, filled as I see thee with the happiness of thinking, of feeling, thou wouldst be too happy if some sorrow did not balance the state of thy fortune, therefore I will overwhelm thee with calamities without number, thou shalt be torn by a thousand enemies, deprived of liberty, of thy property, accused of rapine, of forgery, of imposture, of corruption, of calumny, groaning under the opprobrium of a criminal lawsuit, attacked upon every point of thy existence by absurd, 'they say and tossed about to the scrutiny of public opinion . . ."

Then he prostrates himself before the Supreme Being accepting his whole destiny and saying, "Being of all Beings, I owe to Thee all things, the happiness of existence, of thinking, of feeling. I believe that Thou hast given us the good we enjoy and the evil we suffer in equal measure; I believe that Thy justice has wisely compensated all things for us and that the variety of pains and pleasures, fears and hopes, is the fresh wind which sets the vessel in motion and causes it to advance upon its way. . . ."

In relation to the above Sainte-Beuve says: "I have wished to cite this fresh and happy image which impresses us like a morning breeze, which in spite of everything reached him across the bars of his prison. This was the true Beaumar-chais, truer than he ever painted himself elsewhere.

"In his invocation he continues to address himself humbly to the Supreme Being, begging, since he must have enemies that they be given him according to his choice, with the faults, the stupid and base animosities which he designates, and then with admirable art and vivifying brush, he sketches one after another all his adversaries, giving them an un- mistakable resemblance. 'If,' he says, 'my misfortune must begin by an unforseen attack by a greedy legatee, for a just debt, for an act founded on the reciprocal esteem and the equity of the contracting parties, accord me for adversary, a man, miserly, unjust and known so to be—and he designates the Comte de la Blache so vividly that every one has named him already. It is the same for the counsellor Goëz-man, for his wife, and for their acolytes, but here his ardent spirit outstrips its bounds, it can no longer be contained— at the end of each secondary portrait the name escapes of itself and this name is an additional comic touch, 'Supreme Goodness—Give me Marin! Give me Bertrand! Give me Baculard!

"The whole idea," says Sainte-Beuve, "the manner of its conception and execution, with so much breadth, superiority of gaiety and irony, all with one stroke, one breath, composes one of the most admirable pieces of eloquence which our oratorical literature can offer."

It was by such outbursts as these, that the nation was aroused from the semi-torpor into which it had fallen after the subsidence of the resistance offered to the establishment of the new parliament. With one voice Beaumarchais was hailed as the deliverer of the rights of the people, and the saying, "***Louis*** the ***XV*** founded the parliament which ***fifteen*** Louis destroyed," was the slogan of a new era of public acclaim for justice and equity. In every country of Europe Beaumarchais's memoirs were read, and they excited the liveliest admiration. In the memoirs of Goethe it is told how at a social gathering where those of Beaumarchais were being read aloud, a young woman suggested to the poet that the incident of Clavico might be converted into a drama, where Beaumarchais should come upon the scene. From Philadelphia even came warm expressions of interest, while from every corner of France letters of congratulation, of sympathy and admiration poured upon the hero of the hour.

A few extracts will be sufficient to give an idea of the reigning enthusiasm. The wife of one of the presidents of the ancient parliament, Madame de Meinières, wrote after reading the fourth memoir: "I have finished, Monsieur, that astonishing memoir. I was angry yesterday at the visits which interrupted that delicious reading and when the company was gone, I thanked them for having prolonged my pleasures by interrupting them. On the contrary, blessed forever be le grand cousin, the sacristan, the publicist and all the respectables who have been worth to us the relation of your trip to Spain. You really owe a reward to those people. Your best friends could never have done for you, by their praises or their attachment, what your enemies have done in forcing you to talk about yourself. Grandison, the hero of the most perfect of romances, does not come to your foot. When one follows you to the home of that Cla-vico, that M. Whall's, to the ambassador's, to the King's presence, the heart palpitates and one trembles and grows indignant with your indignation. What magic brush is yours, Monsieur! What energy of soul and of expression, what quickness of esprit! What impossible blending of heat and prudence, of courage and of sensibility, of genius and of grace!

"When I saw you at Madame de Sainte-Jean's you seemed to me as amiable as the handsome man that you are, but these qualities are not what make a man attractive to an old woman such as I. I saw too that you had gifts and talents, that you were a man of honor and agreeable in every way, but I would never have dreamed, Monsieur, that you were also a true father of your family, and the sublime author of your four memoirs. Receive my thanks for the enthusiasm into which your writings have thrown me and the assurances of the veritable esteem with which I have the honor to be, Monsieur, etc.

"Guichard de Meinières. This 18th of February, 1774."

A second letter from the same pen, speaks in even stronger terms.

"Whatever the result of your quarrel with so many adversaries, I congratulate you, Monsieur, to have had it. Since the result of your writings is to prove that you are the most honest man in the world, in turning the pages of your life no one has been able to prove that you have ever done a dishonorable deed, and assuredly you have made yourself known as the most eloquent man, in every species of eloquence which our century has produced. Your prayer to the Supreme Being is a chef-d'oeuvre, the ingenious and astonishing blending of which produces the greatest effect. I admit with Madame Goëzman that you are a little ***malm*** and following her example, I pardon you, because your malice is so delicious. I hope, Monsieur, that you have not a sufficiently bad opinion of me to pity me for having read eight hundred pages when you have written them. I begin by devouring them, and then return on my steps. I pause, now at a passage worthy of Demosthenes, now at one superior to Cicero, and lastly a thousand quite as amusing as Moliere; I am so afraid of finishing and having nothing more to read afterwards, that I recommence each paragraph so as to give you time to produce your fifth memoir, where without doubt we shall find your confrontation with M. Goëzman; I beg you simply to be so good as to notify me by *la* petite *poste* the day before, that the publisher may send copies to the widow Lamarche; it is she who furnishes them to me. I always take a number at a time for us and for our friends, and I am furious always, when, not knowing in time of their publication, I send too late, and word is brought me that I must wait until the next day."

CHAPTER XI

"Après *le* bonheur *de* commander *aux* hommes, *le* plus grand *honneur,* Monsieur, *n'*est-il *pas* de *les* jtiger?"

Preface du *Barbier* de *Seville.*

The Preparation of the Memoirs—Aid Rendered by Family and Friends—The Judgment—Beaumarchais Blâmé Enters the Secret Service of the King—Gudin Relates the Circumstances of the Meeting between the Civilly De-graded Man and Her Who Became His Third Wife—The Père Caron's Third Marriage.

BUT while public opinion was expressing itself so loudly in his favor, the situation of Beaumarchais was in reality cruel in the extreme.

The breaking up of his household had necessitated the separation of the members of his family. His father went to board with an old friend, while Julie retired temporarily to a convent. The two sisters whose acquaintance we made while Beaumarchais was in Madrid, had returned to France, the elder a widow with two children. All of these were dependent upon the generosity of the brother and uncle. Madame de Miron, the youngest sister, had died during the same year, so that it was at the home of the next to the oldest member of the family, Madame Lépine, that the family reunions were held.

M. de Loméiie has drawn an admirable picture of these gatherings, where eager and devoted friends met to discuss, suggest, and criticise with Beaumarchais the composition of his memoirs.

He says: "His coadjutors are his relatives and nearest friends. First of all it is the elder Caron, who with his sev-enty-five years of experience, gives his advice about the memoirs of his son. It is Julie, whose literary aptitudes we are already acquainted with. It is M. de Miron, the brother-in-law of Beaumarchais, **homme** d'*esprit*, of whom we have spoken elsewhere, who furnishes notes for the satirical parts; it is Gudin, who very strong in ancient history, aids in composing several erudite portions and whose heavy and pale prose grows supple and takes color under the pen of his friend. It is a young and very distinguished lawyer named Falconnet who superintends the drawing up by the author of parts where it is as a question of law. It is at last a medical doctor from the Provence, named Gardanne, who especially directs the dissection of the Provençaux his compatriots, Marin and Bertrand."

This is the little phalanx that Madame Goëzman, in her memoirs, calls a "clique infame," and which the ***grand*** Ber-*trand* less ferocious and more reasonable names simply, *la* bande *joyeuse.*

They were in fact very joyful, all those ***spirituels*** bourgeois, grouped around Beaumarchais, combating with him a crowd of enemies, and not without running personal risk, because Julie notably was formally denounced by Goëzman. There was a printed petition of this judge directed especially against her, although it had no consequences. All of them, however, underwent interrogations, confrontations, and verifications, but they came out none the worse for it and their gaiety supported the courage and the ardor of the man to whom they were devoted heart and soul. Beaumarchais, forced to live *en* camp *volant* at the mercy of the sheriffs, of the Comte de la Blacfae and the persecutions of the judge Goëzman, was always on the wing but he came to the home of Madame Lépine near the Palais de Justice to prepare with his friends his means of defense and attack. It is in this house that the elements of each memoir were discussed. All the first draughts were written by the hand of Beaumarchais, all the brilliant portions are rewritten by him three or four times. Like all who wish to write well, he corrects and rewrites many times, he cuts out, amends, concentrates and purifies. If at times he allows himself to be too easily satisfied, he has friends prompt to censure him who do not spare him.

M. de Miron especially criticises in detail and with persistent candor. "Beaumarchais profited from all these aids, so that if his memoirs against Goëzman do not present from the nature of the subject all the interest of the '***Barbier* de *Seville*** or the '***Mariage de* Figaro**,' they are none the less, so far as style is concerned, the most remarkable of all his works, the one where the good qualities of the author are the least mixed with faults. They contain portions of a really finished perfection."

Monsieur de Loménie assures us further, that a certain passage, which is cited at times as being one of the most graceful of the memoirs, is due largely to Julie. He quotes at length the rough draughts of the passage in question as it appeared in its different stages, at first rather dry as written by Beaumarchais, then colored and animated by the brush of Julie, finally very skillfully retouched by her brother. It is where the *plaideur* replies to the attack of Madame Goëzman upon the ancestry and profession of his father. The printed text is as follows:

"You begin your chef-d'oeuvre by reproaching me with the condition of my ancestors; alas madame, it is too true that the last of all united to several branches of industry a considerable celebrity in the art of watchmaking. Forced to pass condemnation on that article I admit with sorrow that nothing can wash from me the just reproach which you make me of being the son of my father.... But I pause, because I feel him behind me, who, watching while I write, laughs while he embraces me. Oh you, who reproach me with my father, you have no idea of his generous heart. In truth, watchmaking aside, there is no one for whom I would exchange him; but I know too well the value of time which he taught me to measure to waste it by similar trifling."

Supported as Beaumarchais was by the constant affection of those nearest to him the loss of his fortune and the dissolution of his household were the least of the calamities weighing upon him. He had known, as we have seen, how to gain the support of the nation at large, but he remained still completely at the mercy of the parliament which he had so hopelessly offended in daring to open up before the whole world those proceedings which it was never intended should be exposed to the light of day. It was of this period that La Harpe says, "Afterwards prosperity came of itself, it was during the combat and the oppression that his glory was gained."

The unique character of this contest as well as its sublimity lies in this, that it is not simply a personal matter in which he was engaged. The blows he dealt so deftly had behind them the force of a nation eager to avenge itself, a nation whose favorite weapon was ridicule. Never was that weapon wielded by "a hand more intrepid and light. It seemed to amuse him to lead before the public so many personages like animals for combat." "Simpletons," says La Harpe, "are by no means rare and they bore us; to put them before us in a way to make us laugh so heartily and so long, to make them amusing to the point of finding pleasure in their stupidity, is surely no common talent, it is that of good satire and good comedy."

This was the talent of Beaumarchais. The public laughed, it is true, but the simpletons thus led forward did not laugh, nor did the chancellor Maupeou. They were waiting, rage in their hearts, for the day of vengeance which was not far off.

Begun in August, 1773, the suit had gone on until February of the following year. "The day of judgment," says Lomenie, "arrived on the 26th of February, 1774, in the midst of universal interest.

" 'We are expecting to-morrow,' wrote Madame du Def-fand to Horace Walpole, a great event, the judgment of Beaumarchais... M. de Monaco has invited him for the evening to read us a comedy *de* sa façon, **which has for the title** le ***Barbier*** de ***Seville***.... The public is crazy over the author who is being judged while I write. It is supposed that the judgment will be rigorous and it may happen that instead of supping with us he will be condemned to banishment or to the pillory; this is what I will tell you to-morrow.'

"Such is the *dose* of interest which Madame du Dcffand takes in people. What a pity for her if the accused had been condemned to the pillory. She would have lost the reading of the *Barbier*. She lost it anyway. For twelve hours the deliberation of the judges prolonged itself. Beaumarchais addressed to the prince of Monaco the following note which belongs with the letter of Madame du Deffand.

" 'Beaumarchais, infinitely sensible of the honor which the Prince of Monaco wishes to do him, replies from the Palace where he has been nailed since six o'clock this morning, where he has been interrogated at the bar of justice, and where he waits the sentence which is very long in coming; but, in whatever way things turn, Beaumarchais who is surrounded by his family at this moment cannot flatter himself to escape them until he has received either their congratulations or their condolence. He begs therefore that the Prince of Monaco will be so good as to reserve him his kindness for another day. He has the honor of assuring him of his very respectful gratitude.

" 'This Saturday, February 26th, 1774.' "

"The evening before the judgment," says Gudin, "he arranged his private affairs, passed the night at work, and went to the gate of the palace before it was day, saw the judges pass before him and submitted to his last interroga-tion. When it was finished and it only remained to the judges to decide, Beaumarchais returned to the home of his sister who-lived near the Palais de Justice. Fatigued from so much labor and very certain that there was nothing left for him to do in that critical time, he went to bed and slept as profoundly as though no one in the universe were occupied with the thought of him. I arrived and found him sunk in a sleep such as only comes to a pure, strong soul, and a truly superior mind, because at such a moment it would have been considered pardonable in anyone to have felt the anguish of anxiety. He slept while his judges watched, tormented by the furies. Divided among themselves, they deliberated in tumult, spoke in rage, wishing to punish the author of the memoirs but foreseeing the clamor of the public ready to disavow them. At last after almost fifteen hours of contradictory opinions and violent debates, they abandoned reciprocally their victims.

"The lady of the fifteen louis was blâmée ***and Beaumarchais was condemned also to*** blâme which seemed a contradiction. The magistrate, husband of the woman, was put out of court which was equivalent to blame for a magistrate, who thus remained incapable, of filling any function of the magistracy.

"I was by his side with all the family when a friend came running, terrified to tell him this absurd judgment. He did not utter an angry word or make a gesture of indignation. Master of all his movements as of his mind, he said, 'Let us see what there yet remains to be done.'"

Loménie says: "The penalty of blâme was an ignominious one which rendered the condemned incapable of occupying any public office, and he was supposed to receive the sentence on his knees before the court, while the president pronounced the words, 'The court blames thee and declares thee infamous.'"

Gudin says, "This sentence had been so badly received by the multitude assembled at the doors of the chamber, the judges had been so hissed on breaking up the audience, although many of them took themselves out of the way by passing through the long corridors unknown to the public, which are called les ***detours*** du ***palais***, they saw so many marks of discontentment that they were not tempted to execute to the letter the sentence which attracted to them only the ***blame*** universel."

Before speaking of the veritable triumph which the public accorded to Beaumarchais in return for this cruel sentence, let us finish with the parliament Maupeou.

"It was not destined," says Loméoie, "long to survive this act of anger and vengeance. In striking with civil death a man whom public opinion carried in triumph, it had struck its own death-blow. The opposition which had slept, now roused, let itself loose upon the parliament with redoubled fury. Pamphlets in prose and verse took on a new virility, the end of the reign assured its fall, and one of the first acts of the new king, Louis XVI was to establish the old parliament." Louis XV died in May, 1774, the old parliament was re-established in August of the same year.

"There were not lacking those," says Bonnefon, "who called the destruction of the parliament Maupeou, the Saint-Bartholomew of the ministers."

The Spanish ambassador, quick at repartee, added, "that in any case it was not the massacre of the Innocents."

But to return to Beaumarchais. "All the gentlemen at court," says Gudin, "all the most distinguished persons of Paris, inscribed themselves at his door. No one spoke of anything but of him."

"It was at the very moment," says Beaumarchais, "when they declared that I was no longer anything, that everyone seemed the most eager to count me for something. Everywhere I was welcomed, sought after; offers of every nature were showered upon me." The Prince of Conti was the first to set the example.

"We are of a sufficiently illustrious house," he said, "to show the nation what is her duty toward one who has de-served so well of his country." He left his name the same day at the door of the man whom the parliament had at-tempted to degrade, inviting him to a princely festival the next day where some forty or more of the greatest personages of the realm were present. The Duke of Chartres showed a like attention. It was in the midst of all these ovations that M. de Sartine wrote to him:

" 'I counsel you not to show yourself any more publicly. What has happened is irritating to many people. It is not enough to be blamed, one must be modest as well. If an order came from the king I should be obliged to execute it in spite of myself. Above everything do not write anything, because the king wishes that you publish nothing more upon this affair.'"

Gudin says: "Determined as was Beaumarchais to break this iniquitous sentence, he was yet conscious that the royal power was a rock against which prudence might well fear to throw herself. He therefore took the wise policy of submitting to the weakness of the king, to obey him and to keep silent."

"Wishing, however, to show to the world," says Lintilhac, "that his silence was not cowardice, he withdrew from France and retired into an obscure place in Flanders."

"It could not be expected," says Bonnefon, "that Beaumarchais would rest tranquilly under the blow of a condemnation which struck him with civil death and ruined his career." His first thought was to appeal for a second judgment. But he feared lest the parliament might confirm the sentence by a second act and foreseeing that it was already doomed, his great desire was to secure from the king a reprieve, which would allow him the right of appeal, no matter how long the period of time elapsed since the decree was issued.

Several days after the judgment he wrote to his friend La Borde, banker at court and particular friend of Louis XV.

"They have at last rendered it; this abominable sentence, chef-d'oeuvre of hatred and iniquity. Behold me cut off from society and dishonored in the midst of my career. I know, my friend, that the pains of opinion should trouble only those who merit them; I know that iniquitous judges have all power against the person of an innocent man and nothing against his reputation. All France has inscribed itself at my door since Saturday! The thing which has most pierced my heart on this sinister occasion is the unhappy impression which has been given the king concerning me. It has beep said to him that I was pretending to a seditious celebrity; but no one has told him that I only have defended myself, that I never ceased to make my judges feel the consequences which might result from this ridiculous suit.

"You know my friend that I always have led a quiet life, and that I should never have written upon public matters if a host of powerful enemies had not united to ruin me. Ought I to have allowed myself to be crushed without attempting self-justification? If I have done it with too much vivacity is that a reason for dishonoring me and my family, and cutting off from society an honest subject whose talents might perhaps have been employed usefully for the service of the king and the state? I have courage to support a misfortune which I have not merited, but my father with his seventy-five years of honor and Work upon his head and who is dying of sorrow, my sisters who are women and weak, their condition is what kills me, and renders me inconsolable. Receive, my generous friend, the sincere expression of the ardent gratitude with which I am, etc.

"Beaumarchais."

A second letter to La Borde, written from his retreat in Flanders, shows that the much desired reprieve had been granted him. He wrote, "The sweetest thing in the world to my heart, my dear La Borde, is the generosity of your sin-cere friendship. Everyone tells me that I have a reprieve; you add to this the news that it is the king's free will that I obtain it. May God hear your prayers, my generous friend!"

To be sure the king had granted the reprieve but he set a price upon this favor. "Judging from the very dexterity which Beaumarchais had displayed in the Goëzman affair," says Loménie, "Louis XV felt that he had need of such skill and promised letters of relief to put him in a position to recover his civil estate, if he should fulfill with zeal and success a difficult mission to which the king attached a great importance. So it was that the vanquisher of the Parliament Maupeou presently went to London in the capacity of secret agent of the king."

But before entering into a consideration of this new phase of adventure, let us ask the faithful historian, Gudin, to relate to us a charming incident which came at the moment of the triumph of Beaumarchais, to add sweetness to its brilliancy. Gudin wrote:

"The celebrity of Beaumarchais attracted to him the attention of a woman endowed with wit and beauty, a tender heart and a firmness of character capable of supporting him in the cruel combats that were destined to come to him. She did not know him at all, but her soul, touched by reading his memoirs, by the fame of his courage, called to that of this celebrated man. She burned with a desire to see him. I was with him when, under the frivolous pretext of busying herself with music, she sent a man of her acquaintance, and of that of Beaumarchais, to beg him to lend her his harp for a short time. Such a demand under such circumstances disclosed her intentions. Beaumarchais comprehended, he replied, 'I lend nothing, but if the lady wishes to come with you I will hear her play and she may hear me.' She came, I was witness to their first interview.

"I already have said that it was difficult to see Beaumarchais without loving him. What an impression must he have produced when he was covered with the applause of the whole of Paris; when he was regarded as the defender of an oppressed liberty, the avenger of the public. It was still more difficult to resist the charm attached to the looks, the voice, the bearing, the discourse of Mademoiselle de Willermawlaz. The attraction of the first moment was augmented from hour to hour, by the variety of their agreeable accomplishments and the host of excellent qualities which each discovered in ,the other as their intimacy increased. Their hearts were united from that moment by a bond which no circumstance could break and which love, esteem, time, and the law rendered indissoluble."

Of the charming woman here described who subsequently became the third wife of Beaumarchais we shall have occasion to speak later. For the present, his situation was such that marriage was out of the question, their union was not solemnized until later. Their one and only daughter, Eugenie, was born in 1777. She was the darling of her father, the source of his deepest happiness and the cause of his crudest suffering. It was for her that we shall find him, old and broken in health, setting himself with almost juvenile vigor, at the time of his return from exile after the Reign of Terror, to gather together the shattered remains of his fortune.

At the moment of his triumph in 1774, flattered, praised, and loved as we have seen him, this condition was offset not only by the judgment of parliament which ruined his career, but by a domestic trouble which was at that moment preparing for him.

His father's health had been so shattered by the terrible strain through which he had been obliged to pass by the succession of calamities which had befallen his son that in the end the vigor of his mind became impaired.

It was thus that shortly before his death in 1775, at seventy-seven years of age, without the knowledge of his son, he united himself in marriage with the woman who had been provided for him, as caretaker. M. de Lom6nie says of this individual, "She was a cunning old maid, who made him marry her in the hope of being ransomed by Beaumarchais.

"Profiting by the weakness of the old man, she had had assigned to her in their contract of marriage, the dowry and the part of a child. However, the elder Caron left no fortune. The portion which he had received from his second wife had gone towards partly covering the advances made to him by his son who in addition gave him a lifetime pension. A written settlement guaranteed Beaumarchais; but the third wife of the elder Caron, speculating upon the celebrity of the son and his repugnance to a suit of such a nature at the very moment when he had scarcely recovered himself from the suit Goézman, threatened to attack the settlement and to make a noise.

"For the first time in his life," continues Loménie, "Beaumarchais capitulated before an adversary and disembar-rassed himself by means of 6,000 francs of the person in question, a person, by the way, very subtle, very daring, and *assez* spirituelle, to judge from her letters.

"Upon the package of documents relating to this affair I find written in the hand of Beaumarchais these words: *'Infamie* de *la vewve* de *mon* père pardonnée (Infamy of the widow of my father, pardoned). It is to the influence of this rusée cammère that we must attribute the only moment of misunderstanding between the father and the son during an intimate correspondence which embraced the last fifteen years of the life of the former; and it must be added that the misunderstanding lasted but a moment, because the letter of the father on his death-bed which has already been cited proves that harmony had been completely re-established between them at the time of the death of the elder Caron towards the end of August, 1775."

CHAPTER XII

"*ll n'y* a *pas* de *conte* absurd *qw'on* ne *fosse* adopter aux *oisifs d'une* grande *vide*, on *s'y* prenant *bien.*"

Le *Barbier* de *Seville,* Act II, Scene VIII

Beaumarchais Goes to London in Quality of Secret Agent of Louis XV—Theveneau de Morande and His Gazetier Cuirasse—The King Dies—Beaumarchais's Second Mission Under Louis XVI—Playing Figaro upon the Stage of Life—Visits the Empress of Austria—Is Imprisoned at Vienna—Addresses Memoir to the King—Confers with the Ministers upon the Recall of the Parliaments.

I

F at the end of a cultivated education and a laborious youth, my parents could have left me an entire liberty as to the choice of a vocation, my invincible curiosity, my dominant taste for the study of mankind and its great interests, my insatiable desire to learn new things, and to form new combinations, would have led me to throw myself into politics." So Beaumarchais had written in 1764, at a time when his intimacy with the diplomatic circle of the court of Madrid had opened up a vista of possible future usefulness in the world of politics and of vast business enterprises, connected with matters of national importance. When his hopes in both these directions had been blighted, we have seen him returning home, bent only upon giving up his appointments at court and retiring with Pauline to the West Indies, there to lead the life of a planter. This dream having likewise dissolved, his next thought was to find consolation in literature. Happy at last in his second marriage, prosperous and rich, his ambition limited itself for a time to the following of a literary career. Suddenly robbed of all these blessings by the untimely death of his wife and infant son, attacked by powerful enemies, forced to defend his honor and his life, we have followed him to where he now stands, a civilly degraded man, powerless in the grasp of overwhelmingly adverse circumstances.

As we already have seen in this narrative, Beaumarchais was no stranger to adversity, whose only effect upon his character seems to have been to rouse him to ever greater and greater efforts to overcome the obstacles that would have seemed to another insurmountable. So in this case we find him turning at once the whole force of his being to outside conditions in order to discover what still remains to be done.

The path which opened before him was one that could have presented itself only under such conditions of abuse of authority and of misrule as characterized the declining years of Louis XV, a condition which allowed justice to be given over into the hands of the infamous parliament of which it has just been question, and which tolerated by the side of the King of France a woman, Madame du Barry, who had begun her career as a girl of the streets.

In the occult diplomacy of the court of Louis XV there was need enough for secret agents, and it was in this ca-pacity that we find our civilly degraded man entering upon that new phase of his career which was so soon to place him where he could take a hand in directing the destinies of nations.

In speaking of this, M. de Loménie has said, "The history of the secret missions of Beaumarchais is instructive if we would attempt to understand absolute governments. The weak side of liberal governments, and the consequences of the abuse sometimes made of liberty, have of late years been sufficiently exposed for it to be interesting to see what went on behind the scenes of absolute power. . . . and to note by what complicated ways an unjustly condemned man was obliged to pass to obtain his rehabilitation, and how in revenge, this same man, stricken with civil death by a tribunal, was able to become the confidential agent of two kings and their ministers, and little by little make himself so useful that he reconquered his civil state and obtained control of a great transaction, one worthy of himself and of his intelligence." This transaction was of course no other than his intervention in the cause of American Independence.

But now in regard to his secret mission, it will be remembered that after the parliament had pronounced its crushing sentence, silence had been imposed upon him by the authority of the King. Strange as it may seem, Louis XV was not unfriendly to the petulant man who had so warmly defended himself. He had followed the suit with interest, had read the memoirs, and even amused himself at the expense of the magistracy, which he had himself established in defiance of the whole nation. The indolence and levity of the King's character showed themselves clearly in this attitude. So long as things lasted *tant* que *lui* he was satisfied to amuse himself in any way that offered, regardless of the future. One day he said to La Borde (first *valet* de *charnbre* of the King and friend of Beaumarchais),,"They say that your friend has a superior talent for negotiation; if he could be successfully and secretly employed in an affair which interests me, his own affairs would be the better for it." The matter which weighed upon the old king, the settlement of which was to be the price of the rehabilitation of Beaumarchais, was one that had been troubling him for more than a year.

There was at this time, established in London, a certain French adventurer, Theveneau de Morande, who, says Lo-menie, "had taken refuge in England, where, speculating upon scandal, he composed coarse libels which he clandestinely introduced into France, and in which he defamed, outraged and calumniated without distinction, every name, more or less known, which presented itself under his pen. He had published amongst other works, under the impudent title of *le* Gazetier cm-rassé, a collection of atrocities, perfectly in accord with the impudence of the title. Profiting from the terror he inspired, he sent from time to time across the Channel, demands for money, from those who feared his attacks. . . . For a manufacturer of this kind, Madame du Barry was a mine of gold; so he wrote to that lady announcing the near publication (except in case of a handsome ransom) of an interesting work of which her life was the subject, under the alluring title of Mémoires ***secrets*** d'une ***femme*** publique. Anyone else but Madame du Barry might have disdained the insults of the pamphleteer, or have brought him to justice before the English tribunals; it can easily be understood that Madame du Barry could take neither of these alternatives. Alarmed and furious, she communicated her anger and her fears to Louis XV."

The King began by demanding George III to give up the adventurer. The English Government had no desire to harbor such a character and replied that if the French King did not wish to pursue legally the pamphleteer, he might arrest him, but only on condition that it was done with absolute secrecy and without arousing the susceptibilities of the English populace. Louis XV then set about preparing for his capture.

Theveneau de Morande was on the alert, and having been warned, he forestalled the King by posing publicly as a persecuted political refugee, placing himself under the protection of the London public. He had not misjudged the temper of the people amongst whom he had sought refuge. Furious at the thought of such a desecration of English law, a band of supporters of Morande lay in wait, so that the secret agents on arriving in London were known and followed. They were on the point of being seized and thrown into the Thames when they learned of their betrayal, and so were obliged to hurry with all possible speed back to France, with their object unaccomplished.

Gloating over his triumph, the unprincipled adventurer hastened on his publication, becoming daily more insolent in his demands. Louis XV sent numerous agents across the channel to attempt to treat with him, but all to no purpose, for the wily Morande, posing now before the public as a defender of public morality, retained the protection of the people and thus.escaped the agents in question. Things were at this pass when the thought occurred to the King of employing the talents of Beaumarchais in terminating this difficult negotiation.

The sentence of the Parliament Maupeou, it will be remembered, had been rendered the 26th of February, 1774; early in March the civilly degraded man started for London, and as his own name was too widely known through his memoirs to admit of secrecy, he assumed that of Ronac, anagram of Caron. The firmness, tact, and above all the persuasiveness of his character, enabled him in a few days completely to gain the confidence of Morande, so that he reappeared almost immediately at Versailles to the unbounded astonishment of the King, bringing a specimen of the libel, and prepared to receive final orders for the termination of the affair. The King sent him back to London in quality of his confidential agent to see that the entire scandalous publication was destroyed by fire, and the future silence of Morande secured. Both objects were speedily accomplished.

Immediately following the destruction of the Memoirs of Mme. du Barry, Beaumarchais wrote to Morande, "You have done your best, Monsieur, to prove to me that you return in good faith to the sentiments and the conduct of an honest Frenchman, from which your heart reproached you long before I did, of having deviated; it is in persuading myself that you have the design of persisting in these praiseworthy resolutions, that I take pleasure in corresponding with you. What difference in our two destinies! It happened to fall into my way to arrest the publication of a scandalous libel; I work night and day for six weeks; I travel nearly two thousand miles. I spend 500 louis to prevent innumerable evils. You gain at this work, 100,000 francs and your tranquillity, while as for me, I do not even know that my traveling expenses will be repaid."

When Beaumarchais arrived in Paris he hastened to Versailles to receive the reward of his activity. He found the old King attacked by a fatal disease, and in a few days he was no more. "I admire," he wrote the same day, "the strangeness of the fate which follows me. If the King had lived in health eight days longer, I would have been rein-stated in the rights which iniquity has taken from me, I had his royal word."

A few days later he wrote to Morande, "Restored to my family and friends, my affairs are quite as little advanced as before my voyage to England, through the unexpected death of the King. I seize the first instant of repose, to write to you and to compliment you, Monsieqr, very sincerely upon your actual condition. Each one of us has done his best; I to tear you from the certain misfortune which menaced you and your friends, and you to prove a return with good faith to the sentiments and conduct of a true Frenchman. . . . There only remains to me for total recompense the satisfaction of having fulfilled my duty as an honest man and a good citizen. . . . What consoles me is that the time of intrigue and cabal is over. Restored to my legal defense the new King will not impose silence on my legitimate reclamations; I shall obtain, by *force* of *right*, and)*by* title *of* justice that which the late King was only willing to accord me as a favor." (Quoted from Lintilhac, **Beaumarchais** et **ses** acuvres, p. 62.)

Here as elsewhere, true to the instincts of his nature, he accepted the inevitable, while looking about him to see what remained to be done. Realizing that the service accomplished for Louis XV could have small interest for the virtuous young monarch just ascending the throne, he had no thought for the moment of pressing for his rehabilitation, but preferred to wait until some opportunity offered for making himself useful, and if possible necessary, to the young King.

In November of the same year, he had the satisfaction of seeing the parliament abolished which had degraded him. More than this, his opinion was sought as to the best means to be employed in the re-establishment of the ancient magistracy. Gudin, in his life of Beaumarchais says, "The ministers were divided in opinion as to the best means to employ in recalling the parliaments; they consulted Beaumarchais, and demanded of him a short, elementary memoir, where his principles should be exposed in a way proper to instruct every clear mind. . . . He obeyed and gave them under the title of—*Idees* élementaires *sur* le *rappel* du *parlement*— a memoir, which contains the most just ideas, the purest principles upon the establishment of that body, and the limitations of its powers. . . ." The Ministers, however, did not dare to follow the simplicity of the principles he laid down. After much discussion the parliaments were recalled, and though the liberties of the people received but slight attention, "Everyone was too flattered by the return of the ancient magistracy, to think of the future."

In the midst of his correspondence with the ministers over this matter of public import, Beaumarchais did not forget his own private interests. He wrote to M. de Sartine, "I have cut out the fangs of three monsters in destroying two libels, and stopping the impression of a third, and in return I have been deceived, robbed, imprisoned, my health is destroyed; but what is that if the King is satisfied? Let him say 'I am content,' and I shall be completely so, other recompense I do not wish. The King is already too much surrounded by greedy askers. Let him know that in a corner of Paris he has one disinterested servitor—that is all I ask.

"I hope that you do not wish me to remain blame by that vile Parliament which you have just buried under the debris of its dishonor. All Europe has avenged me of its odious and absurd judgment, but that is not enough. There must be a decree to destroy the one pronounced by it. I shall not cease to work for this end, but with the moderation of a man who fears neither intrigue nor injustice. I expect your good offices for this important object.

"Your devoted

"Beaumarchais."

Gudin, after quoting this letter, adds "According to the immemorial custom of all courts, they were much more eager to make use of the zeal of a servitor than to render him justice. Nevertheless they repealed the prohibition to play his **Barbier** de **Seville**."

This was near the end of 1774. Already Beaumarchais again had been appealed to, to suppress another scandalous publication, the appearance of which was announced immediately after the accession of Louis XVI to the throne of France. It had for title, *Avis* a *la branche* espagnole *sur* ses *droits* a *la* couronne *de* France, *a* défawt *d'heritiers* (Advice to the Spanish branch, upon its claims to the crown of France in default of heirs.) Although in appearance political, it was in reality a libel directed against the young queen Marie Antoinette. In a memoir addressed to the King after the suppression of the publication, Beaumarchais accounts for its appearance in the following manner, he says, "As soon as your Majesty had mounted the throne, several changes made, several courtiers disgraced, having caused strong resentments to germinate, suddenly there appeared in England and Holland a new libel against you, Sire, and against the Queen. I went with all haste, and an express order of your Majesty augmenting my courage, I followed up the book and the editor to the point of extinction."

"All that was known of this pamphlet," says Loménie, "was that its publication was confided to an Italian named Guillaume Angelucci, who in England went under the name of William Atkinson, and who used a host of precautions to insure his incognito. He had at his disposition enough money to enable him to produce two editions at the same time, one in England and the other in Holland. In order to ensure success to his enterprise and still more no doubt, to heighten the importance of the role he was about to play, Beaumarchais in accepting this second undesirable mission had demanded a written order from the King, bearing the royal signature. This had been refused. Beaumarchais started for London without delay, but had by no means given up the idea of obtaining the written order which seemed to him so important."

"I have seen the Lord Rochford," he wrote to M. de Sartine, "and found him as affectionate as usual, but when I explained to him this affair, he remained cold as ice. I turned and returned it in every way, I invoked our friendship, reclaimed his confidence, warmed his *amour*-propre **by the hope of being agreeable to our King, but I could judge from the nature of his replies that he regarded my commission as an affair of police, of espionage, in a word of** sous-*ordre*.

"You should do the impossible to bring the King to send me an order or mission signed by him, in about the terms which I have indicated at the end of this letter. This need is as delicate, as it is essential for you to-day. So many agents have been sent to London in relation to the last libel, they were often of so questionable a character, that anyone who seems to belong to the same order, cannot expect to be looked upon except with contempt. This is the basis of your argument with the King. Tell him of my visit to the Lord. It is certain that one cannot decently expect that minister, however friendly he may be, to lend himself to the service of my master, if that master puts no difference between the delicate and secret mission with which he honors an honest man, and an order with which a police officer is charged.,,

M. de Sartine seemed to have been convinced, at all events he succeeded in inducing the young king to copy with docility the model which Beaumarchais had drawn up, and which ran as follows:

"The sieur de Beaumarchais, charged by my secret orders, will start for his destination as soon as possible; the discretion and vivacity which he will put into their execution will be the most agreeable proofs which he can giveme of his zeal for my service.

"Marly, July 10, 1774."

Beaumarchais, exultant, wrote at once to the minister, "The order of my master is still virgin, that is to say, it has been seen by no one; but if it has not yet served me in relation to others, it has none the less been of a marvelous help to myself, in multiplying my powers and redoubling my courage."

He even went so far as to address the King personally. He wrote, "A lover wears about his neck the portrait of his mistress; a miser, his keys; a devotee, his reliquary— while as for me, I have had made a flat oval case of gold, in which I have enclosed the order of your Majesty, and which I have suspended about my neck with a chain of gold, as the thing the most necessary for my work, and the most precious for myself."

Satisfied at last in his ambition to have in his possession a written order from the King, Beaumarchais set about arranging with redoubled zeal for the suppression of the publication mentioned before. "He succeeded," says Lo-ménie, "through great supply of eloquence, but also through great supply of money. For 1,400 pounds sterling, the Jew renounced the speculation. The manuscript and four thousand copies were burned in London. The two contractors then betook themselves to Amsterdam for the purpose of destroying the Holland edition. Beaumarchais secured the written engagement of Angelucci, and then free from care, he gave himself up to the pleasure of visiting Amsterdam *en* tourist." . Up to this point the authority of M. de Loménie seems to hold good upon this mission of Beaumarchais, which of late years has given rise to much bitter controversy. "This ob-scure affair Angelucci—Atkinson," says Lintilhac, "has caused as much ink to flow in the last twenty years, as the chefs-d'oeuvre of our author."

We shall not attempt here to enter into the intricacies of this case, and shall scarcely blame our hero, even supposing we should find him playing a bit of comedy, very much a la Figaro, upon the stage of real life; for it is necessary to recall the fact that under the cloak of philosophic acceptance of his fate, Beaumarchais was all the while, at heart, a desperate man. The death of the old King at the moment when he had every reason to expect a speedy restitution to his rights as citizen, had been a cruel blow which left him in a state of inward desperation. When we consider the intense mental excitement in which he had been living from the day of his frightful adventure with the due de Chaulnes, his imprisonment, the loss of his property, the dissolution of his family, the execration of his enemies, the adulation of a nation; when we consider all this and the events immediately following, our wonder is, not that Beaumarchais lost for a time his sense of proportion and the true relation of things, but rather that he had not been a thousand times over, crushed and broken by the overwhelming combination of circumstances against which he had struggled.

There is no doubt that now, at the moment of the termination of his mission, his one idea was to exaggerate to the utmost the apparent value of what he had accomplished, so that it would seem worth the price which he desired for it, in the eyes of the young master whom he served. It was no favor that he wanted; he desired nothing but to be allowed to work, but his rehabilitation he must have at whatever cost. He knew only too well that to the young King it was, after all, a matter of supreme indifference whether or not he, Beaumarchais, regained his civil rights. The affair of the libel even, had scarcely penetrated his consciousness;

that was a matter for the ministers to attend to. Beaumarchais felt, therefore, that something must be done to force himself upon the attention of the royal pair,' both so young and so unconscious, not to say heedless, of the duties of their station; the young Queen thinking of nothing but the amusement of the hour, the King asking only to be relieved from the responsibilities of state and of individual action. How was Beaumarchais then to arouse in them sufficient interest to cause them to give a moment's attention to his wrongs? The spirit of adventure which always animated him, his taste for intrigue, his talent of mis en scene, all combined to aid him in what he undertook. He decided before he returned to France, to present himself therefore before the Empress of Austria, sure that by his talents, his address, and show of fervent zeal in the interest of his Queen, he would win the tender heart of that tenderest of mothers. To give a show of reason to his appearance before the Empress, and to enhance the interest he might arouse, he imagined a wild and romantic story, the heroic part of which he was himself to have acted. On his way down the Danube, he wrote a detailed account of this supposed happening, sending several copies to friends—among others to Gudin, who were asked to inform his extended circle of acquaintances, of this rare new adventure which had befallen him. It may be stated briefly as follows: After having destroyed the libel in London and Amsterdam, and relieved from all further responsibility, he supposed himself suddenly to have discovered that the wily Angelucci had retained a copy of the libel, and that he had gone on to Nuremberg with the intention of there issuing another publication. Furious at this breach of faith, Beaumarchais hurriedly followed after, stopping neither night nor day. He overtook Angelucci in the forest of Neustadt, not far from Nuremberg. The rattling of the chaise attracted the attention of the Jew, who, turning round, recognized his pursuer, and being on horseback, dashed into the forest, hoping thereby to make good his escape. Beaumarchais, however, springing from the chaise, followed after on foot. The density of the forest enabled him to overtake Angelucci, whom he dragged from his horse. In the depths of his traveling sack, the infamous libel was discovered. Then he let Angelucci go. As Beaumarchais was returning to the highway, he was fallen upon by two robbers who attacked him savagely and from whom he defended himself with bravery. He was delivered from them by their taking fright at the noise of the postilion, who, uneasy at the long delay, had come to see what had happened to the traveler.

The latter was found, with face and hands badly wounded. He passed the night in Nuremberg, and next morning, without waiting to have his wounds dressed, he hastened on to Vienna.

So much for the romance what follows is authentic history.

In a *proces*-verbal, under date of September 7, 1774, held by the Burgomaster of Nuremberg, under order of Marie Thérèse, Empress of Austria, the bourgeois Conrad Gruber, keeping the inn of the Coq Rouge at Nuremberg, explained how M. de Ronac arrived at his inn, wounded in the face and hands, the evening of August 14th, after a scene in the woods, and he added "that it was remarked that M. de Ronac seemed to be very uneasy, that he had risen very early in the morning, and wandered all over the house, in such a way that from this and his general manner, it appeared that his wits were a little disordered."

As we said, Beaumarchais immediately hastened on to Vienna. Once arrived in the capital, the question was, how to penetrate to the august presence of the Empress. Absolutely without recommendation of any sort, traveling as an inconspicuous M. de Ronac anyone but Beaumarchais would have renounced so wild and impossible a project from the beginning. In a very lengthy memoir addressed to Louis XVI by Beaumarchais after his return to France, the latter gives a minute account of this most singular adventure. The following extracts will enable us to follow him:

"My first care at Vienna was to write a letter to the Empress. The fear that the letter might be seen by other eyes prevented me from explaining the motive of the audience which I solicited. I attempted simply to excite her curiosity. Having no possible access to her, I went to her secretary, M. le baron de Neny, who, on my refusing to tell him what I desired, and judging from my slashed face, took me for a wild adventurer.... He received me as badly as was possible, refused to take charge of my letter, and would have entirely rejected my advances had I not assumed a tone as proud as his own, and assured him that I made him responsible to the Empress for all the evil which his refusal might make to an operation of the greatest importance, if he did not instantly take my letter and give it to the sovereign. More astonished by my tone than he had been by my face, he took my letter unwillingly, and said that for all that, I need not hope that the Empress would see me. 'It is not this, Monsieur, that need disquiet you. If the Empress refuses me an audience, you and I will have done our duty.' ...

"The next day I was conducted to Schoenbrunn, and into the presence of Her Majesty. ... I first presented to the Empress the order of your Majesty, Sire, of which she perfectly recognized the writing. . . . She then permitted me to speak. . . . 'Madame,' I said, 'it is here less a matter of state interest, properly speaking, than the efforts which black intrigues are making in France to destroy the happiness of the King/ Here I recited the details of my negotiation, and the incidents of my voyage to Vienna.

"At every circumstance, the Empress, joining her hands in surprise, repeated, 'But, Monsieur, where have you found so ardent a zeal for the interests of my son-in-law, and above all, of my daughter?

" 'Madame, I was the most unfortunate man of France during the last reign; the queen in that terrible time did not disdain to show an interest in my fate. In serving her today, I am only acquitting an immense debt; the more difficult the enterprise, the more my ardor is inflamed.

" 'But, Monsieur, what necessity had you to change your name ?'

" 'Madame, I am unfortunately too well known in Europe under my own name to permit me to employ it while undertaking so delicate and important a mission as the one in which I am engaged.'

"The Empress seemed to have a great curiosity to read the work whose destruction had caused me so much trouble. The reading immediately followed our explanation. Her Majesty had the goodness to enter with me into the most intimate details of this subject; she had also that of listening a great deal to what I had to say. I remained with her more than three hours and a half, and I implored her not to waste a moment in sending to Nuremberg' and securing the person of Angelucci. . . .

"The Empress had the goodness to thank me for the ardent zeal which I had shown; she begged me to leave the pamphlet with her until the next day. 'Go and repose your- self she said, with infinite grace, 'and see that you are promptly bled. . . .'"

Whatever pleasing effect the ardor and enthusiasm of Beaumarchais may have produced upon Marie Thérese, it was soon dispelled by the Chancellor Kaunitz, to whom she at once showed the libel, and related the adventure as she had heard it from Beaumarchais. Kaunitz not only pronounced the whole story an invention, but at once suspected that Beaumarchais himself was the author of the libel, and that the Jew Angelucci was a fabrication of his own brain. At the Chancellor's instigation, Beaumarchais was at once arrested and kept in custody until the matter could be cleared up. To continue the narrative as given by Beaumarchais in his report to the King:

"I returned to Vienna, my head still hot with the excitement of that conference. I threw upon paper a host of ob-servations which seemed to me very important relative to the subject in question; I addressed them to the Empress. . . . The same day at nine o'clock I saw enter my room, eight grenadiers, bayonets and guns, two officers with naked swords, and a secretary of the regency bringing me word which invited me to allow myself to be arrested, reserving all explanations. 'No resistance,' said the officer to me.

" 'Monsieur,' I replied coldly, 'I sometimes have resisted robbers, but never Empresses.' I was made to put all my papers under seal. I demanded permission to write to the Empress, and was refused. All my effects were taken from me, knives, scissors, even to my buckles, and a numerous guard was left in my room, where it remained ***thirty*-one *days* or *forty*-five *thousand*, six *hundred* and *forty*** minutes; because, while the hours fly so rapidly for happy people that they scarcely note their succession, those who are unfortunate count time by minutes and seconds, and find it flows slowly when each one is noted separately, . . .

"One may judge of my surprise, of my fury! The next day the person who arrested me came to tranquilize me. 'Monsieur,' I replied, 'there is no repose for me until I have written to the Empress. What happened to me is incon-ceivable. Give me paper and pens or prepare to chain me, for here is surely enough to drive one mad.

"At last permission was given me to write; M. de Sartine has all my letters; read them, and the nature of my sorrows will be seen. ... I wrote, I supplicated—no reply. 'If I am a scoundrel, send me back to France, let me there be tried and judged.

"When, on the thirty-first day of my detention, I was set at liberty, they told me that I might return to France or remain in Vienna, as I wished. And if I should die on the way, I would not have remained another quarter of an hour in Vienna. A thousand ducats were presented to me which I firmly refused. 'You have no money, all your belongings are in France.'

" 'I will give my note and borrow what is absolutely necessary for my journey.'

" 'Monsieur, an Empress does not make loans.

" 'And I accept no favors but from my master; he is sufficiently great to recompense me if I have served him well.'

" 'Monsieur, the Empress will think that you are taking a great liberty to refuse her favors.'

" 'Monsieur, the only liberty which cannot be taken from a very respectful but cruelly outraged man is the liberty to refuse favors. For the rest, my master will decide whether I am right or wrong in this conduct, but as to my decision— it remains as I have said.'

"The same evening I left Vienna, and traveling day and night, I arrived the ninth day, hoping at last fpr an ex-planation. All that M. de Sartine has been willing to say to me is: *Que* voudez-*vous*? The Empress took you for an adventurer. , . .

"Sire, be so good as not to disapprove of my refusal to accept the money of the Empress, and permit me to return it to Vienna. I should, however, be willing to accept an honorable word, or her portrait, or any similar token which I could oppose to the reproach which is everywhere made me of having been arrested in Vienna as a suspicious character. ... I await the orders of your Majesty.
"Caron de Beaumarchais."

The money was subsequently returned, and in its place a valuable diamond ring was sent by the Empress. This ring shone on its possessor's finger, from henceforth, on all occasions of ceremony. As for the suspicions of Kaunitz, which have been shared by many, we can do no more than refer the reader to the special literature on this subject. The story of the brigands is unquestionably an invention, as for proofs of forgery, or real guilt of any kind,—after the most exhaustive investigations, none has ever been found.

In his edition of the History of Beaumarchais, by Gudin, 1888, Maurice Tourneux in a lengthy note points out the fallacies in the story of this adventure as told by Gudin. After speaking of the most recent accusations against Beaumarchais, he says, "But it must be admitted, this is to venture upon a series of very serious as well as practically gratuitous accusations."

Lintilhac does not hesitate to assert that Angelucci did exist, and that not a line of the libel is from the pen of Beaumarchais. As this is the most recent study of the subject which has appeared, it attempts to answer all the arguments set forth by the adversaries of Beaumarchais, and through before unpublished documents, to prove the fallacy of all their conjectures. (See ***Beaumarchais*** et ***ses ceuvres,*** by E. Lintilhac, Paris, 1889.)

What is, however, of vital importance for the life of Beaumarchais, and above all for the very important role which he is about to play in the War of American Independence, is that the adventure just related did not in the least bring upon him the dislike of Marie Antoinette, who had always protected him, or of Louis XVI, or his ministers. On the contrary, he had hardly returned when he found himself summoned to confer with the heads of the government upon the recall of the parliaments. A greater honor could scarcely have been paid to the sound judgment of the man who passed for the wittiest, the most fascinating, in a word the most brilliant man of his time. While conferring with the ministers upon weighty matters of state, Beaumarchais took pains at the same time to obliterate as far as possible from the public mind the impression made by the news of his imprisonment at Vienna. Immediately on his arrival, he launched forth a song which he had composed for this purpose, a song which became at once universally popular, and which renewed the admiration of the people for its author.

The song in question begins with the following stanza:

"*Toujours*, toujours*, il* est *toujours* le *meme*, *Jamais* Robin,
Ne commit *le* chagrin,
Le temps *sombre* ou *serein,*
Les jours *gras*, le carême;
Le matin *ou* le *soir;*
Dites blanc*, dites* noir*,* "Toujours, toujours, *il* est *tou* jours *le* même."

In previous chapters, we have spoken already of the intimacy of Beaumarchais with Lenormant D'Etioles. The latter's fete happening a few days after Beaumarchais's return from Vienna, he suddenly appeared unannounced in the midst of the gay festival, to the unbounded joy of his old friends. As the entertainment progressed, Beaumarchais absented himself for half an hour, returning with a song in dialect, which he had just composed in honor of his host. A young man present sang it before the company. Its success was complete, and along with the one previously mentioned, it soon spread all over Paris. This song contained a verse which recalled in a very pleasing way, the personal affair which was of such great importance to the author, and which had served to make him popular. He was thus kept fresh in the public mind and its sympathetic interest was conserved.

*"**Mes** chers **amis**, pourriez-**vous** m'enseigner*
***J'im** bon **seigneur** don **cha'un** parte?*
***Je** ne **sais** pas **comment** vous **l'**designer*
*** C'pendent,*** on *** dit*** qu'il *** a*** nom *** Charle*** ...*

L'hiver passé j'eut un mandit procéds
Qui m'donna bien d'la tablature.
J'm'en vais vous l'dire: ils m'avons mis exprés
Sous c'te nouvelle magistrature;
Chariot venait, jarni,
Me consolait, si fit; Ami, ta cause est bonne et ronde ...
Est ce qu'on blame ainsi le pauvre monde?"

CHAPTER XIII

Le Barbier De Seville—

"*J'ai* donc *eu* la *faiblesse* autrefois, *Monsieur*, de *faire* des *drames* qui *n'etaient pas* du *bon* genre*; et* je *m'en repens* beaucoup.

"*Presse* depuis, *par* les événements, *j'ai* hasardé *de* mal-é *heureux* mémoires *que* mes *ennemis* n'ont *pas* trouvés *de* bon *style*; j'en *ai* le *remords* cruel.

"*Aujourd'hui* je *fais* glisser *sous* vos yeux, *une* comédie fort *gaie*, que *certains* maitres *de* gout n'*estvment* pas *du* bon *ton*; et *je* ne *m'en* console *point.*

"*Je* ne *voudrais* pas *jurer* qu'il *en* fut *settlement question* dans *cinq* ou *six* siècles; *tant* notre *nation* est inconstante *et* legère."

Preface du Barbier de Seville.

The Character of Figaro—The First Performance of *Le* Barbier *de* Seville—Its Success after Failure—Beaumar-chais's Innovation at the Closing of the Theatre—His First Request for an Exact Account from the Actors— ***Barbier*** de ***Seville*** at the Petit Trianon.

A SIDE from Beaumarchais's participation in the affairs of the War of American Independence, the chief title to glory which his admirers can claim for him is his creation of the character of Figaro.

"Certainly no comic personage," says Gudin, "has more
the tone, the *esprit,* the gaiety, the intelligence, the lightness, that kind of insouciance and intrepid self-confidence which characterizes the French people."

So long and lovingly had Beaumarchais carried about with him this child of his *esprit,* that the two at last practically had become one. Gudin says, "The handsome, the gay, the amiable Figaro, daring and philosophical, making sport of his masters and not able to get on without them, murmuring under the yoke and yet bearing it with gaiety" is no other than Beaumarchais in person. "Welcomed in one city, imprisoned in another, and everywhere superior to events, praised by these, blamed by those, enduring evil, making fun of the stupid, braving the wicked, laughing at misery and shaving all the world, you see me at last in Seville."

"Le Comte—'Who gave thee so gay a philosophy ?

"Figaro—'The habit of misfortune, I hasten to laugh at everything for fear of being obliged to weep.' (*'Le* Barbier *de* Seville,9 Act I, Scene II) or again

"Le Comte 'Do you write verses, Figaro?'

"Figaro 'That is precisely my misfortune, your Excellency. When it became known to the ministers that I sent enigmas to the journals, that madrigals were afloat of my making, in a word that I had been printed alive, they took it tragically, and deprived me of my position under the pretext that the love of letters is incompatible with *l'esprit* des *affaires* "

When Figaro re-appears a few years later, we shall see all his characteristics intensified in proportion as the ex-periences and success of Beaumarchais had heightened his daring and address.

We must not make the mistake however of identifying Beaumarchais with his creation, for to create Figaro re-quired one greater than he. There is undoubtedly a strongly developed Figaro side to Beaumarchais's nature and it is this which always had prevented him from being taken seriously, and which made him an unfathomable being even to those very persons who depended upon and profited most by his rare gifts.

With such limitless resources, such power of combination, such insight, incapable of taking offense at any injury, so generous, forgiving, laughing at misfortune, how could he be taken seriously? With Beaumarchais, as with Figaro, it is the very excess of his qualities and gifts which alarms. As one of his biographers has said, "What deceives is, that in seeing Figaro display so much esprit, so much daring, we involuntarily fear that he will abuse his powers in using them for evil; this fear is really a kind of homage; Figaro in the piece, like Beaumarchais in the world, gives a handle to calumny but never justifies it. The one and the other never interfere except for good, and if they love intrigue it is principally because it gives them occasion to use their *esprit.*"

The first conception of Figaro dates very far back in the history of Beaumarchais. Already before his return from Spain the character was beginning to take form in his mind. Its first appearance was in a farce produced at the Chateau d'Étioles. We have spoken already of its rejection by the Comédie *des* It *aliens,* after it had assumed the form of a comic opera. Made over into a drama, it had soon after been accepted by the Théâtre-Frcmçais.

It will perhaps be remembered that following the frightful adventure with the due de Chaulnes, Beaumarchais had spent the evening of that same day in reading his play to a circle of friends. It had at that time; passed the censor and had been approved. Permission for its presentation had been signed by M. de Sartine, then lieutenant of police, and it was advertised for the thirteenth of February of that year, 1773. The affair with the Duke happened on the 11th, two days before the piece was to be performed. The difficulties which immediately followed were of a nature to cause the performance to be postponed indefinitely.

A year later, however, when the great success of the memoirs of Beaumarchais had made him so famous, "the comedians," says Loménie, "wished to profit by the circumstance. They solicited permission to play the ***Barbier*** de ***Seville.***"

But the police, fearing to find in it satirical allusions to the suit then in progress, caused a new censorship to be appointed, before permission could be obtained. Their report was, "The play has been censored with the greatest rigor but not a single word has been found which applies to the present situation."

The representation was announced for Saturday, the 12th of February, 1774. Two days before this date, how-ever, came an order from the authorities which prohibited the presentation. The noise had gone abroad that the piece had been altered and that it was full of allusions to the suit. Beaumarchais denied this rumor in a notice which terminates thus:

"I implore the court to be so good as to order that the manuscript of my piece, as it was consigned to the police a year ago, and as it was to be performed, be presented; I submit myself to all the rigor of the ordinances if in the context, or in the style of the work, anything be found which has the faintest allusion to the unhappy suit which M. Goëzman has raised against me and which would be contrary to the profound respect which I profess for the par-liament.

"Caron de Beaumarchais"

The prohibition was not removed and the piece was not presented until after the return of the author from Vienna in December, 1774.

"He then obtained permission," says Loménie, "to have his ***Barbier*** played. Between the obtaining of the permission and the presentation he put himself at his ease; his comedy had been prohibited because of pretended allusions which did not exist; he compensated himself for this unjust prohibition by inserting precisely all the allusions which the authorities feared to find in it and which were not there. He reinforced it with a great number of satirical generalities, with a host of more or less audacious puns. He added a good many lengthy passages, increased it by an act and overcharged it so completely that it fell flat the day of its first appearance before the public."

The defeat was all the more striking because of the fame of the author; the public curiosity so long kept in abeyance had brought such a crowd to the first presentation as had never before been equalled in the annals of the theater.

"Never," says Grimm, "had a first presentation attracted so many people." The surprise of himself and his friends was extreme, for Beaumarchais instead of applause received the hisses of the parterre. Anyone else might have been discouraged, or at least disturbed by so unexpected a turn, not so Beaumarchais.

In his own account of the defeat, wittily told in the famous preface to the Barbier, published three months later, he says, "The god of Cabal is irritated; I said to the comedians with force, 'Children, a sacrifice here is neces-sary,' and so giving the devil his part, and tearing my manuscript, 'god of the hissers, spitters, coughers, disturbers,' I cried, 'thou must have blood, drink my fourth act and may thy fury be appeased.' In the instant you should have heard that infernal noise which made the actors grow pale, and falter, weaken in the distance and die away." But Beau-marchais did more than simply renounce an act, he set instantly to work to rearrange and purify the whole play.

"Surely it is no common thing," says Loméiie, "to see an author pick up a piece justly fallen, and within twenty-four hours . . . transform it so that it becomes a charming production, full of life and movement. . . ."

At its second production, "everyone laughed, and applauded from one end to the other of the piece; its cause was completely gained." (Gudin)

What Beaumarchais did, was to restore the piece to about the form which had been approved and signed by the censors.

Some of the best of the satirical portions which are to be found in the printed play, nevertheless, were inserted before the first presentation, these he dared to retain in the final form.

In accounting for its fall, Gudin says, "A superabundance of *esprit* produced satiety and fatigued the audience. Beaumarchais then set about pruning his too luxuriantly branching tree, pulled off the leaves which hid the flowers— thus allowing one to taste all the charm of its details."

As might be expected, the success of the play after its first presentation produced a storm of opposition; critics and journals vied with each other to prove to the public that they had again been deceived. Gudin says, "His facil-ity to hazard everything and receive applause awakened jealousy and unchained against him cabals of every kind."

In the brilliant preface already alluded to, which Beaumarchais published with the play after its success was es-tablished, he allowed himself the pleasure of mocking, not only at the journalists and critics, but at the public itself. "You should have seen," he wrote, "the feeble friends of the *Barbier*, dispersing themselves, hiding their faces, or disappearing; the women, always so brave when they protect, burying themselves in hoods, and lowering their con-fused eyes; the men running to make honorable amends for the good they had said of my piece and throwing the pleasure which they had taken in it upon my execrable manner of reading things. Some gazing fixedly to the right when they felt me pass to the left, feigned not to see me, others more courageous, but looking about to assure themselves that no one saw them, drew me into a corner to ask, 'Eh? how did you produce such an illusion? Because you must admit my friend that you have produced the greatest platitude in the world.'"

Beaumarchais could afford to indulge in such pleasantries, for his piece was not only continuing to draw vast crowds, but it had begun already a triumphant progress over Europe. In St. Petersburg alone it went through fifty representations.

But the revenge of Beaumarchais did not stop here; most of the cuttings which he had been forced to make in the play, the witticisms, jests and tirades were far too good to be lost. He saved them for future use and made the public laugh over and applaud what it first hissed. When Figaro made his second appearance, on the mad day of his marriage, he used them nearly all. Beaumarchais's revenge then was complete. But while waiting for this, he had the audacity to make the comedians themselves mock at their own playing, as we shall see presently.

The story of the **Barbier** de **Seville** is of the simplest: "Never," says Lintilhac, "did any one make a better thing out of nothing."

A young nobleman, the count Almaviva, tired of the conquests which interest, convention, and vanity make so easy, has left Madrid to follow to Seville a charming, sweet, and fresh young girl Rosine, with whom he has never been able to exchange a word owing to the constant oversight of her guardian, the Doctor Bartholo, who is on the point of marrying her and securing to himself her fortune. In the words of Figaro, the doctor is a "beautiful, fat, short, young, old man, slightly gray, cunning, sharp, cloyed, who watches, ferrets, scolds and grumbles all at the same time and so naturally inspires only aversion in the charming Rosine." The count, on the contrary, is a sympathetic figure, who, although disguised as a student and only seen from afar, has already won the heart of the young girl.

Figaro, the gay and resourceful barber to Bartholo has long ago succeeded in making himself indispensable to the latter and to his whole household, while at the same time taking advantage of the avarice and cunning of the doctor and turning them to his own account. It is he who recog-nizes the disguise of the student, his old master, the count Almaviva, loitering under Rosine's window, and offers his services in outwitting the doctor whose arrangements are made for the consummation of his marriage on that self-same day.

It is no easy matter which he here undertakes, for with all his resourcefulness, Figaro has to deal with a suspicious old man, subtle and cunning, who is almost as resourceful as himself.

The count obtains entrance to the house as a music teacher sent by Rosine's usual instructor whom the count announces as ill.

A most amusing scene ensues when Basile, the true instructor, appears, unconscious that he has a substitute and where, by the quick wit of the others, even the old doctor is made to laugh him out of the house, before the situation is spoiled. Basile goes, utterly mystified by the whole proceeding, but carrying with him "one of the irresistible arguments with which the count's pockets are always filled."

The embroglio thickens. Although Bartholo is constantly on his guard and suspicious of everyone, especially of Figaro, the latter succeeds in getting the key to Rosine's lattice from the old man's possession, almost under his very eyes, and then shows it to him, but at a moment when Bartholo is too much taken up with watching the new music teacher to notice the key, or the gesture of Figaro.

In the end, it 'is by the very means which Bartholo has taken ;to outwit the others, that the count succeeds in re-placing him by the side of Rosine, and leading her before the notary, who arrives, after he has been sent for by Doctor Bartholo. The ceremony is concluded, as the doctor arrives on the scene. The fury of the latter is appeased, however, when he learns that he may keep the fortune of Rosine, while the count leads her off triumphant, happy in the "sweet consciousness of being loved for himself."

It is to be sure an old, old story, but made into something quite new by the genius of the author. The situation of Basile in the third act, as already described, is absolutely without precedent, while numerous other scenes offer a *comique* difficult to surpass.

"The style lends wings to the action," says Lintilhac, "and is so full and keen that the prose rings almost like poetry while his phrases have become proverbs."

Perhaps the most remarkable passage of the whole play is that upon slander, which Beaumarchais puts into the mouth of Basile,

"Slander, sir! You scarcely know what you are disdaining. I have seen the best of men almost crushed under it. Believe me, there is no stupid calumny, no horror, not an absurd story that one cannot fasten upon the idle people of a great city if one only begins properly, and we have such clever folks!

"First comes a slight rumor, skimming the ground like a swallow before the storm, *pianissimo*, it murmurs and is gone, sowing behind its empoisoned traits.

"Some mouth takes it up, and *piano*, piano, *it slips adroitly into the ear. The evil is done, it germinates, it grows, it flourishes, it makes its way, and* rinforzando, from mouth to mouth it speeds onward; then suddenly, no one knows how, you see slander, erecting itself, hiss, swell, and grow big as you gaze. It darts forward, whirls, envelops, tears up, drags after it, thunders and becomes a general cry; a public crescendo, a universal chorus of hatred and proscription."

The *Barbier* de Séville *had gone through thirteen presentations when the time arrived for the closing of the theater for the three weeks before Easter. It was a time-honored custom on this occasion for one of the actors to come forward after the last performance was over, and deliver a discourse which was called the* compliment *de* cloture. "*Beaumarchais,*" says Lomenie, "*lover of innovation in everything, had the idea of replacing this ordinarily majestic discourse by a sort of proverb of one act, which should be played in the costumes of the* Barbier" *In explaining the composition of the proverb he says further,* "*It has not been sufficient for Beaumarchais to restore to the Theatre* Français some of the vivid gaiety of the olden time,—he wished for more, he desired not only that the people be made to laugh immoderately, but that one should sing in the theater of **Messieurs** les comédiens *du* roi.*" This was an enormity and essentially contrary to the dignity of the* Comédie *Francaise*. Nevertheless, as Beaumarchais had an obstinate will, the comedians to please him undertook to sing at the first representation the airs introduced into the Bar-bier; but whether the actors acquitted themselves badly at this unaccustomed task, or whether it was that the public did not like the innovation, all the airs were hissed without pity and it had been necessary to suppress them in the next presentation. There was one air in particular to which the author was strongly attached; it was the air of spring sung by Rosine in the third act. "*Quand* dans *la* plaine," etc. The amiable actress, Mademoiselle Doligny, who had created the role of Rosine, little used to singing in public, and still less to being hissed, refused absolutely to recommence the experiment and Beaumarchais had been forced to resign himself to the sacrifice of the air.

But as in everything he only sacrificed himself provision-ally.

At the approach of the day of the *cloture,* he proposed to the comedians to write for them the compliment which it was the custom to give, but on condition that they sing his famous air which he proposed to bring into the compliment, that was to be played by all the actors of the ***Barbier.***

As Mademoiselle Doligny still refused to sing the bit in question, Beaumarchais suppressed the *role* of Rosine, and replaced it by the introduction of another actress more daring, who sang very agreeably, namely, Mademoiselle Luzzi.

This amusing proverb in the style of the ***Barbier*** had a great success and the delicious little spring song as sung by Mademoiselle Luzzi received at last its just applause. In the scene in which it was produced the daring author has dialogued thus:

Scene III

Mlle. Luzzi—"Very well, gentlemen, isn't the compliment given yet?"

Figaro—"It's worse than that, it isn't made."

Mlle. Luzzi—"The compliment?"

Bartholo—"A miserable author had promised me one, but at the instant of pronouncing it, he sent us word to serve ourselves elsewhere."

Mlle. Luzzi—"I am in the secret, he is annoyed that you suppressed in his piece his air of spring."

Bartholo—"What air of spring? What piece?"

Mlle. Luzzi—"The little air of Rosine in the *Barbier de Seville:*

Bartholo—"That was well done, the public does not want any one to sing at the Comédie-Française"

Mlle. Luzzi—"Yes, Doctor, in tragedies; but when did it wish that a gay subject should be deprived of what might increase its agreeableness ? Believe me, gentlemen, Monsieur *le Public* likes anything which amuses him."

Bartholo—"More than that is it our fault if Rosine lost courage?"

Mlle. Luzzi—"Is it pretty, the song?"

Le Comte—"Will you try it?"

Figaro—"In a corner under your breath."

Mlle. Luzzi—"But I am like Rosine, I shall tremble."

Le Comte—"We will judge if the air might have given pleasure."

Mlle. Luzzi sings.

"Quand dans la plaine
L'amour ramène
Le printemps
Si chéri des amants,
Tout reprend l'être
Son feu pénetre
Dans les fleurs
Et dans les jeunes coeurs.
On voit les troupeaux
Sortir des hameaux;
Dans toils les coteaux
Les oris des agneaux
Retentissent; Ils bondissent;
Tout fermente,
Tout augmente;
Les brebis paissent
Les fleurs qui rials sent;
Les chiens fidèles
Veillent sur elles;
Mais Lindor enflame
Ne songe guère

Qu'au bonheur d'être aimé
De sa bergére."

Le Comte—"Very pretty, on my honor." Figaro—"It is a charming song."

Beaumarchais was so far content. He had proved his point and had triumphed over friends and enemies alike. A far more difficult matter remained, however, to be settled. It was one that would have frightened a less intrepid character than that of our author, but obstacles,' as we have seen in many previous instances, only served to strengthen his determination to conquer, which in this instance, as in most others, he did in the end.

When Beaumarchais demanded of the Théâtre-Frcmçais *a statement verified and signed as to his share of the profits from the representation of the* Barbier de Seville, no one knew better than he the magnitude of the innovation which he was committing.

The alarmed comedians, who had never in their lives made out an accurate account and who had not the remotest intention of yielding to the demand, endeavored by every possible means to put him off. The money that they sent and the unsigned memoranda which accompanied it, were all promptly but politely returned with the reiterated statement, most obligingly and cleverly turned and always in some new form, that it was not the money which was wanted, but a verified and signed account which could serve as a model for all future occasions, when it became a matter of business transaction between authors and comedians.

For fifteen years he pursued his object with unfaltering perseverance. Unable to establish a new order of things under the old *regime,* we shall find him in 1791 presenting a petition in regard to the rights of authors to the Assewnblée Nationale.

But to return to the *Barbier* de Seville, let us anticipate a period of ten years and accompany Beaumarchais to a representation of this famous piece played upon another stage than that of the Theatre Français, and by actors very different from the comedians of the king.

It was in 1785. The aristocracy of France, all unconscious of what they were doing towards the undermining of the colossal structure of which they formed the parts, were bent upon one thing only and that was amusement.

From the insupportable *regime* which etiquette enforced, Marie-Antoinette fled the vast palace of Versailles on every possible occasion, seeking refuge in her charming and dearly loved retreat, the ***Petit-Trianon.***

In the semi-seclusion of her palace and its adjoining pleasure grounds, her role of queen was forgotten. It was there that she amused herself with her ladies of honor, in playing at being shepherdess, or dairy maid. Whatever in-genuity could devise to heighten the illusion, was there produced. Innocent and harmless sports one might say, and in itself that was true, but for a Queen of France! A queen claiming still all the advantages of her rank, renouncing only what was burdensome and dull! Innocent she was, of all the crimes that calumnies imputed to her, and of what crimes did they not try to make her appear guilty; but innocent in the light of history she was not. More than any other victim perhaps of the French Revolution, she brought her doom upon herself. The sublimity, however, with which she expiated to the uttermost those thoughtless follies of her youth, enables us to pardon her as woman, though as queen, we must recognize that her fate was inevitable.

But in 1785, mirth and gaiety still reigned in the precinct of the ***Petit-Trianon.*** In August of the year Marie-Antoinette who had always protected Beaumarchais, wishing to do him a signal honor had decided to produce upon the little stage of her palace theater the ***Barbier de Seville.***

In his ***Fin de l'ancien Regime,*** Imbert de Saint-Amand gives the following narration of that strange incident.

"Imagine who was to take the part of Rosine, that pretty little mignonne, sweet, tender, affable, fresh and tempting, with furtive foot, artful figure, well formed, plump arms, rosy mouth, and hands! and cheeks! and teeth! and eyes! (Le Barbier de Séville, Act II, Scene 2). Yes, this part of Rosine, this charming child, thus described by Figaro, was to be played by whom? By the most imposing and majestic of women, the queen of France and Navarre.

"The rehearsals began under the direction of one of the best actors of the Comédie Française, **Dazincourt, who previously had obtained a brilliant success in the** Mariage de Figaro. It was during the rehearsals that the first rumor of the terrible affair of the diamond necklace reached the Queen. Nevertheless she did not weaken.—Four days after the arrest of the Cardinal de Rohan, grand-almoner of France, Marie-Antoinette appeared in the role of Rosine.

"Beaumarchais was present. The role of Figaro was taken by the Comte d'Artois.
...

"A soinée, certainly the most singular. At the very hour when so many catastrophes were preparing, was it not curious to hear the brother of Louis XVI, the Comte d'Artois, cry out in the language of the Andalusian barber, 'Faith, Monsieur, who knows whether the world will last three weeks longer?' (Act III, Scene 5). He the zealous partisan of the old *regime,* he the future émigré, he the prince who would one day bear the title of Charles X, it was he who uttered such democratic phrase as these: 'I believe myself only too happy to be forgotten, persuaded that a great lord has done us enough good, when he has done us no harm.' (Act I, Scene 2)

" 'From the virtues required in a domestic, does your Excellency know many masters who are worthy of being valets?' (Act I, Scene 3)

"Was there not something like a prediction in these words of Figaro in the mouth of the brother of Louis XVI, I hasten to laugh at everything for fear of being obliged to weep'? (Act I, Scene 2)

"Ah, let Marie-Antoinette pay attention and listen! At this moment when the affair of the necklace begins, would not one say that all the maneuvers of her calumniators were announced to her by Basile: 'Calumny, Sir . . .' Beautiful and unfortunate Queen, on hearing that definition of the crescendo of calumny would she not turn pale?

"With this representation of the ***Barbier de Seville,*** ended the private theatricals of the Petit-Trianon. What was preparing was the drama, not the fictitious drama, but the drama real, the drama terrible, the drama where Providence reserved to the unhappy queen the most tragic, the most touching of all the roles . . ." (For the full details of this fatal affair of the diamond necklace, see ***l'amcien Regime,*** by Imbert de Saint-Amand.)

Little did Beaumarchais realize the part he was playing in the preparation for that great drama. The gay ut-terances of his Figaro were the utterances of the mass of the people of France. Through Beaumarchais, the Tiers-État was at last finding a voice and rising to self-consciousness ; it was rising also to a consciousness of the effete condition of all the upper strata of society. Hence the wild enthusiasm with which these productions were greeted, an enthusiasm in which the aristocracy themselves joined, eager as the populace to laugh, for exactly the same reason as Figaro, so that they might not be obliged to weep.

CHAPTER XIV

"0w dit qu'il n'est pas noble aux auteurs de plaider pour le vil mtèrêt, eux qui se piquent de prétendre à la gloire. On a raison; la gloire est attrayante; mais on oublie que, pour en jouir settlement une année, la nature nous condamne à diner trois-cents-soixante-cinq fois; . . . Pourquoi, le fils d'Apollon, l'amant des Muses, incessammant forcé de compter avec son boukmger, négligerait-il de compter avec les coéediens?"
Compte Rendu, par Beaumarchais

Beaumarchais Undertakes to Protect the Rights of Dramatic Authors—Lawsuit with the Comédie Francaise— Founder of the First Society of Dramatic Authors—Jealousies Among Themselves Retard Success—National Assembly Grants Decree 1791—Final Form Given by Napoleon.

WHILE Beaumarchais was enjoying the triumph of his Barbier de Séville, his other affairs were by no means neglected.

Very soon we shall have occasion to accompany him to London on one of the most singular missions of which it is possible to conceive. But before entering into a history of the political and financial operations into which Beau-marchais plunged after his return from Vienna, it is necessary to speak of the very important matter which the suc-cess of the ***Barbier*** emboldened its author to undertake.

As Beaumarchais possessed to such an extraordinary degree the power, as he himself has expressed it, *"de fermer le tiroir d'une affaire,* and instantly to turn the whole force of his mind into a totally different channel, we shall not be surprised to find him at one and the same time undertaking to protect the rights of dramatic authors against the comedians of the king; settling for Louis XVI a matter of occult diplomacy of the old king, Louis XV, which had dragged on for years, and which no one else had been able to adjust; working with unremitting zeal for his own rehabilitation as citizen; pursuing the interests of his suit with the Comte de la Blache, which was still in progress; leading a life in London and Paris which from the point of view of pleasure left little to be desired; and all the while engaged in constant and almost superhuman exertions to stir the French government out of its lethargy in regard to the insurgent American colonies, and later in sending the latter aid, under the very eyes of the English, exposed to constant danger of bankruptcy and ruin.

Unlike Beaumarchais, we are unable to give our attention to so many things at the same time, and we are therefore forced to treat each action separately.

Beginning then with his action against the comedians, it is necessary to state that the custom by which that an-cient and highly honored institution the Théâtre-

Français regulated its accounts with the author whose plays were there produced, permitted of so much obscurity that no attempt was ever made to verify those accounts, so that all the authors practically were obliged to content themselves with whatever the comedians chose to give them.

This condition of affairs had arisen in the following manner. The earliest theatrical representations, since those given in Greece and Rome, were the Mysteries, or Miracle Plays, which were written by the monks, who went about presenting them and who, of course, worked gratuitously. Later, small sums were offered for plays, but it was not until the time of Louis XIV that an author received any considerable sum for a literary production. Even during the reign of this liberal monarch it was the personal munificence of the king that extended itself to the author, rather than any rights which he possessed. That this munificence was quite inadequate is proved by the fact that the "grand Cor-neille," whose sublime genius lifted at one stroke, the literature of France to a height which few nations have surpassed, was allowed to die in poverty and distress.

Finally in 1697, a royal decree had been issued, which gave to the authors of the Theatre François *the right to a ninth part of the receipts of each representation, after the deduction of the costs of the performance and certain rights, the limits of which were not clearly defined. It was stipulated also that if for twice in succession the receipts fell below the cost of performance, from which presentation the author of course received no returns, the piece, which was then termed,* tombée dans les regies, became the property of the comedians. There was nothing said about any future performance of the piece. The comedians thus had it in their power to take it up anew, retaining for themselves the entire proceeds of the performances.

Innumerable abuses had crept in, so that instead of a ninth, it was well proved that often the author received less than a twentieth part of the returns of the play. The position of the comedians was strengthened by the current opinion that it was degrading to the high art of literature to bring it down to a financial basis. Profiting by this and abusing their privileges, the Comédie-Française had gone on confiscating the productions of authors without serious opposition, although their actions had given rise in more than one instance to very serious trouble. Such was the condition of affairs in 1775.

"The richest of the dramatic authors," says Loménie, "Beaumarchais, for whom the theater had never been any-thing but a form of recreation, and who had made a present of his first two plays to the comedians, could not be taxed with cupidity in taking in hand the cause of his brothers of the pen. This is what determined him. We soon shall see him defending, for the first time, the rights of others more than his own, and hazarding himself in a new combat against adversaries more difficult to conquer than those against whom he had fought already; he will conquer nevertheless, but not for many years, and only with the aid of the Revolution will he succeed in getting the better of the kings and queens of the theater, in restraining the cupidity of the directors, and in establishing the rights of authors, until this time so unjustly despoiled.

"To the end of his life he did not cease to demand that the law surround with its protection a kind of property, no less inviolable than other forms, but before his fervid pleadings, completely sacrificed.

"The society of dramatic authors to-day so powerful, so strongly organized, which rightly, or wrongly is sometimes accused of having replaced the tyranny of the actors and directors of the theatre by a tyranny exactly the reverse, do not know perhaps all they owe to the man who was the first to unite into a solid body the writers who up to that time had lived entirely isolated."

Beaumarchais had long lived on terms of intimacy with the comedians of the Théâtre-Frcmçais; that he continued to do so during the years when his suit against them was in progress, is proved by the following letter from Mlle, Doligny, written in 1779.

The letter to which she alludes was in relation to his drama, **Les Deux Amis,** which he very much desired to have brought a second time before the public. The piece, it will be remembered, had never succeeded in Paris. Beaumarchais professed a special fondness for it, however, and desired now to have it revived. The letter of Mlle. Doligny is as follows :

"Monsieur: I do not know how to thank you enough for all that you said of me in the letter which you wrote to the Comédie **on the subject of** Les Deux Amis. All my comrades were enchanted with the gaiety and esprit which shone in your letter. I was more enchanted than anyone, because of your friendship and goodness to me." Then follows a special request in regard to two friends, after which she terminates thus:

"It is your Eugenie, your Pauline, your Rosine, who solicits this; I dare hope that you will pay some attention to their recommendations. Receive the testimony of esteem, of attachment and of gratitude with which I am for life, Monsieur, your, etc.

Doligny."

In 1775, Beaumarchais and the comedians were living on the best of terms as well may be supposed. Never had the Comédie received such fabulous returns from any play heretofore produced. Never had actors entered with more spirit into the views of their author.

"As many times as you please, Messieurs, to give the **Barbier de Seville,** I will endure it with resignation. And may you burst with people for I am the friend of your successes and the lover of my own!—If the public is contented and if you are, I shall be also. I should like to be able to say as much for the critics; but though you have done all that is possible to give the piece to the best advantage and played like angels, you will have to renounce their support; one cannot please everybody."

During the summer the matter of the Barbier de Séville seems to have dropped, owing no doubt to the fact that Beaumarchais was occupied completely with his secret mission and with his ardent addresses to the king in relation to the insurgent colonies. It will be remembered also that it was in August of this same year that the elder Caron breathed his last. We have given already the letter written on his death-bed where the venerable old watchmaker with expiring breath blessed his son who always had been his pride and honor, as well as his devoted friend.

And so to return to the case of the Comédie Française. *In December, 1775, being for a short time in Paris, Beaumarchais addressed himself to the comedians, in a letter the tone and matter of which show that his solicitude as an author had been aroused by a suspicion that they were trying to make his piece* tomber dans les règles, *and so confiscate it, by giving it on a day when some special performance at Versailles was liable to attract thither a large portion of the theater-going public. He wrote in a spirited way demanding that something be substituted for the* Barbier *on that night. The letter, terminates thus, "All the good days except Saturday, the 23rd of December, 1775, you will give me the greatest pleasure to satisfy with the* Barbier, *the small number of its admirers. For that day only, it will be easy to admit the validity of my excuses, recognized by the* Comédie itself. I have the honor to be, etc. "Caron de Beaumarchais."

"In rereading my letter I reflect that the Comédie may be embarrassed for Saturday because all the great tragedians are at Versailles. If that is the reason—Why did you not tell me simply how the matter stood? He who seems strict and rigorous in discussing his affairs is often the man who is the easiest in obliging his friends.—I should be distressed if the Comédie had the smallest occasion to complain of me, as I hope always to have nothing but praise for it.
"Reply if you please.
Paris, December 20th 1775."

Time passed on. As Beaumarchais had given to the comedians his first two dramas, hope was entertained that he would demand no return for his **Barbier.** Early in May, 1776, to their surprise and dismay, came a polite request that an exact account of the part due him as the author be made out and given to him. The play then had been given thirty-two times.

Not wishing to stir up trouble between themselves and their excellent friend, while at the same time unable and unwilling to grant the request, the comedians met the difficulty by a profound silence. "At last," says Beaumarchais in his ***Compte rendu,*** written several years later, "one of them asked me if it was my intention to give the piece to the Comé die or to require the right of authorship? I replied laughing like Sagnarelle: 'I will give it, if I wish to give it, and I will not give it, if I do not wish to give it; which does not in the least interfere with my receiving the account; a present has no merit, excepting as he who gives knows its value.'

"One of the actors insisted and said, 'If you will not give it, Monsieur, tell us at least how many times you desire that we play it for your profit, after that it will belong to us.

" 'What necessity, messieurs, that it should belong to you?'

" 'A great many authors make similar arrangements with us.

" 'Those authors are not to be imitated'

" 'They are very well satisfied, monsieur, because if they do not enjoy the profits of their piece, at least they have the advantage of seeing it played more often. Do you wish that we play it for your profit six, eight, or even ten times ? Speak.'

"The proposition seemed to me so amusing that I replied in the same gay tone, 'Since you permit me, I ask you to play it a thousand and one times.'

" 'Monsieur, you are very modest.'

" 'Modest, Messieurs, as you are just. What mania is it that you have, to wish to inherit from people who are not dead? My piece not belonging to you until it falls to a very low receipt, you ought to desire that it never belong to you. Are not eight-ninths of a hundred louis, more than nine-ninths of fifty? I see, Messieurs, that you love your interests better than you understand them.'

"I laughingly saluted the assembly, who smiled a little on their side because their orator was slightly flushed with argument.

"At last, on January 3rd, 1777, M. Desessarts, one of the comedians, came to my house . . . bringing me four thousand, five-hundred, and six livres as belonging to me from my droits d'auteur for the thirty-two performances of the ***Barbier.*** No account being joined, I did not accept the money, although M. Desessarts pressed me to do so in the most polite way in the world.

" 'There are a great many points upon which it is impossible for the Comédie to give MM. the authors anything but wne cote mat taillée (in lump, without detail)'.

" 'What I require very much more than money,' I replied, 'is une cote bien taillée, an exact account, which may serve as a type or model for all future accounts and may bring at last peace between the actors and the authors.

" 'I see,' he said, 'that you wish to open a quarrel with the Comédie.

" 'On the contrary, Monsieur, nothing would please me so much as to be able to terminate everything to the equal advantage of both parties.' And he took back the money."

Three days later Beaumarchais sent a polite note explaining why he returned the money, and clearly stating the nature of the account which he demanded. Receiving no reply, he wrote again, in the most courteous way, reminding them of their negligence.

The Comédie **then sent a simple memorandum, "following the usages observed by us with Messieurs,** les auteurs," which was without signature.

Beaumarchais at once returned the memorandum, thanking the comedians for their pains, but begging that the memorandum be verified and signed.

Receiving no reply, three days later he sent a second missive, in which he assumed that his first letter had gone astray. "I beg you," he added, "to enlighten me as to this matter and send me your account certified. The messenger has orders to wait." And he ends thus, "I am ill. I have been forbidden all serious affairs for several days; I profit by this forced leisure to occupy myself with this which is not serious at all."

For the ***Comedie,*** however, it was, to say the least, a serious embarrassment. They replied that it was impossible to verify the account except for the receipt taken at the door, "the other elements can only be guessed at."

"The letter," says Beaumarchais, "was garlanded with as many signatures as the memorandum had not."

Assuming that it was their ignorance of affairs that caused the disorder, he undertook to give, in his own inimitable way, a lesson in bookkeeping. The letter begins as follows:

"In reading, Messieurs, the obliging letter with which you have just honored me, signed by a number among you, I am confirmed in the idea that you are very honest people, and very much disposed to do justice to authors; but that it is with you, as with all men who are more versed in the agreeable arts than in the exact sciences, and who make phantoms of the embarrassing methods of calculation, which the simplest arithmetician would solve without difficulty."

Then follows the lesson. The letter ends with, "Eh, believe me, Messieurs, give no more cotes mal taillés to men of letters; too proud to receive favors, they are often too much in distress to endure losses.

"So long as you do not adopt the method of an exact account unknown only to yourselves, you will have the an-noyance of being reproached with a pretended system of usurpation over men of letters which is surety not in the mind of any one of you.

"Pardon that I take the liberty of rectifying your ideas, but it is necessary to come to an understanding; and as you seemed to me in your letter embarrassed to give an exact form to a simple account, I have permitted myself to propose to you an easy method, capable of being understood by the simplest accountant.

"Two words, Messieurs, enclose the whole of the present question; if the account which I returned is not just, rectify it. If you believe it to be exact, certify it; this is the way we must proceed in all matters of business."

"The actors," says Loménie, "did not relish this lesson in accounts given with so much complaisance and politeness. They replied that they would assemble the lawyers forming the council of the Comédie and name four commissioners from their body to examine the case."

"To assemble all the council of lawyers," says Beaumar-chais, "and name commissioners to consult as to whether an exact account should be sent me, duly signed, seemed to me a very strange proceeding."

The comedians were, however, in no hurry to act. The 14th of February, 1777, they wrote to their troublesome friend.

"It is still a question of assembling the council. The circumstance of the carnival joined to the services which we are obliged to perform at court and in the city have prevented the frequent reunion of different persons who should occupy themselves in this affair...."

"I concluded from this letter," says Beaumarchais, "that the Comédie was contented with me, but that the carnival ' seemed a bad time to occupy themselves with business. Letting the comedians, the lawyers, and their council dance in peace, I waited patiently until the end of Lent, but either they were still dancing, or doing penance for having danced, because I heard nothing from them.

"Four months rolled by in a profound sleep from which I was awakened June 1st, 1777." The cause of Beau-marchais's awakening was the sudden discovery that urgent requests from time to time to the comedians to play the ***Barbier*** met with constant refusal.

The 2nd of June he wrote a letter from which we extract the following, "If patience is a virtue, you have the right, Messieurs, to think me the most virtuous of men, but if you take the right to forget that you owe me for two or three years a verified account . . . it is I who have the right to be offended, because there are limits to the patience of even the most absurd. ...."

After a spirited recapitulation of his wrongs he continues, "In a word, Messieurs, you will give the piece, or you will not give it, it is not that which is important to-day. What is important is to put an end to so much indecision. Let us agree that if you accept I shall within eight days receive from you a certified account . . . and when that term has expired, I may regard a silence on your part as an obstinate refusal to do me justice. You will not then object if, making a pious use of my rights as author, I confide the interests of the poor to those persons whose zeal and interests oblige them to discuss these interests more methodically than I, who profess to be always, with the greatest love of peace, . . . Yours, etc.,

"Beaumarchais."

The comedians in their turn awakened by the letter just quoted replied before the expiration of the eight days, promising the much desired meeting. Beaumarchais accepted their proposal with his usual grace and himself fixed the day for the assembly. Fresh difficulties arose. The comedians wrote an apologetic letter asking for a further delay of a few days.

"I thought the comedians very good," wrote Beaumarchais, "to fear that after waiting more than a year for their convenience, I should be offended by a new delay of a few days; I was too used to their manner of proceeding to lose patience at so small a cost. I resolved, therefore, to await the moment when it should please the fugitive assembly to meet. I waited until the 15th of June, when I received a letter from M. le Marechal de Duras...."

"The comedians," says Loménie "brought to the wall had solicited the support of the duke, who intervened and begged the claimant to discuss the matter with him. As Beaumar-chais demanded nothing better, he hastened to offer to the Duke of Duras the same lesson in bookkeeping which he had vainly offered to the comedians.... Beaumarchais wrote to him:

" 'You are too much interested, M. le Maréchal, in the progress of the most beautiful of the arts, not to admit that if those who play the pieces gain an income of twenty-thousand livres, those who thus make the fortune of the comedians should be able to draw from it that which is absolutely necessary. There is no personal interest, M. le Marechal, in my demand; the love of justice and of letters alone determines me. The man whom the impulsion of a great genius might have carried to a renewal of the beautiful chefs-d'oeuvre of our masters, certain that he cannot live three months from the fruits of the vigils of three years, after having lost five in waiting, becomes a journalist, a libellist or debases himself in some other trade as lucrative as degrad-ing.'"

M. de Loménie continues, "After a conversation with Beaumarchais, M. de Duras seemed to enflame himself with ardor for the cause of justice. He declared that it was time to finish with the debates where authors are at the discretion of the comedians. He proposed to substitute for the arbitrary accounts a new regulation where the rights of the two parties shall be stipulated in the clearest, the most equitable manner. He invited Beaumarchais to consult with several dramatic authors, and to submit to him a plan. To this Beaumarchais replied that in a question which interested all equally, everyone who had written for the Théâtre-Français had a right to be heard and that all must be assembled."

The duke consented and the first society of dramatic authors was founded by a circular, dated June 27th, 1777, in which Beaumarchais invited all to a dinner.

"To unite men," says Loménie, "who up to that time had been in the habit of living isolated and jealous lives, was something far from easy, even when invoking them to a common interest."

In order that the reader may judge of the obstacles which this new phase of his enterprise presented, we subjoin two letters of La Harpe, published by M. de Loménie, in reply to the invitation of Beaumarchais.

"If the end," says Loménie, in speaking of the first of these letters, "announced a man unwilling enough to treat with his fellows, the beginning seemed equally to indicate a little annoyance that another than himself should have been given the lead with the consent of M. de Duras."

"M. le Marechal de Duras," wrote La Harpe, "has already done me the honor, Monsieur, of communicating to me, and even in great detail, the new arrangements which he projects, and which tend, all of them toward the perfection of the theater, and the satisfaction of authors. I am none the less disposed to confer with you and with those who like you, Monsieur, have contributed to enrich the theater, upon our common interests and on the means of ameliorating and assuring the fate of dramatic authors. It enters into my plan of life necessitated by pressing occupations never to dine away from home but I shall have the honor of coming to you after dinner. I must warn you, however, that if by chance, M. Sauvigny or M. Dorat are to be present, I will not come. You know the world too well to bring me face to face with my declared enemies. I have the honor to be with the most distinguished consideration, Monsieur, etc.
"De la Harpe."

Beaumarchais, a little embarrassed because he had also invited Sauvigny and Dorat, replied to La Harpe by the following letter: "You have imposed upon me, Monsieur, the unpleasant task of informing you that MM. Sauvigny and Dorat do me the honor of dining with me to-day. But in a common cause, permit me to observe to you that in all countries it is the custom to set aside private quarrels.

"I shall be only too happy, if seconding my pacific views, you do me the honor to come and forget in the pleasure of an assembly of men of letters all of whom honor you, small resentments which exist perhaps only through misunderstanding.

"Do not divide us, Monsieur. We are none too strong with all our forces united against the great machine of the Comédie. We dine at three, and I shall flatter myself that you are coming even until three-fifteen—so anxious am I to have you with us.

"I have the honor to be, etc.
"Beaumarchais."
To which La Harpe replied:

"It is absolutely impossible, Monsieur, ever to find myself with two men whose works and whose persons I equally despise; one of them, Dorat, insulted me personally . and the other is an unsociable and ferocious madman whom no one sees, and who is always ready to fight for his verses. You feel, Monsieur, that this means to fight for nothing. I cannot conceive how you can class these among les phis honnétes gem de la litterature.

"I beg you to accept my excuses, and my sincere regrets. I take very little account of quarrels where *amour-propre* alone is concerned, but I never forget real offenses.

"I have the honor to be . . . etc.
"La Harpe."

"It was necessary to get on without La Harpe," says Loménie, "at least for this first meeting, because I see by another note of his that at the next meeting, where Beau-marchais no doubt sacrificed to the irascible academician on that day Dorat and Sauvigny, for he accepted the invitation for dinner and wrote in a more joyful tone.

" 'Your invitation leading me to suppose that the obstacles which kept me away no longer exist, I willingly con-sent to join you towards five o'clock. It is not that I renounce the pleasure of finding myself, glass in hand, with a man as amiable as you, Monsieur, but you are of too good company not to have supper and I admit that it is my favorite repast; thus I say with Horace, *"Arcesse vel vmperiwm fer."*

" 'I have the honor to be—etc.
" 'La Harpe.'

On the third of July, 1777, twenty-three dramatic authors found themselves gathered together around the table of Beau-marchais. If several had absented themselves from personal jealousies, others had stayed away through indifference. Collé, **homme spiritual** and author famous in his time, replied in a letter flattering to Beaumarchais but refusing all participation in the work of the society. Absent at that time from Paris, he wrote, "I avow, Monsieur, with my ordinary frankness that even had I been in Paris I should not have had the honor of finding myself at your assembly of MM. the dramatic authors. I am old and disgusted to the point of nausea with that ***troupe royale.*** For three years I have seen neither comédien ***nor*** comédiennes.

De tons ces gens-ld,
J'en ai jusque-lh.

I do not any the less, Monsieur, desire the accomplishment of your project, but permit me to limit myself to wishing you success, of which I would very much doubt if you were not at the head of the enterprise, which has all the difficulties which you can desire because you have proved to the public, Monsieur, that nothing is impossible to you. I have always thought that you disliked that which was easy. "I have the honor to be, etc.
"Collé."

A second invitation had no better success. The old poet answers in the same vein, "M. Collé thanks M. de Beaumar-chais for his remembrance. He begs him anew to be so good as to receive his excuses for the affair of the comedians. He is too old to bother himself with it. Like the rat in the fable, he has retired into his Holland cheese and it is not likely that he will come out to make the world go otherwise than she is going. For fifteen years he has been saying of the impolite and disobliging proceedings of the comedians, that verse of Piron in Callisthène, *'From excess of contempt I have become peaceable.* A force de mépris je me trowve paisible.

"M. Collé compliments M. de Beaumarchais a thousand and a thousand times."

Diderot, the founder of the new school of literature, also refused his concurrence.

"Vows voilà, Monsieur," he wrote, "at the head of an in-surgence of dramatic poets against the comedians . . . I have participated in none of these things and it will be possible to participate in none that are to follow. I pass my life in the country, almost as much a stranger to the affairs of the city as forgotten of its inhabitants. Permit me to limit myself to desires for your success. While you are fighting, I will hold my arms elevated to heaven, upon the mountains of Meudon. May those who devote themselves to the theater owe to you their independence, but to speak truly I fear that it will be more difficult to conquer a troup of comedians than a parliament. Ridicule does not have here the same force. No matter, your attempt will be none the less just and none the less honest. I salute and I embrace you. You know the sentiments of esteem with which I have been for a long time, Monsieur, yours, etc.
"Diderot."

Most of the authors had responded with enthusiasm to the appeal of Beaumarchais. A few lines from a letter of Cham-fort will serve to show the spirit which animated many of them.

He says, "One can flatter one's self that your esprit, your activity and intelligence will find a way to remedy the principal abuses which must necessarily ruin dramatic literature in France. It will be rendering a veritable service to the nation and join once more your name to a remarkable epoch. ... I hope, Monsieur, that the états-génératiuc de l'art dramatique, which to-morrow is to come together at your house, will not meet with the same destiny as other states-general, that of seeing all our miseries without being able to remedy any. However it be, I firmly believe that if you do not succeed, we must renounce all hope of reform. For myself, I shall have at least gained the advantage of forming a closer bond with a man of so much merit, whom the hazards of society have not permitted me to meet as often as I should have desired.

"I have the honor to be, etc.
"Chamfort."

"After the dinner," says Loménie, "they proceeded to the election of four commissioners charged to defend the interests of the society, and to work in its name at the new regulations demanded by the duke of Duras. Beaumarchais, originator of the enterprise, naturally was chosen first. Two Academedians, Saurin and Marmontel, were joined to him, and besides them Sedaine, who, without being yet a member of the Academy, enjoyed a very justly acquired reputation.

"This assembly of ***insurgents,*** to use the term of Diderot, recalled in a way the group of colonies who just one year before at the same time of the year, had declared their independence, but it was easier to conquer the English than the comedians.

"These latter, learning of the action of the authors, assembled on their side, called to their aid four or five lawyers, and prepared to make a vigorous resistance."

In very truth the troubles of Beaumarchais were only beginning, nor did these troubles come from the comedians alone; after the first few meetings complete discord reigned among the authors themselves, so much so that anyone but Beaumarchais would have given up in despair. The details of this disheartening undertaking have been given fully in the ***Compte rendu,*** published with the works of Beaumarchais. They have interest for us only so far as they reveal the character of this many-sided man.

Overwhelmed with enterprises of every sort, with losses and disasters that from time to time brought him to the verge of ruin, he still maintained the cause of men of letters with unfaltering perseverance, and this notwithstanding the bickerings, the petty jealousies, the ingratitude of the most interested in the result of the undertaking. Those appointed joint-commissioners with him left to him all the work. When anything went wrong all the blame fell back on his shoulders; nevertheless, with his usual philosophy he forgave and forgot everything but the end which he kept constantly in view.

At last, in the spring of 1780, a sort of arrangement was reached which was indeed an improvement on the regulations of the past, though still far from satisfactory.

In honor of the reconciliation, authors and comedians were invited to dine together at the house of the man who for so long had been trying to bring peace between them. It was not long before a rumor was afloat that Beaumarchais had gone over to the side of the comedians. His colleague, Se-daine, hastened to inform him in a thoughtless fashion of the reproaches which were being made by some of those for whom he had sacrificed so much of his repose. The tone of the letter of Sedaine was light and flippant. Beaumarchais, hurt to the quick, replied in the following words:

"Paris, this 3rd of May, 1780.
"I have not at once replied, my dear colleague, to your letter because the heat which mounted to my head would not have permitted me to do so with proper moderation. I have passed my entire life in doing my best, to the sweet murmur of reproaches and outrages from those whom I have served; but perhaps nothing ever

has hurt me so much as this. Let others do better, I will congratulate them. . No human consideration can retain me any longer in the following of this very ungrateful, dramatic literary association. I salute, honor and love you.

"I realize in re-reading my scribbling that my head is still hot, but I recommence in vain. I find myself less master of myself than I could wish."

"Sedaine," says Loménie, "recognizing that he had been, in the wrong, replied by an affectionate letter which proved that if the author of **Le Philosophe sans le Savovr** loved gossip, he was at heart an excellent man."

"Yes, my dear colleague," he wrote, "your head was still hot when you replied. Perhaps something in my letter hurt you, because the reproaches which I had heard uttered had angered me. I cannot, however, believe that you have taken for my sentiments that which I reported of your ungrateful and unreasonable **confreres.** Nevertheless, excepting three or four, the rest do us justice, and it is to you that we pass it on. If I said anything which pained you, I very sincerely beg your pardon. It is for you to be moderate, it does you more honor than me, who am older than you. Continue your beautiful and excellent services; finish your work, and do them good in spite of their ingratitude. This affair terminated to our honor by you, I will beg them to assemble at my house and they will order me to join myself to a deputation to go to thank you for all your pains. This is all we can offer you now. They will do it, or I shall separate myself from them for the rest of my life, who have only need of repose and your friendship.

"I embrace you with all my heart, and let us leave the evilly disposed for what they are."

The debates, however, were not over, for the next ten years the- struggle continued with Beaumarchais always in the lead.

"At last," says Loménie, "the Revolution came to put an end to the old abusive privileges of the Théâtre-Français, and the usurpation of the directors of the theaters of the provinces. Following a petition drawn up by La Harpe, Beaumarchais and Sedaine, representing the society of dramatic authors and under the influence of numerous memoirs pub

www.bookjungle.com email: sales@bookjungle.com fax: 630-214-0564 mail: Book Jungle PO Box 2226 Champaign, IL 61825

The Codes Of Hammurabi And Moses
W. W. Davies

QTY

The discovery of the Hammurabi Code is one of the greatest achievements of archaeology, and is of paramount interest, not only to the student of the Bible, but also to all those interested in ancient history...

Religion   ISBN: *1-59462-338-4*   Pages:132   *MSRP $12.95*

The Theory of Moral Sentiments
Adam Smith

QTY

This work from 1749. contains original theories of conscience amd moral judgment and it is the foundation for systemof morals.

Philosophy   ISBN: *1-59462-777-0*   Pages:536   *MSRP $19.95*

Jessica's First Prayer
Hesba Stretton

QTY

In a screened and secluded corner of one of the many railway-bridges which span the streets of London there could be seen a few years ago, from five o'clock every morning until half past eight, a tidily set-out coffee-stall, consisting of a trestle and board, upon which stood two large tin cans, with a small fire of charcoal burning under each so as to keep the coffee boiling during the early hours of the morning when the work-people were thronging into the city on their way to their daily toil...

Childrens   ISBN: *1-59462-373-2*   Pages:84   *MSRP $9.95*

My Life and Work
Henry Ford

QTY

Henry Ford revolutionized the world with his implementation of mass production for the Model T automobile. Gain valuable business insight into his life and work with his own auto-biography... "We have only started on our development of our country we have not as yet, with all our talk of wonderful progress, done more than scratch the surface. The progress has been wonderful enough but..."

Biographies/   ISBN: *1-59462-198-5*   Pages:300   *MSRP $21.95*

The Art of Cross-Examination
Francis Wellman

I presume it is the experience of every author, after his first book is published upon an important subject, to be almost overwhelmed with a wealth of ideas and illustrations which could readily have been included in his book, and which to his own mind, at least, seem to make a second edition inevitable. Such certainly was the case with me; and when the first edition had reached its sixth impression in five months, I rejoiced to learn that it seemed to my publishers that the book had met with a sufficiently favorable reception to justify a second and considerably enlarged edition. ..

QTY

Reference   ISBN: *1-59462-647-2*   Pages: 412   MSRP $19.95

On the Duty of Civil Disobedience
Henry David Thoreau

Thoreau wrote his famous essay, On the Duty of Civil Disobedience, as a protest against an unjust but popular war and the immoral but popular institution of slave-owning. He did more than write—he declined to pay his taxes, and was hauled off to gaol in consequence. Who can say how much this refusal of his hastened the end of the war and of slavery?

QTY

Law   ISBN: *1-59462-747-9*   Pages: 48   MSRP $7.45

Dream Psychology Psychoanalysis for Beginners
Sigmund Freud

Sigmund Freud, born Sigismund Schlomo Freud (May 6, 1856 - September 23, 1939), was a Jewish-Austrian neurologist and psychiatrist who co-founded the psychoanalytic school of psychology. Freud is best known for his theories of the unconscious mind, especially involving the mechanism of repression; his redefinition of sexual desire as mobile and directed towards a wide variety of objects; and his therapeutic techniques, especially his understanding of transference in the therapeutic relationship and the presumed value of dreams as sources of insight into unconscious desires.

QTY

Psychology   ISBN: *1-59462-905-6*   Pages: 196   MSRP $15.45

The Miracle of Right Thought
Orison Swett Marden

Believe with all of your heart that you will do what you were made to do. When the mind has once formed the habit of holding cheerful, happy, prosperous pictures, it will not be easy to form the opposite habit. It does not matter how improbable or how far away this realization may see, or how dark the prospects may be, if we visualize them as best we can, as vividly as possible, hold tenaciously to them and vigorously struggle to attain them, they will gradually become actualized, realized in the life. But a desire, a longing without endeavor, a yearning abandoned or held indifferently will vanish without realization.

QTY

Self Help   ISBN: *1-59462-644-8*   Pages: 360   MSRP $25.45

www.bookjungle.com email: sales@bookjungle.com fax: 630-214-0564 mail: Book Jungle PO Box 2226 Champaign, IL 61825

www.bookjungle.com email: sales@bookjungle.com fax: 630-214-0564 mail: Book Jungle PO Box 2226 Champaign, IL 61825

QTY

	Title	ISBN	Price
☐	**The Rosicrucian Cosmo-Conception Mystic Christianity** by *Max Heindel*	1-59462-188-8	$38.95
	The Rosicrucian Cosmo-conception is not dogmatic, neither does it appeal to any other authority than the reason of the student. It is: not controversial, but is: sent forth in the, hope that it may help to clear...	New Age/Religion Pages 646	
☐	**Abandonment To Divine Providence** by *Jean-Pierre de Caussade*	1-59462-228-0	$25.95
	"The Rev. Jean Pierre de Caussade was one of the most remarkable spiritual writers of the Society of Jesus in France in the 18th Century. His death took place at Toulouse in 1751. His works have gone through many editions and have been republished...	Inspirational/Religion Pages 400	
☐	**Mental Chemistry** by *Charles Haanel*	1-59462-192-6	$23.95
	Mental Chemistry allows the change of material conditions by combining and appropriately utilizing the power of the mind. Much like applied chemistry creates something new and unique out of careful combinations of chemicals the mastery of mental chemistry...	New Age Pages 354	
☐	**The Letters of Robert Browning and Elizabeth Barret Barrett 1845-1846 vol II** by *Robert Browning* and *Elizabeth Barrett*	1-59462-193-4	$35.95
		Biographies Pages 596	
☐	**Gleanings In Genesis (volume I)** by *Arthur W. Pink*	1-59462-130-6	$27.45
	Appropriately has Genesis been termed "the seed plot of the Bible" for in it we have, in germ form, almost all of the great doctrines which are afterwards fully developed in the books of Scripture which follow...	Religion/Inspirational Pages 420	
☐	**The Master Key** by *L. W. de Laurence*	1-59462-001-6	$30.95
	In no branch of human knowledge has there been a more lively increase of the spirit of research during the past few years than in the study of Psychology, Concentration and Mental Discipline. The requests for authentic lessons in Thought Control, Mental Discipline and...	New Age/Business Pages 422	
☐	**The Lesser Key Of Solomon Goetia** by *L. W. de Laurence*	1-59462-092-X	$9.95
	This translation of the first book of the "Lernegton" which is now for the first time made accessible to students of Talismanic Magic was done, after careful collation and edition, from numerous Ancient Manuscripts in Hebrew, Latin, and French...	New Age/Occult Pages 92	
☐	**Rubaiyat Of Omar Khayyam** by *Edward Fitzgerald*	1-59462-332-5	$13.95
	Edward Fitzgerald, whom the world has already learned, in spite of his own efforts to remain within the shadow of anonymity, to look upon as one of the rarest poets of the century, was born at Bredfield, in Suffolk, on the 31st of March, 1809. He was the third son of John Purcell...	Music Pages 172	
☐	**Ancient Law** by *Henry Maine*	1-59462-128-4	$29.95
	The chief object of the following pages is to indicate some of the earliest ideas of mankind, as they are reflected in Ancient Law, and to point out the relation of those ideas to modern thought.	Religion/History Pages 452	
☐	**Far-Away Stories** by *William J. Locke*	1-59462-129-2	$19.45
	"Good wine needs no bush, but a collection of mixed vintages does. And this book is just such a collection. Some of the stories I do not want to remain buried for ever in the museum files of dead magazine-numbers an author's not unpardonable vanity..."	Fiction Pages 272	
☐	**Life of David Crockett** by *David Crockett*	1-59462-250-7	$27.45
	"Colonel David Crockett was one of the most remarkable men of the times in which he lived. Born in humble life, but gifted with a strong will, an indomitable courage, and unremitting perseverance...	Biographies/New Age Pages 424	
☐	**Lip-Reading** by *Edward Nitchie*	1-59462-206-X	$25.95
	Edward B. Nitchie, founder of the New York School for the Hard of Hearing, now the Nitchie School of Lip-Reading, Inc, wrote "LIP-READING Principles and Practice". The development and perfecting of this meritorious work on lip-reading was an undertaking...	How-to Pages 400	
☐	**A Handbook of Suggestive Therapeutics, Applied Hypnotism, Psychic Science** by *Henry Munro*	1-59462-214-0	$24.95
		Health/New Age/Health/Self-help Pages 376	
☐	**A Doll's House: and Two Other Plays** by *Henrik Ibsen*	1-59462-112-8	$19.95
	Henrik Ibsen created this classic when in revolutionary 1848 Rome. Introducing some striking concepts in playwriting for the realist genre, this play has been studied the world over.	Fiction/Classics/Plays 308	
☐	**The Light of Asia** by *sir Edwin Arnold*	1-59462-204-3	$13.95
	In this poetic masterpiece, Edwin Arnold describes the life and teachings of Buddha. The man who was to become known as Buddha to the world was born as Prince Gautama of India but he rejected the worldly riches and abandoned the reigns of power when...	Religion/History/Biographies Pages 170	
☐	**The Complete Works of Guy de Maupassant** by *Guy de Maupassant*	1-59462-157-8	$16.95
	"For days and days, nights and nights, I had dreamed of that first kiss which was to consecrate our engagement, and I knew not on what spot I should put my lips..."	Fiction/Classics Pages 240	
☐	**The Art of Cross-Examination** by *Francis L. Wellman*	1-59462-309-0	$26.95
	Written by a renowned trial lawyer, Wellman imparts his experience and uses case studies to explain how to use psychology to extract desired information through questioning.	How-to/Science/Reference Pages 408	
☐	**Answered or Unanswered?** by *Louisa Vaughan*	1-59462-248-5	$10.95
	Miracles of Faith in China	Religion Pages 112	
☐	**The Edinburgh Lectures on Mental Science (1909)** by *Thomas*	1-59462-008-3	$11.95
	This book contains the substance of a course of lectures recently given by the writer in the Queen Street Hall, Edinburgh. Its purpose is to indicate the Natural Principles governing the relation between Mental Action and Material Conditions...	New Age/Psychology Pages 148	
☐	**Ayesha** by *H. Rider Haggard*	1-59462-301-5	$24.95
	Verily and indeed it is the unexpected that happens! Probably if there was one person upon the earth from whom the Editor of this, and of a certain previous history, did not expect to hear again...	Classics Pages 380	
☐	**Ayala's Angel** by *Anthony Trollope*	1-59462-352-X	$29.95
	The two girls were both pretty, but Lucy who was twenty-one who supposed to be simple and comparatively unattractive, whereas Ayala was credited, as her Bombwhat romantic name might show, with poetic charm and a taste for romance. Ayala when her father died was nineteen...	Fiction Pages 484	
☐	**The American Commonwealth** by *James Bryce*	1-59462-286-8	$34.45
	An interpretation of American democratic political theory. It examines political mechanics and society from the perspective of Scotsman James Bryce	Politics Pages 572	
☐	**Stories of the Pilgrims** by *Margaret P. Pumphrey*	1-59462-116-0	$17.95
	This book explores pilgrims religious oppression in England as well as their escape to Holland and eventual crossing to America on the Mayflower, and their early days in New England...	History Pages 268	

www.bookjungle.com *email:* sales@bookjungle.com *fax:* 630-214-0564 *mail:* Book Jungle PO Box 2226 Champaign, IL 61825

QTY

The Fasting Cure *by Sinclair Upton*　　　　　　　　　　　　　　　　**ISBN:** *1-59462-222-1*　**$13.95**
In the Cosmopolitan Magazine for May, 1910, and in the Contemporary Review (London) for April, 1910, I published an article dealing with my experiences in fasting. I have written a great many magazine articles, but never one which attracted so much attention...　*New Age/Self Help/Health Pages 164*

Hebrew Astrology *by Sepharial*　　　　　　　　　　　　　　　　**ISBN:** *1-59462-308-2*　**$13.45**
In these days of advanced thinking it is a matter of common observation that we have left many of the old landmarks behind and that we are now pressing forward to greater heights and to a wider horizon than that which represented the mind-content of our progenitors...　*Astrology Pages 144*

Thought Vibration or The Law of Attraction in the Thought World　　**ISBN:** *1-59462-127-6*　**$12.95**
by William Walker Atkinson　　　　　　　　　　　　　　　　　　　*Psychology/Religion Pages 144*

Optimism *by Helen Keller*　　　　　　　　　　　　　　　　　　**ISBN:** *1-59462-108-X*　**$15.95**
Helen Keller was blind, deaf, and mute since 19 months old, yet famously learned how to overcome these handicaps, communicate with the world, and spread her lectures promoting optimism. An inspiring read for everyone...　*Biographies/Inspirational Pages 84*

Sara Crewe *by Frances Burnett*　　　　　　　　　　　　　　　　**ISBN:** *1-59462-360-0*　**$9.45**
In the first place, Miss Minchin lived in London. Her home was a large, dull, tall one, in a large, dull square, where all the houses were alike, and all the sparrows were alike, and where all the door-knockers made the same heavy sound...　*Childrens/Classic Pages 88*

The Autobiography of Benjamin Franklin *by Benjamin Franklin*　**ISBN:** *1-59462-135-7*　**$24.95**
The Autobiography of Benjamin Franklin has probably been more extensively read than any other American historical work, and no other book of its kind has had such ups and downs of fortune. Franklin lived for many years in England, where he was agent...　*Biographies/History Pages 332*

Name	
Email	
Telephone	
Address	
City, State ZIP	

☐ Credit Card　　　　☐ Check / Money Order

Credit Card Number	
Expiration Date	
Signature	

Please Mail to:　Book Jungle
　　　　　　　　　PO Box 2226
　　　　　　　　　Champaign, IL 61825
or Fax to:　　　630-214-0564

ORDERING INFORMATION

web: *www.bookjungle.com*
email: *sales@bookjungle.com*
fax: *630-214-0564*
mail: *Book Jungle PO Box 2226 Champaign, IL 61825*
or PayPal *to sales@bookjungle.com*

Please contact us for bulk discounts

DIRECT-ORDER TERMS

**20% Discount if You Order
Two or More Books**
Free Domestic Shipping!
Accepted: Master Card, Visa,
Discover, American Express

www.ingramcontent.com/pod-product-compliance
Lightning Source LLC
Chambersburg PA
CBHW080537170426
43195CB00016B/2586